21st Century Yakuza

CLARENDON STUDIES IN CRIMINOLOGY

Published under the auspices of the Institute of Criminology, University of Cambridge; the Mannheim Centre, London School of Economics; and the Centre for Criminology, University of Oxford.

RECENT TITLES IN THIS SERIES:

Drugs, Race, and the Politics of Modern Slavery Law: When Enemies Become Victims
Koch

Outsourcing Crimmigration Control: Digital Borders, the IOM, and Biometric Statehood
Singler

Facial Recognition Surveillance: Policing and Human Rights in the Age of Artificial Intelligence
Fussey and Murray

Domestic Violence in Pakistan: The Legal Construction of 'Bad' and 'Mad' Women
Kamal

Transforming Justice Responses to Non-Recent Institutional Abuses
McAlinden, Keenan, and Gallen

Mafia Expansion: The 'Ndrangheta in Established Democracies
Hauser

Constructing Victimhood: Beyond Innocence and Guilt in the Transitional Justice
Lawther

Crime and Civilization: The Birth of Criminology in the Early Nineteenth Century
Kivivuori

Palestinian Political Organizations in Israeli Prisons
Bernstein

21st Century Yakuza

Death of Japanese Organised Crime

MARTINA BARADEL

OXFORD
UNIVERSITY PRESS

OXFORD
UNIVERSITY PRESS

Great Clarendon Street, Oxford, OX2 6DP,
United Kingdom

Oxford University Press is a department of the University of Oxford.
It furthers the University's objective of excellence in research, scholarship,
and education by publishing worldwide. Oxford is a registered trade mark of
Oxford University Press in the UK and in certain other countries.

Published in the United States of America by Oxford University Press
198 Madison Avenue, New York, NY 10016, United States of America.

British Library Cataloguing in Publication Data
Data available

Library of Congress Control Number: 2026935777

ISBN 9780198876212

DOI: 10.1093/9780191987755.001.0001

Printed and bound by
CPI Group (UK) Ltd., Croydon, CR0 4YY

The manufacturer's authorized representative in the EU for product safety is
Oxford University Press España S.A. of Parque Empresarial San Fernando de Henares,
Avenida de Castilla, 2 – 28830 Madrid (www.oup.es/en or product.safety@oup.com).
OUP España S.A. also acts as importer into Spain of products made by the manufacturer.

MIX
Paper | Supporting
responsible forestry
FSC® C013604
FSC
www.fsc.org

Series Editors Preface

The Clarendon Studies in Criminology series aims to provide a forum for outstanding theoretical and empirical work in all aspects of criminology and criminal justice, broadly understood. The Editors welcome submissions from established scholars, as well as manuscripts based on excellent PhD dissertations. The series was inaugurated in 1994, with Roger Hood as its first General Editor, following discussions between Oxford University Press and Oxford's then Centre for Criminological Research. It is edited under the auspices of three centres: the Institute of Criminology at the University of Cambridge, the Centre for Criminology at the University of Oxford, and the Mannheim Centre for Criminology at the London School of Economics. Each supplies members of the Editorial Board and, in turn, the Series General Editor or Editors.

In *21st Century Yakuza: Resilience and Downfall of Japanese Organised Crime*, Martina Baradel offers a remarkably insightful and authoritative analysis of how the yakuza governs — and what happens when that governance begins to collapse. Drawing on extensive fieldwork across multiple settings and levels of affiliation, she reconstructs how yakuza groups enforce discipline, structure obligations, and generate legitimacy, and traces with precision how those capacities have been eroded under sustained legal, policing, and market pressure. The result is a richly detailed account of the Japanese yakuza as a system of governance — and a major contribution to how we understand criminal authority more broadly.

But this is not only a book about the yakuza. It is also a book about the state, and about what repression does to criminal organisations over time. Japan's legal and economic architecture sits at the centre of the analysis, but the patterns that emerge are wider: how criminal groups govern illicit markets, how they maintain authority, and how — or whether — they adapt to regulatory change. In answering these questions, Baradel makes a contribution that will matter to scholars of mafias and organised crime well beyond the Japanese case. We are delighted to welcome the book into the Clarendon Studies in Criminology series.

Paolo Campana and Kyle Treiber
General Editors
Institute of Criminology, University of Cambridge
April 2026

Contents

Theorising yakuza decline

A festival of fading power

On an autumn afternoon in 2023, as I approached the yakuza headquarters that I usually visit in Tokyo, I was taken aback to find the street bustling with the vibrant stalls of a *matsuri*, a festival, which seemed unusual for the season. The air was rich with the aroma of *yakisoba*, and vendors energetically beckoned to the passersby. I made my way to the familiar four-storey building, easily identifiable to the trained eye as a yakuza office by the multiple CCTV cameras aimed at its entrance. The yakuza, Japanese organised crime groups that operate under a system of formal state designation and regulation, are permitted to maintain offices, but prohibited from displaying signs bearing their names. They exist in this visible anonymity, very present to those that know about them and forgotten by the rest. After I had rung the bell and announced my name, a young man came to open the door for me in his usual navy suit. 'Welcome,' he said, bowing. 'Long time no see,' I replied formally. We climbed the stairs to the boss' office. As always, I waited for him to knock on the door and announce me, then I went into the elegant room. The green leather sofas were positioned around a low marble table, and Japanese paintings and statues decorated the room. The boss, a tall, elegant man in his sixties, was sitting at his desk at the far end of the room, but stood up as I entered. 'What a lovely *matsuri* you have out front!' I remarked after exchanging the usual pleasantries. 'We organised it to give something back to the community. I want them to enjoy the neighbourhood.' He suggested we take a stroll through it, so he summoned a few men and we went out to the festival escorted by them. The head of the stallholders promptly came over to greet us and guide us through the stalls. We had some sweets and participated in children's games. We played *takaratsuri*, a game in which participants pull on a string from a bundle, each string being attached to a hidden prize. We then played *shateki*, where players use an air gun to shoot at small prizes

21st Century Yakuza. Martina Baradel, Oxford University Press. © Martina Baradel 2026.
DOI: 10.1093/9780191987755.003.0001

placed on shelves. The irony of playing this game with a yakuza boss while his men were around us was not lost on me. The boss vigilantly ensured the stallholders were not cheating the customers; he checked that the prizes were of decent quality and that the food was fresh, asking questions of both the head of the stallholders and vendors. Several locals approached with their children to greet the boss, who, kindly smiling, reminded them to be good and behave. We distributed the small prizes we had won to the children, while greeting people and chitchatting. This experience gave me a firsthand view of the group's tangible influence and integration within the neighbourhood—a dynamic I had only previously heard about from those within the yakuza, but which was neglected in recent official accounts. The yakuza are known to be the main actors in the Japanese underworld: they not only try to exert monopolistic control over territories and markets, particularly illegal markets, but they also engage with local communities and politics, are embedded in the social fabric, and provide services to both legal and illegal actors. This scene reveals what the yakuza are fighting to preserve: their role as community governors, embedded and legitimate. Yet these performances of governance are no longer sufficient to secure their survival.

While the yakuza in the twentieth century have developed into a complex organisation with tens of thousands of members, in recent years they have seen a dramatic decline in their membership and influence. Their survival is threatened by recent external developments (i.e. the increased scope of the laws and controls, a less amicable relationship with society at large, and greater competition from other forms of crime) as well as internal issues (ageing, lack of new recruits, intra-gang fighting). At the moment, they seem to be a dying species. The membership of the yakuza has dropped from 82,600 in 2009 to less than 18,800 members as of 2025 (NPA, 2025). Their finances appear to be under enormous stress; Japanese newspapers and media have increasingly been reporting about destitute yakuza members struggling to survive (Asahi Shinbun, 23/05/2017; NHK, 28/05/2018; Tetsu, 16/08/2023). As their numbers and finances have weakened, internal cohesion has also fractured; the biggest and most influential yakuza group, the Yamaguchi-gumi, split in 2015 and a low-intensity war has ensued for ten years, leading to more splits into different groups. The decline of the yakuza is not merely a story of crime suppression; it is also about what happens when a mafia organisation begins to die. While existing scholarship has identified the causes of mafia decline—repression, competition, market change—we know far less about the process of organisational death and what comes after. This raises broader questions about how governance in illicit markets is established, maintained, and eroded, as well as the role the state plays in that process. What happens when entrenched criminal regimes collapse? Do they get replaced, absorbed, or leave a vacuum? And what are the consequences for order, violence, and the communities left behind? In other words: what happens when a mafia begins to die?

This book makes three core arguments. First, that regulatory saturation can suppress criminal groups but may leave behind unfilled governance voids that the state will not necessarily fill. Second, that mafias do not vanish but rather they reconfigure, retaining certain governance functions even as their operational structures shrink. Third, that mafia decline does not produce successors capable of monopolistic governance: rather than being replaced, they are surrounded by a mosaic of looser, trade-oriented and predatory actors with whom they coexist.

Theoretical framework of the book

The idea that some criminal groups act not merely as market participants, but as regulators or 'governors' of the underworld was first articulated by Thomas Schelling (1971), who distinguished between actors who engage in crime as one among many, and actors who, on the other hand, attempt to dominate the illicit domain by exercising power, enforcing rules, and asserting control over criminal activities. Building on this insight, scholars such as Gambetta (1993), Chu (2000), Varese (2001), and Hill (2003) have conceptualised mafias as a specific subset of organised crime: groups that do not simply trade in illegal goods and services but seek to regulate markets and enforce their monopoly through violence and reputation. They aim to control both territory and markets through the provision of private protection, regulating the production and distribution of goods and services.

Mafia groups need to invest in a special set of resources, which are not necessarily available to illegal producers and traders, such as violence (Varese, 2025), which is necessary to maintain the monopoly and the reputation of a group capable of enforcing decisions (Gambetta, 1993; Campana and Varese, 2013). In this sense, mafias resemble states in their function of offering governance services, with the optional use of violence. When there is ineffective state policing or when the state's representatives have decided to withdraw from certain areas and markets, mafias can grow in size and complexity, such as in the case of Japan in the twentieth century (Varese, 2017). Similarly, intervention of the state can explain the emergence, growth, transplantation, and demise of criminal organisations (Catino, 2019; Gambetta, 1993; Hauser, 2025; Lessing, 2017; Skarbek, 2014).

Mafias tend to emerge as providers of governance or private protection in contexts where the state fails to adequately safeguard property rights. During abrupt transitions from planned to market-based economies, as seen in Italy, Japan, the Soviet Union, and Hong Kong, the volume of social and economic transactions expands rapidly, placing sudden and intense pressure on state institutions to regulate and enforce newly created property rights. In the absence of effective state capacity, criminal organisations can step in to fill this institutional void (Gambetta, 1993; Varese, 2001; Hill, 2003).

Just as mafias can emerge as governance providers, they can also decline. Over time, a group that once operated as a governance-type organisation may gradually lose this capacity and transitions into a conventional illicit enterprise, functioning merely as a trader in illegal markets. Conversely, under certain conditions, a criminal enterprise originally focused on trade may expand its role and begin to perform governance functions over a specific market or community. As Varese (2017) notes, the scope of criminal governance is not fixed: it can contract, evolve, or even disappear altogether depending on changing institutional, economic, or social conditions.

Scholars have explained the decline of mafias with a combination of institutional, legal, and market-related factors. In Italy, sustained state repression through the use of anti-mafia legislation, enhanced investigative powers, and aggressive asset seizure regimes has significantly weakened traditional criminal organisations (Paoli, 2003; Calderoni, 2011). In particular, the implementation of direct anti-mafia strategies following the 1992 assassinations of judges Giovanni Falcone and Paolo Borsellino is widely seen as having been relatively effective (Jamieson and Violante, 1999; Schneider and Schneider, 2003; Paoli, 2007). These efforts combined legislative reform, enhanced law enforcement coordination, and civil society mobilisation. Key innovations included longer investigative timeframes, expanded use of wiretapping and entrapment, legal recognition of state witnesses, and the criminalisation of mafia-facilitating activities (Vigna, 2006). Similarly, in cities such as New York and Amsterdam, for example, the introduction of Racketeer Influenced and Corrupt Organizations (RICO) Act-style legislation to criminalise mafia association, alongside administrative tools aimed at increasing transparency (e.g. the appointment of trustees in industries infiltrated by organised crime) has been credited with diminishing the influence of criminal networks (Jacobs et al., 2001; Huisman and Nelen, 2007). In the United States, demographic shifts, urban governance reforms, increased federal oversight, and more robust legal frameworks have also played a role in curbing corruption and limiting mafia infiltration at the local level (Reuter, 1995).

In Russia, the so-called 'extinction' of the Russian mafia resulted from a convergence of structural transformations that undermined the foundations of criminal governance. Three key developments were decisive. First, competition: the liberalisation of the protection market in the 1990s, combined with mass redundancies from state coercive institutions, led to the emergence of a vast private security sector staffed by ex-MVD (Ministry of Internal Affairs) and KGB (Committee for State Security) officers. These new actors provided more competent and legitimate forms of protection, crowding out mafia groups from their core economic function (Volkov, 2002). Second, the consolidation of state authority under Putin, characterised by the centralisation of executive power, the appointment of security personnel to high-level posts, and the revitalisation of state arbitration and fiscal systems, reasserted the state's monopoly over violence and dispute resolution (Taylor, 2011; Kryshtanovskaya and White, 2003). Finally, as criminal leaders began to capitalise their protection services into legal ownership, they gradually distanced themselves from overt violence, rebranding as businessmen and integrating into the formal economy (Volkov, 2002). This shift marked the decline of mafia governance in Russia through absorption, legalisation, and replacement by other forms of coercive authority.

In other cases, the decline of mafia-type organisations has been attributed to structural changes in criminal markets and their inability to adapt accordingly. Indeed, not all criminal markets favour hierarchical, territorially embedded organisations: some reward instead flexibility, anonymity, and decentralised coordination. Zhang and Chin (2003) show how the Chinese Triads were gradually sidelined as they failed to capitalise on emerging opportunities in human trafficking and heroin smuggling. These transnational smuggling markets rely on short-lived, low-visibility networks that are difficult to monopolise or control, making the Triads' rigid structure and overt presence a disadvantage. Smuggling operations typically rely on short chains of dyadic relationships that form and dissolve quickly, making them difficult to monopolise or regulate. In this context, the Triads' rigid hierarchy and overt presence became liabilities, resulting in what the authors describe as a 'structural deficiency' compared to more fluid criminal networks composed of unaffiliated actors.

Recent scholarship has further refined our understanding of how different types of criminal activity shape network structures, a distinction that becomes crucial for understanding how the yakuza have reorganised under pressure. Breuer and Varese (2023) find that trade-oriented groups, such as drug traffickers, tend to be more centralised in their network structures than governance-oriented mafias, which are comparatively less centralised and more reliant on reputation and symbolic authority. Morselli, Giguère, and Petit (2007) similarly observe that short-term, transactional criminal networks often prioritise efficiency over security, resulting in centralised and clustered structures coordinated by flexible entrepreneurial actors. In contrast, ideologically motivated groups or those with governance ambitions adopt sparse, long networks with minimal exposure. Calderoni's (2012) analysis of two 'Ndrangheta drug trafficking networks also reveals that despite a lack of formal hierarchical control, the groups exhibited clear task differentiation, status markers, and strategic positioning of leaders, demonstrating how cultural and kinship ties substitute for formal structure. Finally, Morselli and Roy (2008) highlight how criminal activity often unfolds in chain-like transactional arrangements, where flexible, loosely structured processes are more likely to emerge and persist than rigid hierarchies. Across these studies, a pattern emerges: the nature of the activity (production, trade, or governance) shapes the organisational form, with governance-oriented groups requiring long-term cohesion and enforcement capacity, while trade-type groups prioritise adaptability and speed (Varese, 2025).

While Japan has long been a focal point for sociological studies of crime, the scholarship has largely concentrated on the structure of policing (Ames, 1981; Bayley, 1991; Miyazawa, 1992); the criminal justice system (Foote, 1992; Johnson, 2002); and the features that sustain low levels of crime (Komiya, 1999; Leonardsen, 2004). These works have paid limited attention to the role of organised crime groups in structuring illegal markets or regulating violence. Research on the yakuza has typically focused on historical development, socio-legal status, and economic functions. Kaplan and Dubro (2003) offered a journalistic overview of the history of the yakuza, exploring the ties with politics and the economy; Hill (2003) applied the property right theory of mafia emergence (Gambetta, 1993; Varese, 2001) to the yakuza, exploring its rise and the 1991 law which introduced a formal system of designation and administrative controls over yakuza organisations; Milhaupt and West (2000) analysed the logic of 'private ordering' through which yakuza mediated business disputes in the absence of effective legal enforcement; Siniawer (2008) demonstrated how violence practitioners, sometimes affiliated with yakuza gangs, were embedded within national politics and nationalist movements in early modern Japan. Yet no study examined the yakuza as providers of criminal governance, tracing their decline through sustained empirical access to members and affiliates.

This book addresses that gap by offering an integrated analysis of the yakuza's governance function, the processes that have dismantled it, and how they are trying to survive. Grounded in extensive fieldwork across multiple regions and levels of affiliation, it reconstructs how yakuza groups enforced discipline, structured internal obligations, and generated external legitimacy, and how these capacities have been eroded by legal exclusion, policing, and market regulation. The book is not only about the yakuza: it is also about the role of the state and of repression on mafia activity and structure. The Japanese case is situated within a comparative framework that draws on scholarship on mafia emergence and decline, including the Sicilian mafia, the 'Ndrangheta, the Russian vory, the Hong Kong Triads, as well as gangs and other forms of organised crime. The book places the yakuza and Japan's legal and economic architecture at the centre of the analysis, while identifying broader patterns in how criminal groups govern illicit markets, maintain authority, and adapt—or fail to adapt—to regulatory change. It also presents the first comprehensive account of the yakuza as a system of governance, and of what happens when such a system begins to collapse under sustained repression. By tracing both the transformation of illegal trade and regulation, and the internal reorganisation of groups themselves, the book offers a detailed empirical portrait of how mafias adapt, fragment, or recede. As the first ethnographic account of a semi-legal mafia in decline, it makes a theoretical contribution to the study of mafias and organised crime: the Japanese case challenges assumptions about visibility, institutionalisation, and decline, and reveals how criminal authority is negotiated not only through violence and profit, but also through law, culture, and the shifting boundaries of state tolerance.

Building on this literature, the book puts forward three core arguments.

The first is that regulatory saturation can dismantle criminal organisations, but leaves pockets where their governance remains preferred or necessary. Japan's unique model of non-penal repression, based on administrative exclusion, social stigmatisation, and market isolation, has been effective in shrinking yakuza activity and membership. Organised crime benefits from poorly regulated markets in which the state is unlikely to intervene, even where law enforcement is otherwise strong. The yakuza historically thrived in semi-legal markets—such as hostess clubs, pachinko parlours, and segments of the sex industry—where regulatory ambiguity enabled them to operate on both the legal and illegal ends of the spectrum. Given their vulnerability to police oversight and weak contractual enforceability, the entrepreneurs who populate these markets often turn to private protection. As Lessing (2021) argues, criminal governance can, under certain conditions, serve state interests by controlling spaces that are otherwise difficult to regulate, thereby contributing to social stability or even to forms of state-building. The yakuza exemplify this dynamic. Their monopolistic control over the Japanese underworld historically contributed to lower levels of predatory violence, greater cooperation with law enforcement, and deeper entrenchment in legal markets. However, regulatory saturation, while effective in several semi-legal markets, could not reach the interstices where formal law remains unused—entertainment districts where police involvement is avoided, long-standing protection relationships, and fully illegal markets beyond state jurisdiction.

The second argument is that mafias can survive institutional decline by contracting to core governance functions. The Japanese case offers a unique variation on this theme. As yakuza groups are not criminalised per se, they have long operated as quasi-legal entities, enjoying higher visibility and a degree of social legitimacy—partly due to the connection to, and embodiment of, traditional Japanese values. They were able to establish monopolies over illicit markets while maintaining low levels of inter-group violence. Even as yakuza syndicates lose formal power, territory, and visibility, they continue to exert influence through symbolic capital, reputation, and informal mediation. Decline does not imply disappearance, but reconfiguration. The argument is that when confronted with effective state intervention, mafias react by contracting: they shrink their organisation to a core of trusted members to minimise legal risk, and delegate criminal activities to non-affiliated actors, including former members. Even if it would be more profitable to shift towards trade activities, these groups retain their core function, governance, which can persist even if diminished. This persistence reflects a combination of organisational identity (yakuza define themselves as territorial governors rooted in tradition), practical constraints (governance networks cannot be easily converted into trade operations), and strategic calculation (while trade offers short-term profit, governance preserves the long-term organisational structure and authority that enables survival).

The third argument is that the decline of a mafia does not automatically produce a successor capable of monopolistic governance. The decline of a governance-providing organisation may attract new actors, but these groups rarely take its place. Governing illicit markets requires specialised skills, legitimacy, and social embeddedness—attributes that cannot be developed overnight. The groups that emerge in the wake of a declining mafia are typically oriented towards trade-type activities or predatory activities, rather than governance. They are not direct competitors of the declining mafia, but opportunistic actors operating in looser, more modular formations. Rather than being replaced, the yakuza often co-exist with or subcontract tasks to these emergent groups. This leads to a blurring of boundaries between old and new actors. The criminal underworld becomes more fragmented, and at the same time, there is a shift away from monopoly governance towards transactional criminality.

Structure of the book

The book is based on extensive fieldwork with current and former member of the yakuza, current and former members of non-yakuza criminal networks, former prisoners, the police, lawyers, and prosecutors. This unique access calls for a detailed methodology chapter (Chapter 1), which explores the challenges of doing fieldwork in Japan in the context of organised crime. Although the situation of Japan is rare, this chapter also speaks to broader debates on ethnography with organised crime groups. It calls for a more honest approach to fieldwork, arguing that reflections on fieldwork should be aimed mainly at developing feasible strategies to engage with informants. It highlights how many requirements imposed by universities and ethics committee do not take into consideration the reality of the field, especially with current and former members of organised crime, and are either unfeasible or harmful for the relationship that the researcher needs to establish with their informants.

Chapter 2 charts the historical development of the yakuza's core function: governance. Rather than focusing solely on criminal enterprise or violence, it reconstructs how yakuza groups emerged as providers of order, protection, and dispute resolution in spaces where the state was absent, ineffective, or complicit. From their mythical roots in premodern trade and labour brokerage, to their entanglement with postwar black markets and state actors, yakuza syndicates developed institutionalised systems of regulation that resembled forms of authority more than outlawry. Yet governance has never been their exclusive domain. Even before the tightening of law enforcement and the re-regulation of key markets in the 2010s, many yakuza members pursued trading-type activities, albeit independently.

Chapter 3 examines the structure, codes, and rituals of the yakuza. While previous studies have often referenced yakuza ideology, none have provided a comprehensive description of its core elements and ceremonies. This chapter offers an analysis of the yakuza's internal and external structure, which has evolved into a particularly complex organisation due to their unique legal status. Furthermore, it explores the rituals and celebrations of the yakuza. Rather than being merely performative, these rituals serve concrete functions; they promote cooperation within the groups, establish common knowledge about the organisation, and enforce adherence to specific behaviours (Catino, 2015). Additionally, the chapter addresses one of the fundamental values of mafia groups, and of the yakuza in particular: masculinity. It explores the role of women in the yakuza through the unique case of Nishimura Mako, one of only two living women formally affiliated with the criminal syndicates. Several in-depth interviews with Nishimura show that a woman's ability to play an active role is contingent on formal affiliation and the capacity to exercise violence independently. Despite this, the role of women remains peripheral, never ultimately rising to a position of power.

Prior the tightening of anti-yakuza regulations in 2010 to 2011, the approach of the Japanese police to the yakuza has been unorthodox: rather than criminalising the autochthonous criminal syndicates, the Japanese government has regulated them while maintaining what can be defined a collaborative approach. Against this backdrop, Chapter 4 examines the effect of increasingly severe anti-yakuza laws in the past thirty years. It gives a complete and updated description of the laws and ordinances that regulate the yakuza, with a focus on the 2010–2011 Yakuza Exclusion Ordinances (Bōryokudan Haijōjōrei), after which the size of yakuza membership has dramatically decreased. Furthermore, the chapter shows how visibility is crucial to the social legitimacy of criminal governance, and how, as the yakuza's presence diminishes under Japan's legal pressures, so too does their authority. The role of the penal system is examined in relation to its disruption potential of the yakuza membership.

Chapter 5 examines how market regulation led to the expulsion of the yakuza and significantly impacted several markets in which they were involved. At its core, the decline of the yakuza reflects the progressive closure of the grey zones in which they operated – through the redefinition of property rights, the introduction of exclusion clauses across regulated industries, and the formalisation of markets previously characterised by institutional ambiguity. Where the state intervened directly, as in labour brokerage and the fish market, the yakuza were expelled. Where markets remain in a grey area, such as prostitution, night-time entertainment, and gambling, they retain influence, though under increasing pressure. In outright illegal markets, such as drug trafficking, the yakuza continue to function as governance providers, while other groups and individuals act as traders. Where markets have migrated to digital platforms, by contrast, the anonymity inherent in online transactions prevents territorial control, allowing yakuza members to participate only as private entrepreneurs rather than governance providers.

Chapter 6 explores how the yakuza reorganised themselves to maintain their core function of governance while delegating trading-type activities to other criminal networks. The discussion highlights the yakuza's strategic delegation of various business operations to non-yakuza actors and networks as a means to circumvent increasingly aggressive law enforcement measures. This reorganisation has allowed the yakuza to preserve a degree of influence and operational capabilities despite the heightened legal pressures. By outsourcing trading activities, the yakuza ensure that they remain the central figure in the criminal underworld, while reducing their direct involvement in activities that attract significant law enforcement attention.

Taken as a whole, the book examines how the yakuza's decline is reshaping Japan's criminal landscape. It traces the transformation of the yakuza from territorially embedded brokers of governance to players in a fragmented game with emerging actors. It explores how legal repression, market regulation, and social isolation have dismantled much of their formal power, yet have failed to fully destroy their influence. At the same time, it interrogates the limitations of state intervention and the unintended consequences of regulatory overreach, asking not only what happens to a mafia under sustained repression, but also how it fragments, recedes, and adapts in ways that allow parts of it to endure. Each Chapter contributes to a broader inquiry into what happens when a criminal organisation loses its capacity to govern, interrogating not only how a mafia comes to die, but what survives.

1
Doing fieldwork with the yakuza

Introduction

This chapter outlines the methodology used in the book while reflecting on the challenges and strategies of conducting fieldwork with organised crime. Although Japan's context is unique due to its criminal syndicates' semi-legal status, the insights presented here offer valuable lessons applicable to a broader range of settings.

There are two main issues for ethnographers studying criminal groups. The first is a problem of the characterisation of the object of the study, which is often vague, and secondly, the difficulty in safely penetrating such organisations (Varese, 2021). The dilemmas that arise when studying organised crime appear, at least in theory, somewhat minimised in the case of the yakuza. Yakuza groups are recognised and designated by Public Safety Commissions across Japan, their members are registered, and, overall, they are a visible and well-defined organisation. Despite increased anti-yakuza regulations over the past decade, making contact with the yakuza remains possible because they are not fully criminalised. This visibility differentiates them from other 'hidden populations' (Heckathorn, 1997) and offers a unique opportunity to study organised crime in a more direct manner.

This research is based on two distinct fieldwork periods. The first was conducted between 2017 and 2018 during my PhD at Birkbeck, University of London, which included a six-month stay at Risshō University (Tokyo). The second fieldwork took place while I was a Marie Skłodowska-Curie fellow at the University of Oxford, during which I was hosted at Nagoya University from March 2022 to December 2023. During both fieldwork periods, I used my personal and professional networks to be introduced to, and interview, former and current yakuza members, active yakuza bosses and high-ranking members, non-yakuza criminals and former prisoners. In the text, such interviews are marked with a C. Moreover, I interviewed journalists (indicated with a J); bar owners, personal acquaintances who worked in yakuza-related night-time entertainment, and the ex-lawyer of the biggest yakuza group (marked with a V); a prosecutor, a police chief, and around twenty

21st Century Yakuza. Martina Baradel, Oxford University Press. © Martina Baradel 2026.
DOI: 10.1093/9780191987755.003.0002

between unit chiefs and police officers (indicated with a P). Having studied and worked in both Tokyo and Shizuoka prefecture before my PhD, I was able to rely on pre-existing networks of people that I had built over time. After getting in touch with a respondent, I would set a time and date for the interview, which generally took place in a public space. My previous experiences in Japan helped me break the ice with the interviewees, who were curious about why I was interested in this marginalised group in Japanese society. My appreciation for Japanese food and spirits, allied with my delusional conviction that I am a great singer at karaoke bars, also proved to be helpful in that I was able to take part in the social gatherings and dinners that play an important function in terms of social bonding. Since both the language in which an interview is conducted and the use of dialects can affect people's understanding of the questions and thus the answers they give, my fluency in Japanese was useful for both removing this immediate access issue and allowing me to conduct all the interviews without the help of an interpreter. People who are involved in the yakuza might use a peculiar jargon, but knowing that I am a foreigner they always made an effort to speak clearly and in standard Japanese. Being an avid consumer of yakuza films, I was accustomed to some of the typical yakuza sayings,[1] and was taught many more. Initially, I recorded the interviews, but eventually decided against it for reasons discussed below. Depending on the respondent, I either took notes during the interview or immediately afterwards. Interviews were then coded and categorised by topic for easy reference. I ensured the validity of my analysis by using techniques such as member checking (asking participants to verify my findings if I met them more than once), triangulation (using multiple sources or methods to cross-check data), and peer debriefing (discussing my findings with colleagues or mentors).

The major academic accounts of the yakuza that are based on fieldwork are David Stark's PhD thesis *The Yakuza: Japanese Crime Incorporated* (1981), and Peter Hill's *The Japanese Mafia: Yakuza, Law, and the State* (2003). In 1979, Stark carried out a unique observational study of the operations of a yakuza group. He was able to visit their offices daily and participated in their activities and ceremonies. He describes in painstaking detail the internal order, the membership and recruitment, the economic activities,

[1] Common yakuza expressions include saying that someone who has left the group has 'washed his feet' (*ashi o arau*), someone released from prison has 'graduated from university' (*daigaku wo sotsugyō shimashita*), and someone sent into enemy territory to provoke conflict is referred to as a 'bullet' (*tama*).

and the dispute-resolution mechanisms within the group. In 1998, Hill carried out fieldwork in Japan, interviewing active and retired yakuza members, criminologists, police officers, and policymakers. Arguably, Hill's and especially Stark's experiences in conducting fieldwork differed from mine due to the introduction of new anti-yakuza regulations in recent years, in particular the 2010–2011 Yakuza Exclusionary Ordinances (*Bōryokudan Haijojōrei*), which aim at preventing contact between the yakuza and civilians. During his fieldwork in the 1970s, Stark easily gained access to the daily operations of a yakuza group, spending entire days with them at their offices and at their celebrations. While I regularly visited yakuza offices, at this juncture, it is not possible to spend whole days with a group, as the yakuza, under increased police scrutiny, have to rely on higher levels of secrecy. However, while some groups were more cautious and only took me to quiet restaurants, others openly paraded in the areas they control, introducing me to business owners and other customers without any restrictions.

Epistemology

The ethnographic method in sociology is often associated with the Chicago School, which has produced a vast array of significant studies on crime and deviancy, such as *The Gang: A Study of 1,313 Gangs in Chicago* (Thrasher, 1963), *Organized Crime in Chicago* (Landesco, 1968), and *The Hobo* (Anderson, 1923). However, as Varese (2021) points out, these studies rely heavily on secondary sources. A modern ethnography of organised crime emerged only with the publication of *Street Corner Society* by William Foote Whyte in 1943, or more precisely with the publication of the second and following editions, which included increasingly detailed methodological appendixes. There, Whyte clearly states his epistemological position, which opposes the postfoundational or postmodern view that there is no objective truth to be observed, and that the researcher can only provide subjective works of fiction whose primary goal is to be convincing enough (Geertz, 1988). In other words, according to this perspective, there is nothing to be represented; rather, the researcher creates works of fiction in the process of investigation (Clifford and Marcus, 1986). Truth is 'the best idea we currently have about how to explain what is going on' (Rorty, 1979: 385). In the influential *The Consequences of Modernity*, Giddens (1990) argues that postmodernity is marked by a recognition that 'nothing can be known with certainty, since all pre-existing "foundations" of epistemology have been shown to be unreliable' (ibid. 46). That is, everything that we know, or think is true, could and eventually will be discarded and reformulated as we gain new and better knowledge. In particular, sociological knowledge does not work like natural sciences, where knowledge can be simply accumulated; it creates knowledge that is repetitively fed into social reality and actively reconstructs it (ibid.).

Whyte, on the other hand, believes that there is 'the objective (what is out there to be observed) and the subjective (how the researcher or others interpret the observed phenomena)' (Whyte, 1993: 366). This distinction is not clear-cut: the researcher cannot observe everything, but only behaviour that is significant to the research question. Whyte's approach subscribes to the Western rationalist tradition and is based on the belief 'that there is a mind-independent external reality, that language refers to objects and events and does not just communicate meaning, and that empirical support can lend a degree of truth-value to sentences about the world' (Varese, 2022: 227). This book adopts Whyte's stance, which Varese (2022) refers to as rigorous ethnography, emphasising the existence of an objective reality that warrants investigation. Recognising that researchers may carry personal biases, it is crucial to identify and mitigate these biases whenever possible, as discussed in the following section. As an external observer not embedded in the Japanese underworld, my insights are limited to what I can directly observe and what is conveyed to me. By acknowledging these limitations and employing methods such as triangulation, cross-checking, and diverse sources, this book aims to provide an accurate and honest portrayal of the contemporary yakuza.

If, through fieldwork, we can find explanations, we should have a theoretical focus from which we start and a set of questions in mind when we enter fieldwork. One strand of qualitative research argues that by doing this, we risk imposing a preconception on the subject and influence participants (Bryman, 1988). Whyte enters the field with a question in mind, which he revises if the evidence suggests it should be modified (Varese, 2022); he delays making theoretical inferences. Being flexible is indeed necessary, and contact with the field should determine what should be investigated. After an initial formulation of plans, the researcher builds on observations and refines the question (Bryman, 2012). In the case of my own two fieldwork periods, the first was aimed at researching the situation of the yakuza, and was more open in its approach. The second focused on the aftermath of yakuza decline and had a more definite objective: to understand the effects of state intervention on yakuza governance, starting from the assumption that yakuza's primary function is to govern certain markets. My aim was to understand how the state goes about fighting the yakuza, whether these efforts can be effective, and what unfolds once they are. However, I did not put all the pieces of the puzzle together until the end of the fieldwork, and subsequently, in a coherent formulation after my return to Oxford. The necessity of such a prolonged process takes us back to another central point of Whyte (1993), made also by others (see Varese, 2022), that is, the importance of lengthy fieldwork. This allows the impact of the researcher to be minimised, for them to gain trustworthiness, and also allows the researcher to capitalise on their intuitions and observations, reformulate questions and hypotheses, and be able to test them. In the case of this book, the two fieldwork periods allowed for extensive research, and many hypotheses and assumptions were changed along the way.

Positionality and being a woman in the field

Researchers have long reflected on how the intersection of gender, ethnicity, social class, and social capital can influence the relationship between the researcher and the researched (Hobbs and Antonopoulos, 2014), as the researcher–participant relationship in fieldwork is often conditioned by the researcher's personal characteristics including gender, race, and age (Dewalt and Dewalt, 2002; Ladson-Billings, 2003; Wax, 1979). Feminist researchers have played a significant role in redefining the field, emphasising and challenging the power dynamics embedded in knowledge production, particularly the role and position of the researcher and how they influence the research and its outcomes (Pillow, 2010). Assessing positionality is a necessary exercise for researchers embarking on fieldwork to honestly evaluate their position relative to the participants. However, scholarship has highlighted how statements on positionality in some cases have become exercises in narcissism, where researchers, through the continuous confession of their own privilege, contribute to the reinforcement of hierarchies between people (Gani and Khan, 2024). Patai, in strong terms, warns about the 'methodological self-absorption' (1994: 69) that characterises much of the discourse on reflexivity in the field. Amidst the extreme personalisation of research, where the other is merely a mirror to reflect oneself, academics' 'pretense that the world's ills are set right by mere acknowledgment of one's own position' (ibid. 67) serves to establish one's credential in the academic field but rarely improves the quality or ethics of the research itself.

While being aware of one's own position in the field is crucial for conducting fieldwork, I concur that many of the statements researchers include in their academic outputs benefit the researcher more than the participants. In ethnography, the researcher is the primary 'tool' of research, and inevitably information is filtered through their values. However, I believe that more candid and honest reflections are necessary to counter long and self-absorbed positionality statements. More importantly, such reflections are necessary to conduct fieldwork efficiently. While it is crucial to acknowledge how certain immutable characteristics of the researcher influence participants' perceptions, this acknowledgement should primarily serve to inform strategic fieldwork management. For example, understanding the yakuza's specific views on women or white Europeans is necessary, inasmuch as this awareness should be leveraged to develop an effective fieldwork strategy for engaging with participants. The researcher's attitude, personality, and flexibility play a crucial role in building relationships with participants.

In particular, being a woman in a male-dominated world such as that of the yakuza and the police requires thorough reflection. There is the perception that female fieldworkers will be denied access or face considerable problems when working in either sensitive areas with a track record of poorly protecting women's rights or in fields that are deemed to be dangerous. Indeed, several studies have reported sexual harassment from male counterparts in the field (see Kloß, 2017; Hanson and Richards, 2017; Mügge, 2013). Although the prevailing wisdom is that a female researcher will encounter far greater problems than men when conducting first-hand research in areas perceived as dangerous for women, researchers have shown how women may even enjoy easier access than their male counterparts (Schwedler, 2006). The behaviour of participants towards male and female researchers might be different, but for women it is more common to receive more private details from the informants, who may feel more at ease talking to them (Barnes, 2025; Wong, 2019).

In the case of the present research, many people associated to the yakuza have an old-fashioned way of dealing with women, which could be described as a form of benevolent sexism. Of course, this applied only to certain 'respectable' women. Towards others—particularly those exploited in sex trafficking and the sex industry—their attitudes reflected what can only be described as hostile sexism (Glick and Fiske, 1996). At the beginning of my fieldwork, when discussing potential meetings with both active and ex-yakuza members, I was often told that because I was a young woman, I had nothing to worry about as the yakuza are never aggressive towards women.

Indeed, my status at the antipodes of a senior man in the yakuza granted me a position as an outsider that facilitated the meetings, as I was perceived as unthreatening and as having no stake in their business. A Japanese man, as the usual comment went, would have a different kind of relationship with them altogether. Indeed, he would carry different social expectations into the encounter—assumptions about hierarchy, obligation, and shared cultural codes that shaped the relationship in ways my outsider status avoided. Moreover, my citizenship also had its benefits during my encounters as conversations about Italy often broke the ice with many of the participants. However, one quickly realises that, despite being helpful in certain respects, this attitude is in fact far from flattering as it stems from the interviewees' perception that female researchers are neither harmful nor competent enough in their field of study. That is to say, despite the sensitivity of the information my informants were willing to provide, there was at times a lingering feeling that they were doing so because my presumed incompetence would prevent me from doing anything with it. Of course, such patronising attitudes are nothing new for female researchers studying social groups that are especially patriarchal, which tends to be the case with criminal groups: Rawlinson, for example, reported how the 'mix of courtesy and condescension' exhibited by a Russian director of a criminal protection racket who she was trying to interview left her feeling humiliated, both as a woman and a researcher (Rawlinson, 2008a).

Nevertheless, researchers can strategically engage with these perceptions to facilitate access and candor. Gurney (1991) argues that being a female researcher is thus a double-edged sword, in the sense that women are perceived as being less threatening, and thus participants are more willing to welcome them into their world, while, simultaneously, they are perceived as being less professional, which, in turn, may jeopardise the data they collect. I do not agree with the second proposition as the fact that female researchers are framed as being less capable of using the data they collect may actually encourage the respondent to talk even more candidly. However, such sexist attitudes are not the sole province of individuals directly involved with the yakuza: biting my tongue and forcing myself to smile have proven to be necessary coping mechanisms on numerous occasions with people from different sectors. For example, on several occasions I was asked whether I had put on weight since our previous meeting. The comments were delivered matter-of-factly, as casual observations rather than insults. In a conventional professional setting such remarks would be considered inappropriate; here, however, they formed part of an interactional style in which women's bodies were treated as legitimate topics of commentary. I responded with humour, joking that any change was the inevitable consequence of good Japanese food, or that my tattoos prevented me from going to the gym, thereby diffusing the remark and easing the conversation. These exchanges might seem trivial but were instructive: by showing that I could accommodate this mode of interaction without visible offence, I signalled familiarity with their communicative norms while retaining control over the tone of the encounter and sustaining rapport. The ethical issues female researchers encounter also pertain to 'the extent to which they can and should behave in a way that betrays their own values, which may only serve to reaffirm the values of a society they would normally hold up for criticism' (Rawlinson, 2008b: 299–300). However, this does not only apply to women, as I will explore in the following section.

Betraying personal values

Ethnographers often have to face several ethical and moral problems in the field (Clarke, 1975; Ellis, 2007; Etherington, 2007) but often avoid discussing how they solved them (Clark, 2012; Fabian, 1991). There are occasions when the researcher must decide whether to stick to their values and compromise the success of the fieldwork, or whether to use a more flexible approach. These situations require a passive or active participation. In the former, which can also be described as a 'conformity' dilemma (Berik, 1996), the researcher has to agree to take part in rituals and manifestations that do not align with their personal values, but that do not require active participation. For instance, I became acquainted with several former yakuza members who had turned Christian, and gathered other former yakuza members and prisoners in their congregations. Although not religious myself, I had to sit through religious services, baptisms, and prayer meetings, in order to conform and meet new informants. However, my presence was enough to show my commitment and they never tried to actively evangelise me. For female researchers, a common issue is whether to ignore or endure sexist behaviour to avoid losing sources (Piacentini, 2004). For instance, how should one reply to a respondent who in private correspondence sends ostensibly funny videos that are predicated on sexist stereotypes? In this instance, the researcher, on the one hand, wants to develop a good relationship with the participant to benefit her study, but, on the other hand, she is not willing to respond positively towards a video that goes against everything she believes in. Ignoring the message or responding with a simple thumbs up were my strategies of choice. On other occasions, I had to passively listen to misogynistic jokes and remarks, but I was not forced to take part in them and I could decide whether to smile or to pretend not to have heard.

However, the researcher is faced with a more difficult choice when she has to choose whether to actively go against a value that she holds dear, such as not eating meat for ethical reasons. In most cases, it was possible for me to choose a suitable menu option, without having to explain my dietary restrictions, which would have led to long discussions about the health benefits of eating meat. However, there have been cases in which the choice was not available. One night I was invited out for dinner with high-ranking officials of a yakuza group in Okinawa. Being excited to meet them for the first time, and knowing that a vegetarian option is usually available, I had not told them in advance about my dietary restrictions. Two men and one of the bosses picked me up near my hotel and we drove to the elegant restaurant they had exclusively booked for our dinner. Another boss joined us, and as I was waiting for the menu, he asked enthusiastically if I knew what *agū* was. As I often go to Okinawa, I had heard about it, but pretended not to know. The boss excitedly explained that it was a type of pork that comes from a breed of pig native to Okinawa, raised with great care, and whose meat is known for its well-marbled texture and rich flavour. They had ordered the best *agū* for me, and were looking forward to me trying it. I timidly said that I do not eat a lot of meat, but that I was more than happy to have all the vegetables that would come with it. The room went silent. The boss changed his expression instantly, saying sternly: 'No way. Then we are going to a different restaurant to eat what you prefer.' He was trying to offer the best hospitality, so it would have been incredibly rude to refuse the well-planned banquet that they had so kindly organised. I broke the tension with a laugh and assured him that the fact I do not usually eat meat would make the occasion all the more special. When they presented me with a huge dish of finely cut pork, I had to fight against my morals to take the first bite, but I have to admit it was one of the best flavours I have ever tasted.

The researcher who is faced with moral and ethical dilemmas in the field must make quick decisions to solve them in a way that is not damaging to themselves, while being aware that an inflexible attitude can have a negative impact on participants. On these occasions, general ethical guidelines are not very helpful. Although one's core values might be challenged in fieldwork, researchers should try to have as little impact on the field as possible. I strongly believe that animals do not need to be harmed for human consumption if there is an alternative, but fieldwork is not the place to lecture others about it. A brief, light-hearted remark is usually sufficient to convey one's stance on personal values. I believe in gender equality, but it is fruitless for me to try to convince men who have strong sexist convictions that adultery and exploitation of certain categories of women are not acceptable. While these behaviours should not be condoned, openness, kindness, and acceptance, coupled with appropriate detachment and non-judgement, are the only attitudes conducive to effective fieldwork.

Dealing with ethics in fieldwork

Both fieldwork periods were preceded by extensive and rigorous reflections on the ethics and dangers of doing fieldwork with groups involved in organised crime.[2] Ethics protocols are invaluable in helping the researcher understand the implications of their research and ensuring that participants are aware of their rights and are not harmed by the interview process. However, it is also important to be realistic and flexible when conducting fieldwork with present and former members of criminal groups. Presenting information sheets and informed consent forms, meticulously prepared to comply with ethics guidelines, is not always advisable. It can either make the researcher look disconnected from the reality in which participants live, or it might even come across as a performative act to establish dominance. This might alienate the participant, who may see the paperwork as intimidating, and it can ultimately compromise the fieldwork. The first time I met with a yakuza boss during my PhD fieldwork, I made the mistake of immediately presenting him with my paperwork for reading and signing. He glanced at it and said, 'We can do this later', which was a polite way of saying that he would not sign any documents. I still remember that afternoon as the most humbling episode in my fieldwork: I acted as an inexperienced researcher (which I undoubtedly was), mechanically repeating the protocol I had learnt at university. I soon realised that with that gesture I had created a distance, but the boss forgave my clumsy attempt and I was able to restore a friendly atmosphere with the following conversation. Members of the police had a similar reaction and ultimately, all refused to sign any paperwork. In their case, I learnt that as civil servants they were not supposed to sign any documents. Often, participants who were

[2] This research was approved by the ethics commissions of Birkbeck, Risshō University, the University of Oxford, Nagoya University, and the European Commission.

willing to sign the consent forms did not read the information sheet, or read it as if forced, again creating impatience and frustration. So it is important to be flexible: relying too much on rules can reduce ethics to a pedantic attitude of rule-following, and, in many cases, breaking the rules that were established by ethics boards does not necessarily result in unethical conduct (Haggerty, 2004). Although obtaining written consent is always preferable, when doing fieldwork with current and former members of organised crime, or other vulnerable participants such as prisoners, clear and concise oral consent is often the best approach to inform participants of the research background, its aims, and their rights. When I handed out copies of the paperwork to participants, I often found these later, abandoned on a table. It was more efficient to give a business card, telling participants to contact me with any questions or in case they wished to withdraw their consent.

Another point that required careful consideration before the fieldwork was whether or not the conversations would be recorded. Varese (2001) and Hamill (2010) caution against the use of tape recorders during interviews, as they might inhibit participants from talking freely. I decided at first to record interviews, after obtaining consent from the respondents, since I was concerned about missing out details or not understanding some expressions. However, I found that taking notes during the interview or immediately afterwards was more feasible in practice: conversations with yakuza members in particular tended to be lengthy and wide-ranging, making continuous recording impractical. As noted by Hamill (2010) in her fieldwork in Northern Ireland, asking too many questions is counterproductive. Instead of a rigid question-and-answer format, I allowed the conversation to flow naturally, while keeping in mind key topics of interest to make sure that we would touch on them. This method often yielded unexpected insights and made the conversation more enjoyable for the respondents. Depending on the respondent, as they spoke, I would take notes in a mix of English, Italian, and Japanese, and later I would systematise them in English on my laptop. If I could not take notes, I would write down the contents of the conversations as soon as I got home so that my memory would not fail me.

Interviews took place in a variety of settings, wherever participants felt more at ease: restaurants, bars, cafés, yakuza offices, police headquarters, law offices, churches, and charities. When at restaurants and cafés with current and former yakuza members, the ethical issue of who is paying the bill becomes a pressing one. In the case of Japan, being the only woman and the youngest person, it would be considered extremely rude if I paid for men my senior. Furthermore, even if I had wanted to make the gesture, the bills never arrived at the table, they were settled separately. I became aware that this arrangement was not universal when, in conversation with a Japanese journalist about yakuza members we both knew, he asked whether I ever paid during such meetings. I replied that I had never even seen a bill; he noted that, in his case, it was typically split. This exchange suggested that, while hospitality towards a researcher was certainly part of the equation, my age, gender, and foreign status also shaped how these interactions were structured. When I was with journalists or researchers, we offered alternately to buy food or a round of drinks.

Within the panorama of entrepreneurialisation and bureaucratisation of universities (Fisher, 2009; Ovetz, 1996), it has become apparent that the increasing requirements of ethics assessments and procedures have little to do with the safety of the researcher or the rights of the participants, but are mostly related to the increased need of universities to avoid any kind of legal liability from the fieldwork. Ethics reviews have recently been under scrutiny for their increasing grip on research, with the imposition of restrictive regulations to the point where they are being accused of restricting academic freedom to protect their reputation (Hedgecoe, 2016). Researchers are asked to respond to imagined risks that are not likely to occur, and are asked to undergo a pervasive scrutiny for activities that, in a related field like journalism, would raise no ethical concerns (Haggerty, 2004). The scrutiny under which researchers are placed and the extensive self-reflecting reports required for external evaluation add significant labour to the research process, often disproportionate to the benefits they provide. Despite claims of cultural sensitivity, ethics committees, which cannot always fully grasp the nuances of every research context, may impose procedures that undermine the rapport crucial for effective participant engagement. Asking participants from certain backgrounds to read and sign long information sheets and consent forms written in academic jargon harms the dignity of participants and breaks the trust with the researcher. Requirements for achieving gender balance in the respondents' pool in a field that is entirely populated by men constitute a further unrealistic expectation that many researchers have been facing. Achieving it at any cost would mean paradoxically going against the principle of data minimisation, which prescribes collecting only necessary data. Ethics requirements are an important way to reflect on fieldwork and ways to ensure participants will not be harmed by participating in it, but it may be unrealistic, and sometimes inappropriate, to mechanically apply standard procedures in sensitive fieldwork settings, such as those involving organised crime.

Anonymity

Anonymising participants is often a central requirement for doing research. While journalists also provide anonymity to confidential sources, anonymity in academia is the starting assumption: informants should be anonymised unless explicit permission has been provided. Haggerty (2004) poses the bizarre case of a journalist and an academic interviewing a prominent author, in which only the academic who wants to name the author would have to undergo the ethics review and obtain formal consent. In criminological research, anonymity is the default position, but it carries many fundamental issues, such as making it hard to judge the external validity of the work and fact-checking, losing important contextual information, and undermining internal validity (Varese, 2022). In *The Mafia of a Sicilian Village 1860–1960* (Blok, 1974), anonymity protocols are strict to the point of anonymising the name of the village in which fieldwork takes place. However, the village has a unique ethnic composition that creates special dynamics that, for the sake of anonymity, are ignored in the book, and makes it difficult to evaluate findings of the research (Varese, 2021, 2022). Extreme anonymisation might therefore take away precious context and be counterproductive to the point that it skews existing data.

Hamill (2010) anonymises participants but discloses the name of the place or the organisation to which each participant belongs, demonstrating that relevant details can be revealed without posing risks to the researcher or the participant. This book takes the same approach. Anonymising to the point of making a place and its people unrecognisable does not give the reader the necessary context, risks missing out important details, and hinders the reader from checking material against other sources. As for the current research, anonymity was granted to almost all participants. When reassuring them that they would be anonymised, several participants noted that they would not mind having their name in the book, and a few insisted on it. This echoes Lusthaus (2018), who found that several former cybercriminals he interviewed expressed a desire to be named. In this book, however, naming individuals would not have added analytical value and a decision was made to anonymise participants wherever possible. Exceptions were made where anonymisation was either impossible or unnecessary: for instance, it would have been useless to anonymise one of the only two living women to have been an active member of the yakuza, Nishimura Mako, or the most famous legal adviser to the Yamaguchi-gumi, Yamanouchi Yoshio, as they would have been recognised instantly with a simple search online. In order to make the text readable without having to remember participants' names, they will still be referred by their profession rather than their name, which is available in the appendix. While specific details of the places will not be given, name of cities or prefectures will be indicated where useful. Data on the participant's gender or the city in which a group was based were also not anonymised as they are relevant information for the story.

Getting and keeping in touch

Researching criminal groups often requires using the social networks of the respondents (Atkinson and Flint, 2004). I was able to reach informants via introductions from other participants, who often offered to make the connection spontaneously—most notably Japanese journalists and researchers specialising in organised crime, who had established relationships across different syndicates and regions. On two occasions, I was able to reach two informants simply by emailing them. In the case of the yakuza, high-ranking members refrain from introducing high-ranking members from other groups. For them, meeting with a researcher from a foreign university is a matter of pride that they prefer to keep exclusive. Once, I asked a boss in Tokyo if he could introduce me to a yakuza boss in Nagoya as I was living there. Nagoya is the stronghold of the Kōdō-kai, the most influential group of the Yamaguchi-gumi. The boss in Tokyo is from another prominent syndicate, with friendly relations to the Kōdō-kai. To my request, he replied, alarmed, 'Has something happened? Do you need help with some situation?' I explained that I was fine and I just wanted to meet someone working in Nagoya. He said he could help me with anything else, except introducing me to other bosses.

Given that talking to the yakuza is now more difficult than in the past, I could not make a selection of groups I wanted to talk to. However, since I talked to anyone who was willing to talk to me, I was able to meet with current and former members of different groups. As for their ranking, I mainly spoke with active high-ranking members, but sometimes I was able to talk to the members who accompanied them. Most of the participants were male: yakuza affiliation has traditionally been closed for women, and, indeed, it is only in very rare instances that women take full part in the operations of criminal syndicates. However, I was able to interview on multiple occasions Nishimura Mako, one of the only two known women to have undergone the affiliation ceremony of the yakuza and to have become a fully fledged member (Baradel, 16/01/2024, see Chapter 3). Similarly, researching organised crime in Japan is a predominantly male domain, a fact which was strongly reflected in the researchers, journalists, and police officers that I met. All participants were aged between late 20s and 70s. Regarding the geographical spread, the interviews were conducted in Tokyo and the surrounding areas, in Osaka, Nagoya, Kyūshū, and Okinawa.

Prior to beginning my fieldwork, Hirosue Noboru, an author and researcher on the yakuza, warned me about the questions one should not ask active or former yakuza members. Above all, *yubitsume* (the self-inflicted practice of severing one's own fingertip as an act of repentance or punishment) is a sensitive topic, and thus interviewers should avoid asking any questions about the circumstances that led to this. This is because it is highly likely that a participant who is missing one or more of their fingertips made a mistake deemed to be serious enough to warrant the amputation of their finger, and, as such, would be embarrassed at having to recount the episode. However, on multiple occasions, the participants offered explanations about the circumstances that led to the practice and even explained to me the best techniques to amputate fingertips. I was also instructed to avoid directing questions on income and drugs to active criminals, unless—and this often happened—the respondent willingly introduced the topic. The reasons for not asking directly about criminal activities were twofold: on the one hand, this places the researcher in an uncomfortable position towards both the participant and the law; on the other hand, although it is undoubtedly useful to possess such information, there is no way to corroborate this data, and, in fact, it is highly likely that participants would provide incorrect information about such sensitive topics. Current and former members often volunteered information about their criminal activities, without giving specific details, while being reluctant to disclose their involvement in inflicting physical harm on another person.

The way a method is deployed is also of paramount importance. Researchers must pay due care to the respondent's mental and emotional state during an interview, especially when the topic being discussed is as sensitive as one's criminal past (or present). During the interviews, I tried to maintain a respectful and non-judgemental attitude. As many scholars have noted, it is of utmost importance not to exhibit a horrified or amazed reaction when participants are recounting the unethical behaviour they have engaged in (Varese, 2001; Wong, 2019). Former members of the yakuza who had abandoned their career in the syndicate to become priests were particularly willing to confess their past wrongful actions. For these individuals, their new faith deepened their perception of the crimes they had committed, especially those who inflicted violence against other people. Many of the participants who used to be involved in criminal activities were eager to explain the reasons why they initially joined the yakuza, which were often connected to a sense of abandonment and loneliness, and the humanity that emerged out of their accounts was often disarming. As for the people who were criminally active at the time of the interview, they were careful enough not to disclose anything too incriminating, but were happy to talk about methods to protect their territory, or to force shop owners to pay protection money. In that case, I remembered that these are organisation dynamics that the individual decides to take part in, but not for his own enjoyment, and I refrained from assigning moral values to these behaviours. After talking for long hours with participants about their personal lives and hardships, my view has increasingly become that there are people who make bad choices, but there are not intrinsically bad people, and that people who cause hurt are often the first to be suffering.

Providing details of the individual biography of the researcher is a common strategy for negotiating access (Hobbs, 2001), therefore one must be prepared to share parts of their own lives with their informants. Although in the literature this is often described as a practice that tends to occur between women, scholars have noted that male participants can also expect the disclosure of information from researchers (Russell, Touchard, and Porter, 2002), which proved to be the case in my own fieldwork. Given the sensitivity of the topic, and in an effort to establish a trusting relationship with my informants, prior to the interviews, I shared details about myself and my research with them. This was particularly the case with high-ranking members of the yakuza, who often organised preliminary meetings in public spaces such as cafés or restaurants to talk casually about what I do, and other general topics. During these meetings, a reversed dynamic occurs where the participant evaluates the researcher. In such instances, attempting to steer the conversation towards research-relevant topics can be futile and even detrimental. The willingness of researchers to share personal information is pivotal in negotiating their engagement. Often, informants will divulge details about their group once they feel comfortable, whether during the initial meeting or subsequent interactions.

Dealing with the police

Studies on organised crime ordinarily rely on the valuable assistance of police agencies to gather information on criminal groups and their activities.

In the case of the ethnography that forms the basis of this book, it proved easier to get in touch with a yakuza boss than it did with the police. Fieldwork with Japanese police has been conducted by several scholars in the past (see Ames, 1981; Bayley, 1991; Miyazawa, 1992), who all reported on the relative ease with which they gained access to the agency. On the other hand, Stark (1981), because of the unprecedented access he had to a yakuza group, could not talk to the police, as he was warned by the boss of the group he studied. Hill recounted that he was easily able to get in contact with 'serving officers at nearly all levels within the police hierarchy' (Hill, 2003: 3), both amongst the Iwate prefectural police and the National Police Agency (NPA) in Tokyo. In this regard, my experience was markedly different. After having met and talked to a member of the NPA at an international conference, who appeared eager to help me in any way that she could, I left the event promising that I would be in touch once the fieldwork started. I messaged soon after my arrival in Japan, but despite some promising initial correspondence and after having agreed to refer me to someone in the relevant office, she subsequently stopped replying to my emails altogether. I sought advice from research-active professors and from independent researchers and was told that recently it had become very difficult to get in touch with members of the NPA, especially in regard to yakuza-related affairs. A common explanation for this was that, as we were approaching the 2020 Tokyo Olympics, the government and the police were reluctant to spread news about the yakuza, irrespective of whether it was good or bad, as any publicity would just draw attention to the issue, which had otherwise practically been forgotten, especially on the international stage where news on the yakuza is hardly ever translated and broadcast.

I was luckier in my second fieldwork period, when my then supervisor, Federico Varese, introduced me to a high-ranking police officer at the NPA in Tokyo, who then became a prefectural chief of police. This police officer was instrumental in granting me access to the prefectural Organised Crime division and Narcotics and Firearms division that he oversaw. Having received their superior's permission, the officers were very cooperative and helpful in answering all my questions, and they put in extra effort to prepare materials and presentations with information not available to the general public. Furthermore, with the introduction of a researcher, I was also able to talk to an officer at the National Centre for the Removal of Organised Crime (NCROC), an organisation dependent on the police. I approached the police and NCROCs in other prefectures, but the interviews typically began with officers reading from publicly available national reports. When

I posed questions that went beyond the context of these reports, their response would be that they could only provide information contained within the report itself. While an initial reaction may be frustration, it is important for researchers conducting fieldwork in Japan to consider the significant role that hierarchy plays in Japanese organisations. Even though many individuals might be willing to assist, their ability to do so often depends on their receiving approval from their superiors. Establishing trust and building connections through personal introductions, flexibility, and persistence are necessary to navigate the bureaucratic challenges encountered during such research, even though sometimes the only chance to gain access is through a lucky encounter.

Danger and obstacles in the field

Criminological fieldwork is often seen as a 'risky' (Monaghan, 2006) and 'dangerous' fieldwork (Jacobs, 2006, see also Belousov et al., 2007; Lee-Treweek and Linkogle, 2002; van Uhm, 2016), which requires stepping out of one's comfort zone (Monaghan, 2006). Indeed, many ethnographies of organised crime have highlighted the dangers for researchers: Sánchez Jankowski (1991) mentions that he had to undergo a 'fighting test' to get access to the gangs, and he was subsequently hurt twice. Barnes (2025) recalls many occasions on which shots were fired near him when he was carrying out ethnographical studies in Brazil.

One of the questions I am often asked when talking about my research, is whether I have ever felt scared or in danger. I reply that I felt anxious only once. I was given an appointment to meet a yakuza boss at 15:00 in a busy shopping centre in Tokyo. This was the first encounter I had with an active high-ranking member of the yakuza. I thought he would meet me there and then we would go to a nearby café. Although he had been introduced to me by an authoritative journalist, the meeting made me nervous, but I felt reassured that he had chosen a public space for the encounter. As I sat on a bench in the shopping centre, I was approached by two men in elegant navy suits, who asked me my name and said that they would take me to their boss. Still thinking we would walk there, I was taken aback when they escorted me out and pointed to a big black car. 'We will drive you there, please get in the car.' I was at a crossroads: either leave and never meet the yakuza boss, or trust them. I climbed into the backseat. I decided to trust them for a simple reason: their reputation. Indeed, reputation is one of the crucial assets for a criminal group, and for the yakuza, it is particularly significant as they enjoyed a good reputation for decades prior to the anti-yakuza measures of the last thirty years. Furthermore, I was confident that this group had no interest in harming me and that the introduction from the journalist meant that there was virtually no chance something bad could happen. I wanted to show that I trusted them, since without trust between researchers and participants, the researcher cannot rely on the information gathered and the informant may withhold potentially important information. This is particularly true when researchers engage with marginalised groups, or outsiders, as the willingness to share with a researcher is necessarily based on trust and an honest rapport (Brunson and Pegram, 2015). On this occasion, my trust proved not to be misplaced, we met at a café and the meeting took place without incident.

Doing fieldwork with people who are involved in active criminal groups undoubtedly carries risks, but such risks have also been exaggerated to paint the researcher as a hero (Wong, 2015; Varese, 2022). In the case of Japan, the risk is sometimes inflated by journalistic accounts. Given that yakuza membership is not illegal, and, most importantly, that the yakuza have always prided themselves on being a group that does not engage in violence against common citizens, conducting fieldwork with criminal groups in Japan presents less risk of physical danger to researchers. There has been a tendency to overstate the risks of dealing with the yakuza on the part of some foreign journalists who exaggerate the danger they encountered in the field. This tendency has made Japanese journalists working on the yakuza wary of extending their trust to foreign researchers. I experienced this with one of the most important journalists in the field, who at first refused to meet with me. When I finally gained his trust, he explained his position: in the past, he had been generous with a famous foreign journalist but found that his trust had been misplaced as the journalist gave an unrealistic and biased picture of the Japanese criminal underworld. With time and experience, I came to understand very well what he meant.

An additional hurdle for academics conducting research on the yakuza in Japan is the lack of institutional support. In the best-case scenario, there is a general lack of interest, while in the worst-case scenario, Japanese universities display explicit hostility towards such research. Criminology is not widely popular in Japan and studies on organised crime remain severely limited, resulting in a scarcity of guidance, supervision, and expertise in this area. The introduction of the 2010–2011 Yakuza Exclusionary Ordinances has further complicated matters, as any form of engagement with the yakuza can lead to sanctions. Universities are particularly wary of potential liability associated with researchers contacting current or former yakuza members and other criminals, actively discouraging research in this field. Once again, personal networks remain the primary means for navigating these challenges. I was fortunate to find hosts in both Risshō University and Nagoya University who supported my work, trusted my skills, and believed in the value of academic freedom.

Reliability and relaying messages

When conducting fieldwork, one of the main issues is the reliability of the data collected (Englander, 2012). In particular, doing interviews with active members of organised criminal groups who have numerous motives not to tell the truth about themselves, makes this matter even more pressing. Chin (2007) in his fieldwork in the Golden Triangle, talks at length about how participants' deceit influenced his work. It is not uncommon for researchers carrying out fieldwork with offenders and prisoners to have to confront the assumption that the participants in their study cannot be trusted in what they say. The experiences of researchers talking to active and former offenders is often characterised by the eagerness and openness of their participants' accounts (Waldram, 2007); indeed, Jacobs (2006) points out how, on different occasions, offenders gave unsolicited accounts of sensitive information and serious crimes they had committed because they needed to get it off their chest. Not being able to talk to their peers, criminals often turn to researchers because the social distance between them allows them to talk freely. Indeed, both respondents who are still offenders and those who used to engage in criminal activities are especially eager to share their own version of the facts when it is made clear that the researcher has no power over them and no reason to harm them (Waldram, 2007).

Although reliability is always a problem when conducting in-depth interviews, it is particularly relevant in studies involving criminal actors whose accounts cannot be cross-referenced. Triangulation is often used in criminology as a reliable method for enhancing the validity of the data collected, either through the use of multiple methods of triangulation—such as written documents, follow-up or group interviews, CCTV pictures and video footage, accounts from other people (Bernasco, 2011)—or multiple triangulations—actor triangulation or triangulation of context (Hamill, 2010; Lindegaard and Bernasco, 2018). In the event that time and monetary constraints do not allow for such a thorough triangulation process, a more informal way to check the validity of the stories collected involves observing patterns in the responses of different participants, as conducted by Zhang and Chin in their study (2003).

It is not easy for criminals to communicate, and they often have to find ways to convey their message to the right recipient without attracting unwanted attention. They might do so with costly signals (e.g. killing, fighting) or through more conventional signals and trademarks (Gambetta, 2009). Unlike other criminal groups, the yakuza, due to their unique legal status, face fewer communication restrictions and have capitalised on this by disseminating their messages through films, magazines, and manga. Across these media, the yakuza consistently portray themselves as custodians of traditional Japan, adhering strictly to an ancient and coherent set of principles, defining their organisational structure and ideology across all yakuza groups. As explored in subsequent chapters, the yakuza maintain a strong self-image, a cohesive mission, and a robust value system that they aim to communicate to the world.

However, the signalling cost for the yakuza has notably increased in the past thirty years, while their avenues for self-expression have greatly reduced. Speaking to friendly journalists and researchers has become a crucial way for the yakuza to convey their perspective during what they perceive as a period in which they are often misunderstood. Informants have a vested interest in shaping researchers' interpretations of reality, knowing that academics can retell and endorse their stories with objectivity. Ethnographic seduction describes both intentional and unconscious strategies of persuasion deployed during fieldwork in studies of violence and conflict. Seduction aims to put the ethnographer at ease and divert their gaze away from critical inquiries, while at the same time fostering a sense of deep understanding of participants' lives. However, this approach can sometimes lead researchers to avoid asking critical questions for fear of disrupting rapport (Nordstrom and Robben, 1995).

The high-ranking yakuza members I met had great conversational experience and flair. They were used to mediating, giving speeches, and persuading. Ethnographic seduction, in their case, extended beyond verbal signals to include receptions in their offices and upscale restaurants, visits to festivals, and sharing of videos and images—all strategically designed to impress. However, I eventually found a pattern: recurrent tropes, such as embeddedness with the population, kindness, discipline, and talks of a heroic remote past were usually indicative of a seductive argument. Even people who were formerly involved with the yakuza adhered to this script, acknowledging past missteps such as drug use, violence, and abuse, yet asserting a strong ideological foundation for their yakuza careers. Conversely, participants who were not formal yakuza members did not justify their past actions morally. However, the yakuza are not the only group with a message for the public; the police also use strategic signals to send their message to the public and the research community as well, highlighting their authority, efficiency, and commitment to public safety.

Other sources

This book used a vast array of official sources. These include reports such as the White Papers of the Police (*Keisatsu Hakusho*), the White Paper of Crime (*Hanzai Hakusho*), the Report on the Situation of Organised Crime (*Soshiki Hanzai no Jōsei*), and aggregated statistics by the Portal Site of Official Statistics of Japan (e-Stat, Ministry of Justice). Furthermore, I had access to a wealth of publications closely aligned with the yakuza, which warrant a more detailed explanation.

First and foremost, magazines such as *Jitsuwa Jidai*, *Bull*, and their special editions served as invaluable resources until they were discontinued in 2019. *Jitsuwa Jidai* (referenced in the text as JJ followed by month and year of publication), renowned for its coverage of criminal and controversial topics, featured detailed articles and reports on yakuza news, conflicts, leadership changes, and opinion pieces. It provided comprehensive narratives, interviews with underworld figures, and investigative reports, making it a significant source for understanding the yakuza's evolution. Hill (2003), who also made use of these sources, notes that they are often disparaged by Japanese criminologists. In my experience, the majority of criminologists in Japan ignore, or at worst belittle, the study of the yakuza *in toto*, regardless of the sources, but the few that give it enough dignity, agree that these magazines do hold some value. Suzuki Tomohiko, former editor of *Bull* and prominent yakuza journalist, vouched for the reliability of the information reported in these magazines. It is important to note that these publications did not investigate criminal plans or scandals involving the yakuza but reported on them as a legitimate organisation. Consequently, the yakuza not only welcomed these magazines but also supported their publication by providing information to the journalists.

Bull, a similar magazine from the same publisher, features articles akin to those in *Jitsuwa Jidai* but also includes more general content on politics, the economy, and manga. Both magazines were widely purchased by yakuza members to stay informed about leadership changes, conflict dynamics, alliances, and other pertinent matters. However, they were also popular among regular office workers. As confirmed by Suzuki, office workers often saw resemblances between their companies and yakuza groups: the vertical hierarchy, the stubborn boss, the rules, the long work hours, and socialisation through drinking were all relatable topics. Simultaneously, these workers could perceive their lives through the lens of a criminal syndicate, imbued with danger and heroism, tapping into the excitement their daily work lacked. As well as the monthly issues, there were special editions where a single topic would be extensively covered, such as special issues on a specific criminal organisation or a particular conflict.

Although many manga are centred on fictional yakuza stories, specific series of manga, such as those published by Bamboo Comics, exclusively featured real-life stories of yakuza bosses or yakuza conflicts, or nonfictional tales of events within the yakuza world, in a positive light. Additionally, there are manga that convey the ideology and code of rules of the yakuza to the everyday company worker. For instance, in '*Yakuza ni manabu shidōryoku*' ([Leadership skills that can be learned from the yakuza] Yamadaira, 2003) a senior office worker well-versed in the yakuza world shares tales of yakuza life with his struggling co-workers, to help them overcome their challenges in a manner consistent with traditional Japanese, or yakuza, values.

A particularly unique source is the *Ninkyō Daihyakka*, the comprehensive encyclopaedia of *ninkyō*.[3] This book was published in 1983 by Fujita Gorō, a yakuza-turned-writer. Only a handful of copies are available on the market, but I was fortunate enough to find a copy in good condition in a small old bookshop in Osaka. This copy included an addendum in which the author corrected mistakes from the first and only edition. With a red fabric cover and the title in golden characters, the book contains complete family trees of yakuza groups active at the time of writing. It also includes detailed descriptions of the yakuza's ideology, its Chinese origins, rituals, and rules of traditional gambling games.

[3] *Ninkyō* refers to the code of honour that the yakuza abides by. See Chapter 2 for a detailed explanation.

Limitations

This book contains several limitations, common to research on organised crime. The book's empirical core is based primarily on qualitative fieldwork conducted in Japan, focusing on the yakuza and their socio-economic entanglements. While this approach enabled in-depth and sustained engagement, the number of people I was able to speak with is necessarily limited. Access to criminal and law enforcement actors is difficult, and both yakuza and police interviewees had clear stakes in how they were represented. Their accounts, therefore, offered partial and often strategic visions of the situation, and not all information could be cross-verified. The strong ideology and rhetoric of the yakuza often came through in interviews with active and former members, and obfuscated accounts of their groups. The book also prioritises the perspective of actors operating within or adjacent to the yakuza, which may not fully capture the experiences of victims or marginalised communities affected by organised crime. Specific figures on yakuza activities and those of other criminal groups are unavailable. At the time of writing, the yakuza consists of twenty-five syndicates active across Japan, and although they share rules and codes of behaviour, providing a comprehensive account of the yakuza as a whole remains nearly impossible. Local markets and dynamics shape the yakuza in different ways: a yakuza member from Tokyo differs significantly from one in the countryside due to different markets, levels of integration with local communities, and relationships with law enforcement. I tried to present an overarching description of the yakuza while highlighting local nuances where possible, but the complexity and regional diversity of the yakuza is inevitably compromised. Finally, while the study touches on transnational developments, its primary focus remains domestic.

However, the book makes a significant contribution to a field that has been largely ignored since Hill's *The Japanese Mafia* (2003). Since his account, the Japanese criminal landscape has changed dramatically: the yakuza have experienced a considerable decline in membership and influence, while new criminal actors and networks have emerged. This book explores how market reform and third-party regulations have forced the yakuza out of several markets, and examines how the yakuza have adapted to these challenges while maintaining their core governance function. Additionally, it provides the first academic account of the new panorama of the Japanese criminal underworld, where the yakuza are no longer the only players.

2

Illicit authorities

A history of yakuza governance

Introduction

During one of my visits to a yakuza office a few years ago, the boss spent the afternoon recounting the origins of his group, proudly tracing its lineage back to the Meiji period (1868–1912). It was not just a nostalgic exercise. For him, the history of his group mattered as it was the proof that he was not the boss of a street gang, but of a serious and traditional organisation. For many yakuza members, the history of the yakuza is not distant folklore or nostalgic myth-making, but evidence that legitimises the yakuza's place in the contemporary world. Though the syndicates as we know them today crystallised in the aftermath of the Second World War, they rightly claim much older roots, linking themselves to gamblers, peddlers, and other marginal figures of early Japan. Similarly to other mafias, they originated in the premodern period, before the state consolidated its monopoly on violence or regulation (Paoli, 2002).

This chapter offers a historical reconstruction of the yakuza's evolution with a particular focus on their governance function, defined here as the capacity to regulate behaviour, resolve disputes, enforce norms, and stabilise markets, often in ways that supplement or substitute state functions. It asks not merely what the yakuza have done over time, but what kind of order they have produced, in what types of spaces, and with what degrees of legitimacy. Drawing on criminal governance scholarship, it frames the yakuza not simply as purveyors of violence or illicit goods, but as actors embedded in the governance of social and economic life (see Arias, 2006; Lessing, 2021; Moncada, 2021). Like other criminal groups operating in institutionally weak environments, the yakuza have historically stepped in to mediate conflicts, enforce informal property rights, allocate market access, and manage territory, particularly in spaces where state regulation was absent or contested. The yakuza also built and maintained authority through embeddedness in local communities, reciprocal relations with business actors, and strategic

21st Century Yakuza. Martina Baradel, Oxford University Press. © Martina Baradel 2026.
DOI: 10.1093/9780191987755.003.0003

alliances with political and police institutions. As Varese (2001, 2011) has shown, mafias that endure do so not because they impose violence efficiently, but because they provide services that are socially necessary, politically tolerated, and economically valuable. The yakuza fit this model, as their presence in urban and industrial life was not only visible, but institutionalised through networks of collusion, as well as state and social tolerance.

At the heart of this chapter is a question of historical scope: how far back does the governance function of the yakuza extend? Were the *bakuto* (gamblers, a group which also included labour contractors and hoodlums) and *tekiya* (itinerant peddlers of medicines and small commodities) of the Tokugawa period (1603–1868) already functioning as regulators, or did the capacity to govern only emerge as the modern state matured in the Meiji (1868–1912) and postwar periods? This question requires us to consider when and how coercive actors become political actors, when violence becomes rule-making, and when organised crime ceases to be an exception to order and begins to participate in its production.

By examining the long history of the yakuza, this chapter aims to contribute to broader debates on the nature of criminal governance and its relationship to state formation. The argument unfolds chronologically, tracing how governance functions first emerged in fragmented form, expanded through urbanisation and political alliance, and became territorially institutionalised, showing that yakuza governance was not a postwar phenomenon but a recurring response to the same conditions—institutional weakness, demand for informal order, and state tolerance of extra-legal authority.

Early formations and yakuza mythology

Even the yakuza have their historians. The most famous of these is undoubtedly Fujita Gorō, an ex-yakuza who published the *Ninkyō Daihyakka* (Comprehensive Encyclopedia of Chivalrous Organizations), a detailed book that merges historical facts and yakuza mythology. While these origin narratives do not provide reliable historiography, they can reveal how governance, protection, and moral authority became central to the yakuza's own self-understanding. The first part of the book tells the history of the yakuza in its most embryonic form, that of gamblers and peddlers in Japan. It starts in the Nara period (710–784) where, in the capital of Nara, an East market and West market were established, and the city governor would control trade in the city. There were additional markets controlled directly by the imperial court, such as that of Tsubaki (Yamato), Azu (Izu), and Mikō (Kawachi). In peripheral regions, markets popped up in strategic nodes, at important crossroads or in populated areas with fisheries. Mountain populations lacked access to salt and fish, and island dwellers lacked grain, necessitating the rise of itinerant merchants who connected disparate economies. These included seaborne traders (*ama*), mountain people (*sanjin*), and vagabonds (*furōnin*), whose nomadic lifestyles laid the groundwork for early non-sedentary commercial networks. From these vagabonds emerged the *kagushi*, itinerant merchants considered precursors to the *tekiya*. A parallel lineage arose from itinerant woodworkers, who were in high demand during the construction of feudal castles and residences. Like *bakuto*, woodworkers elaborated a moral code (the *kobiki jingi*) which prescribed proper conduct when staying as guests, and which was later adopted by gamblers and itinerant merchants (Fujita, 1983). By developing their own moral codes and embedding themselves in the logistical and social infrastructure of itinerant commerce, these early groups facilitated trade and contributed to the informal ordering of marginal economies, a developmental trajectory that Fujita suggests anticipates some of the functions that would later characterise more formalised yakuza syndicates.

Another important figure in the mythology of the yakuza is the *machi-yakko* or 'town servants', widely regarded as precursors to later yakuza formations. Emerging in the early Tokugawa period, the *machi-yakko* were local vigilantes who defended townspeople from abusive samurai and *hatamoto* (direct retainers of the shogunate), and whose activities laid the groundwork for the development of urban-based groups claiming to act in the name of justice and protection (J1). Fujita reports this part of history as well. After the Battle of Sekigahara (1600), Tokugawa Ieyasu, founder and first shogun of the Tokugawa shogunate, implemented a strategic redistribution of authority: he granted actual political power to the *fudai daimyō* (hereditary vassals loyal to the Tokugawa before the battle) without assigning them significant landholdings, while awarding land but withholding power from the *tozama daimyō* (those who had not been early Tokugawa allies). This arrangement generated discontent across both groups, destabilising early Tokugawa alliances. During this period, some *hatamoto* exploited their status to act with impunity against rural communities. In response, self-defence alliances—composed largely of servants and lower-status individuals—emerged, such as that under the leadership of Ōshima Ippei. When members of the group began retaliating against injustice, the shogunate viewed their defiance, and particularly their prioritisation of peer loyalty over hierarchical allegiance, as a potential threat to the feudal order. In 1612, Ōshima was executed by crucifixion alongside 300 of his followers. He is nevertheless remembered as the founding figure of Tokyo's *kyokyaku* (chivalrous outlaws), laying the foundation for the rise of the *machi-yakko*.

By the late seventeenth century, the *machi-yakko* often operated as intermediaries in urban labour markets, including the running of employment agencies, and towards the end of the century they were replaced by official fire-fighting brigades, which were also tasked with maintaining urban security. In 1718, magistrate Ōoka Tadasuke issued a directive granting a group of street vendors the right to carry swords and batons, thus granting them some limited authority. This formal extension of regulatory power was later applied to licensed gamblers as well. This genealogy, linking self-defence, honour, and protection of the population, is central to the mythology through which the yakuza retrospectively legitimise their origins. While it captures certain patterns of social organisation and informal authority, it should be understood more as a narrative of symbolic lineage than as a verifiable historical truth (Iwai, 1963).

It is commonly held that the groups of *bakuto* and *tekiya* in the Tokugawa era (1603–1867) are the predecessors of the yakuza (Hill, 2003; Iwai, 1963). Yet, as Hill (2003) argues, their emergence as a mafia-type organisation occurred only when private protection became central to their activities. From this perspective, the yakuza only began to take on such characteristics towards the end of the Tokugawa period, and it was not until the late Meiji period (1868–1912) that they consistently functioned as groups offering private protection. At the beginning of the Tokugawa period, gambling was strictly prohibited but the restrictions eventually relaxed and gamblers started to organise themselves in groups. By the end of the Tokugawa period, the state weakened as merchants accumulated immense economic power, creating a growing tension with a debt-ridden samurai class that nominally remained at the top of the social hierarchy (Sheldon, 1983). With many areas effectively unpoliced, gambling groups operated with increasing impunity. *Bakuto* leaders also became increasingly prominent figures outside of the gambling world, expanding into the booming construction sectors (Iwai, 1963). Shirayanagi Shūko (1916, in Iwai, 1963: 41) argues that the most famous *bakuto* leaders emerged from regions in which local administrations were powerless, further proving their role as alternative rights-enforcers and dispute-mediators. The origins of the *tekiya* are more disputed: given the nature of the trade, these groups were likely to be interested in limiting competition and organising spaces, and indeed some of their leaders were appointed to organise markets and open air trade in specific areas (Hill, 2003). However, there are no written records indicating with certainty their early organisation (Iwai, 1963).

These dynamics suggest that the yakuza's roots lie not just in criminality but in the organisation and regulation of certain areas of society. Both *bakuto* and *tekiya* were operating within and around the economic structures of their time, tolerated and sometimes mobilised by local authorities to enforce order where the state could not. These groups exhibited patterns that resemble, in embryonic form, what later scholarship would call governance functions. While modern syndicates have portrayed their origins in terms of chivalry and patriotic duty, the historical record suggests that their legitimacy rested on the practical function they performed, especially in the Tokugawa period, when these groups were scattered, locally embedded, and lacked any form of national coordination or unified political vision.

Meiji restoration: new cities, new yakuza

Since the beginning of the nineteenth century, economic development and political integration weakened the social divisions of the Tokugawa era, which were fortified by the racial, linguistic, and cultural homogeneity of a long-isolated Japan. These changes were manipulated by the newly formed Meiji regime, which aimed to cultivate a 'traditional' view of society based on a uniform social structure, institutionalised principles of morality—duty, obligation, hierarchy—and loyalty to the emperor (Hunter, 2013). At the same time, the Meiji government was determined to bring Japan from feudalism to modernity. It introduced new legal codes, property rights, and centralised power in the hands of the government (Varese, 2014). However, the rapid introduction of new legal codes and property rights outpaced the government's enforcement capacity, creating a vacuum that groups like the yakuza filled by offering rights enforcement and dispute mediation (Milhaupt and West, 2000) in sectors such as prostitution, entertainment, and construction industries (Iwai, 1963).

The organisation of Japanese cities, and, in turn, their residents, changed dramatically at the turn of the twentieth century: they became places of industrial development and grew in size to accommodate increased migration from the countryside. These changes profoundly affected the organisation of the yakuza. As Miyazaki states: 'The modern yakuza is born out of the modern city' (Miyazaki, 2008: 42). Above all, the prototype of the 'new' form of the yakuza came to be modelled on the 'great bosses' (*dai-oyabun*) that emerged in the context of the Wakamatsu harbour in Kitakyūshū city, such as the famous Yoshida Isokichi. The Meiji administration based its plan for economic growth on expanding the army and strengthening the industrial sector, which gave great impetus to the coal industry. The extracted coal needed to be transported by boat, as the railway system was still underdeveloped, so autonomous boatmen organised themselves into *gumi* (groups) to gain leverage with the mine owners. Yoshida soon became one of the boatmen's leaders, and often frequented gambling dens, where he came into contact with local yakuza. The tremendous impetus given to the local economy by the Russo–Japanese war of 1905 attracted many people from the surrounding territories and placed immense pressure on the city. The police were not strong enough to maintain social order since they were a relatively young institution, and so figures like Yoshida organised groups to provide self-defence, that gradually evolved into structured yakuza organisations. By mediating disputes among labourers, gambling circles, and local residents, he consolidated authority across overlapping social spheres. He also gained popularity because he successfully mediated disputes between yakuza groups and different interest groups in the world of sumo, a sport that was very popular at that time. Indeed, starting with the promotion of sumo events in his region, Yoshida's group gradually began to take control over the entertainment sector. Popular entertainers and artists were considered an underclass of outsiders, and thus it was only natural for the yakuza to act as their management. As entertainment became ever-more popular, this sector quickly became an important source of income for the yakuza. Furthermore, extra-legal arbitration of disputes was common, and usually entrusted to *kaoyaku* (influential men, or 'bosses'), who were ostensibly adhering to the code of chivalry known as *ninkyō*. So, at the turn of the century, these *ninkyō* organisations became the prototype for modern yakuza groups. The *oyabun-kobun* (father/boss-son/members) structure of the labour organisation was converted into the *oyabun-kobun* relationship of the *ninkyō* groups, and these groups soon became an important socio-economic force in their own right (Miyazaki, 2008). The trajectory of Yoshida and his contemporaries illustrates a broader pattern: where rapid urbanisation outpaced institutional capacity, informal leaders with coercive resources and social embeddedness stepped into the resulting vacuum, consolidating authority that was simultaneously economic, social, and proto-political.

At the beginning of the Meiji period, gamblers were often involved with social unrest. For instance, during the rural uprisings of Chichibu in 1884, *bakuto* played leading roles in organising and mobilising impoverished farmers. Known figures like Inoue Zensaku and Iizuka Morisaburō were instrumental in rallying discontented peasants under the guise of mutual aid and resistance to debt oppression. Their local reputation, hierarchical networks, and ability to intimidate or persuade made them effective organisers. But gambling groups were not nationally coordinated, and there were both groups aligned with the government, supporting the state and acting as informal enforcers, as well as groups aligned with the opposition movements. The authorities, alarmed by the political agenda together with the capacity for violence of these groups, carried out a crackdown on gamblers in 1890, under the Dajōkan Proclamation No. 1, which established regulations for punishing gambling offenders. However, the weakening of the gambler groups due to the great roundup was only temporary. During the economic boom surrounding the First Sino–Japanese War (1894–1895) and the Russo–Japanese War (1904–1905), these groups began to revive (Ino, 2000). The structure of their operations also evolved. Whereas they had previously focused almost exclusively on gambling, they began to operate within, and exercise control over, several markets, such as the red-light districts, the entertainment industry, and particularly industrial capital sectors like construction and mining. Within these sectors, they became involved in procuring cheap labour, managing workers, and enforcing harsh labour conditions (Iwai, 1963). In the red-light districts, their work typically involved running the door operations, serving as bodyguards, or monitoring the prostitutes who would often try to escape. In the entertainment sector, they began to manage and control performances held within their territories and collect 'greeting fees', which later evolved into organising and managing shows themselves. In construction and mining, their roles included providing labourers, preventing runaways, supervising worksites, managing lodging facilities, and controlling makeshift barracks (*takobeya*). Naturally, these roles brought them into connection with emerging corporate interests, and from there, it was a short step to building ties with local political circles, which eventually extended into national political connections (Ino, 2000).

Thus, the economic development that followed the reorganisation of the Japanese economy provided manifold opportunities for yakuza groups, who were already involved in the construction industry and the docks. Gamblers and peddlers remained heavily involved in their respective businesses, even though gambling in the open air was less and less tolerated, which led *bakuto* gangs to become more marginalised within society (Kaplan and Dubro, 2003). At the same time, peddlers received legal authorisation to open fixed stalls in the commercial streets of cities. This decision allowed *tekiya* gangs to expand into the city operating alongside, and increasingly blending with, legitimate shopkeepers (Mizushima, 1986). The revitalisation of the Japanese economy that followed the Meiji restoration was a period of significant expansion for the yakuza, as the array of new business activities meant heightened demand for extra-legal forms of protection, especially in a period when democratic institutions were in their embryonic form (Hill, 2003).

The Meiji period also reconfigured the political landscape in ways that drew yakuza into new alliances. Indeed, the new social order resulted in many ex-samurai feeling discontented over their lessened social role and the new regime's disregard of tradition. This discontent quickly became a breeding ground for militarism and patriotism, especially in areas where the samurai community was larger, such as Fukuoka in Kyūshū. In recognition of this, Toyama Mitsuru, who was himself a member of an impoverished samurai family, founded the Gen'yōsha (Dark Ocean Society) in 1881. The group's members were employed as government officials' bodyguards, goons for local politicians, as well as skilled labourers (e.g. carpenters and plumbers), and soon became a paramilitary force for Japanese politicians who used them to intimidate and harass their political adversaries and labourers. This new politically oriented yakuza assimilated with the traditional gambler and peddler groups. This process was also facilitated by the fact that, although the *bakuto* and *tekiya* did not have a well-defined political ideology, there were numerous similarities with ultranationalists (i.e. romanticisation of the past, worship of the Emperor and Shintō gods, structure, hostility towards the left and foreigners), which, in turn, led to a unification of politics and activities between the yakuza and rightists (Kaplan and Dubro, 2003; Siniawer, 2012).

During the Meiji restoration, the yakuza established close relationships within both the business and political spheres. They grew closer to ultranationalist movements, due to similarities in their ideologies and methods of accumulating wealth, while some groups even transformed into political and paramilitary groups. Moreover, taking advantage of the impetus that the new government had given to the national economy, they increasingly mixed with legitimate businesses (Mizushima, 1986), showing themselves to be suitably adroit at mingling with all sectors of society. It is thus possible to pinpoint within this historical juncture the consolidation of the connection between the yakuza and the power elites, particularly with respect to those on the right, which, in turn, allowed the yakuza to maintain a privileged position in the underworld for decades to come.

Territorial governance

The structural relationships within a yakuza group are strictly regulated by the relationship of the boss and the subordinates, elder and younger brothers. Respect for the relationships, rules, and unity is reinforced through the rituals, as will be shown in Chapter 3. These internal dynamics are overshadowed in favour of group unity when viewed from the outside. Each family must maintain solidarity, morality, and activity as a group. The authority of the boss and the group was traditionally expressed by the area they govern, named *nawabari* from the old custom of delimiting one's territory with a rope (*nawa*). The concept of *nawabari* is based on three ideas: a certain amount of land, the right to control it exclusively and arbitrarily, and a sharp delimitation that distinguishes between the inside and outside of the territory (Iwai, 1963). As reported in a 1890 article from the newspaper *Yomiuri Shinbun*, *bakuto* groups were highly territorial, and imposed borders between the areas (*nawabari*) of different groups. They employed ex-samurai to serve as professional enforcers, attempting to exert authority and taking on police-like functions (Yomiuri Shinbun, 19/02/1890).

In the *bakuto* tradition, the area controlled by the family is also known as *shima* (island) or *shimori* (defend to death). The boss had overall control of the gambling dens in that area and earned his living from the taxes of the dens, as well as the temple and other activities in the group's territory. He distributed the dens to his subordinates and had them manage them, and all members of the group received a percentage according to their level in the group. *Tekiya* territory was referred to as *niwaba* (garden grounds) and it pertained to the right to occupy certain roads or open spaces and set up stalls (Fujita, 1983). Because *tekiya* were typically responsible for itinerant activities like festivals and street stalls, they did not impose fixed taxes. Instead, event organisers had to notify the group and pay a usage fee. While the *tekiya* did not own the territory, they administered it by obtaining permits (*kamei-ryō*, or family name fees) through negotiations with police, temples, or shrines. These permits were then subleased to affiliated vendors. Affiliation with a strong family ensured better stall locations, prompting even independent vendors to enter into 'temporary assistance' agreements to secure access. *Tekiya* bosses became de facto territorial lords, monopolising specific areas under the group's name. They would also distribute these locations to their direct subordinates who, in turn, would collect protection money (e.g. refuse collection fees, space fees, miscellaneous fees, or duty fees) from vendors who relied on them. In Tokyo, all permanent street stalls were removed in 1951, altering the operational framework of the *tekiya*. In turn, *tekiya* deepened their influence in entertainment districts, transitioning into roles such as security for cafés, cabarets, and markets, or managing pachinko prizes. Since they differed in nature, the *bakuto* and *tekiya* could co-exist in the same territory. Furthermore, unlike the *bakuto*, the *tekiya* did not have clearly defined territorial boundaries. Multiple groups could co-exist within the same area, sharing the territory through mutual agreements.

Traditionally, within the territory, power is exercised at the discretion of the boss, and each group maintains their own livelihood based on the private benefits derived from their assigned zones. Territories are of utmost importance: expanding one's area of influence increases the boss's revenue, enhances authority, and elevates the position of the members, making territorial expansion the collective goal of the group. Yakuza norms explicitly acknowledge this dynamic. One principle holds that: 'only by protecting one's territory can we protect the boss's life'. In this sense, life does not only mean physical existence, but also survival as a yakuza group. Such principles create latent tensions between groups that, without regulation, can escalate into mutual destruction. Another motto states 'even a modest boss has his domain, and if other bosses wish to use it, they must negotiate access'. Territorial boundaries are mutually recognised and enforced, and violations invite sanctions from the entire community (Iwai, 1963).

One of the most enduring of these practices, particularly in the Kantō region, is *kashijima/karijima*. The practice involves renting out (*kashi*) or borrowing (*kari*) one's territory (*jima*). This system originally fulfilled a dual function: managing expansion pressure on one side and protecting declining groups on the other. The groups with an increasing membership must increase their revenue because new members need to earn their wages and pay the group fee. Since they cannot take over parts of the market that are already controlled by other senior members of their own group, they are likely to expand to new territories controlled by other yakuza groups, which will retaliate even if the controlling group is in decline. To prevent this from happening, yakuza groups whose membership is on the rise rent territory from yakuza groups whose membership is in decline. By doing so, the rising gang pays for the land they rent, and at the same time increases their business, securing a way to earn money for new gang members. On the other hand, the declining group preserves its position in a territory that might otherwise be lost. Although the group that rents their territory loses protection money from businesses in the area, they receive regular rent in return. Furthermore, if the territory is taken by force, the hierarchical relationships between yakuza groups could shift. With this system, the declining group does not lose face in the underworld (JJ2014/5; JJ2014/6).

These practices point to a system of territorial governance that was practically effective and durable. Rather than relying solely on violence, yakuza groups developed mechanisms for managing competition, preserving hierarchy, and resolving disputes through negotiation and recognised convention—a degree of institutional sophistication that is rarely observed in other mafia-type groups, and that helps explain the longevity of their organisation.

Taishō democracy and militarist years: the yakuza in the House of Representatives

Although Japan participated only marginally in the First World War, postwar inflation nevertheless hit the country hard. While inflation rose, rice prices quadrupled from their prewar level. This rise was beyond the margins of inflation, and popular discontent quickly gave rise to revolts and protests, which began in July 1918 in the Toyama prefecture, but soon spread all over the country, involving 700,000 protesters. Since the police were unable to repress these outbursts of violence, the government eventually had to deploy the army to stop the riots, which they did successfully by mid-September. Yakuza groups displayed two different types of behaviour at this time. Some groups sided with rice farmers and acted as private protectors of their interests, while others confronted the enraged population. In some cases, the police even turned to local yakuza bosses to help suppress the protests (Iwai, 1963; Siniawer, 2008).

As Japan entered the 1920s and 1930s, the social unrest of the previous decade gave way to a new political climate marked by the rise of nationalist organisations. Although these groups varied in ideology, they were united in their rejection of leftist currents inspired by the Russian Revolution. Many of these groups had strong connections with the criminal underworld: the yakuza in particular were visibly involved with the Dai Nihon Kokusuikai (Greater Japan National Essence Association) and the Dai Nihon Seigidan (Greater Japan Justice Association). The founding of these two groups in 1919 and 1922, respectively, in both cases through the direct participation of yakuza bosses, can be understood as the precise moment in which yakuza forces became institutionalised and recognised as a socially acceptable force (Siniawer, 2008). The Kokusuikai was the creation of Toyama

Mitsuru and Tokonami Takejirō, the Minister of Home Affairs, and was the successor of the abovementioned Gen'yōsha. It was based on the same ultranationalist ideology but had an altogether more violent edge. Members of the Kokusuikai (which amounted to 60,000 gangsters, labourers, and ultranationalists) were deployed against strikers and subversives, with the full backing of the police, the Home Office, and high-ranking military officials (Kaplan and Dubro, 2003). According to Iwai (1963), the Kokusuikai, in particular, were established by *bakuto* members, but were directly backed by Prime Minister Hara Takashi, and by the army. In the 1920s and 1930s, the yakuza were still not formally considered criminal syndicates, and therefore political parties could fully collaborate with them without being accused of collaborating with criminal groups (despite the fact that many of the methods used by these groups were illegal). Using the yakuza rather than the police brought clear advantages, insofar as the yakuza could be arbitrarily directed against any perceived enemy without the constraints of legal accountability. In this way, the Kokusuikai were able to advance their particular ideological, political, and financial agenda, while, simultaneously, singlehandedly repressing all forms of opposition (Siniawer, 2012).

Given the popularity of many yakuza leaders (and the fact that yakuza were not reticent about using violence to achieve their goals), democratic elections represented an opportunity through which to secure higher-level political roles for the yakuza. Yoshida Isokichi, the yakuza boss from Kyūshū whose ascent to power was described above, eventually made it to the House of Representatives. Even in his role as a politician, he was painted by his fellow Diet members as a chivalrous man and an example for future politicians to emulate. Despite both his role as a mediator in his community and his (often exaggerated) reputation, he did not hesitate to join in physical scuffles in the Diet, nor did he shy away from deploying his henchmen on the political floor. A colleague of Yoshida from a similar background was Hora Sennosuke: the two of them had long careers in local and national politics and were emblematic of the widespread acceptance of the yakuza at the highest circles of national politics (Siniawer, 2008). The example of Yoshida illustrates the intermediary role played by early yakuza leaders across labour, politics, policing, and commerce. At different points of his career, and often concurrently, he was a yakuza boss and a parliamentarian, a representative of labourers and leader of a self-defence force that acted as a surrogate police force, and a businessman in the flourishing entertainment sector. This entanglement of the yakuza with politics, society, and economy suggests that the distinction between these bodies was far from clear-cut, which reinforced the perception of the yakuza as just another form of social organisation upon which one could rely if needed. The high levels of visibility of yakuza groups, and particularly some of their representatives, is emblematic of the level of acceptance they achieved through their far-right political activism, which only served to bring the yakuza and politics even closer together (Mizushima, 1986).

In the Taishō period (1912–1926), the yakuza transitioned from loosely territorial actors with an ideological affinity for nationalism into explicitly political enforcers serving state interests. Far from operating in opposition to the state, they were increasingly mobilised to suppress strikes, intimidate leftist organisers, and neutralise dissent. In doing so, they provided the state with a means of coercion that bypassed legal constraints: they acted as criminal enforcers, but for the government. This arrangement offered the advantage of maintaining formal distance, while simultaneously reinforcing the yakuza's public legitimacy.

The yakuza at war: colonial expansion and comfort women

Throughout the 1930s, democracy in Japan continued to wane as rightist groups such as the aforementioned Kokusuikai posed an increasing threat to democratic institutions through attacks on politicians and industrialists. The yakuza supported the cause of the militarist and ultranationalist factions by providing manpower and coercive capacity. As the Japanese government started its colonial expansion with the 1931 invasion of Manchuria, some yakuza groups took advantage of the war efforts to magnify their influence, by sending men to occupied regions in Manchuria and China to take part in so-called 'land development' programmes (Kaplan and Dubro, 2003). The Opium Law of 1924 granted control of opium supply to the Japanese government (Kingsberg, 2014), and some yakuza groups assisted the Opium Monopoly Bureau, which was operating to make profits while at the same time weakening the public through opium addiction. Japan had already started smuggling morphine into China during the First World War: Japanese agents would buy the drug in the United Kingdom and sell it in North China, where it quickly replaced the declining use of opium. After the war, the Japanese would buy the opium in India and refine it in Kobe through ports employing Japanese officials to circumvent the ban imposed by the International Convention (Arduini, 2016). The opium produced in China was also smuggled in Japan for domestic use, as many newspaper articles of the time reported (Kingsberg, 2014).

The majority of yakuza groups were focused on expanding their financial base at home through the capitals and assets brought in by the colonial expansion. Most yakuza groups operated solely at a local level, in their towns and neighbourhoods of origin: a very lucrative market was the organisation of labour in port cities. For instance, before the war the Yamaguchi-gumi acquired most of its power by becoming the winning faction in the fight over contracts and territories in the city of Kobe.

The attack on Pearl Harbour in 1941 and Japan's subsequent involvement in the global conflict led yakuza members to a crossroads: either join the war effort or be treated as traitors. The imprisonment of prominent yakuza figures did not lead to the complete dismantling of yakuza operations or alliances; in fact, it helped them form particular connections that would prove to be essential in postwar Japan. The most significant of these fortuitous scenarios was undoubtedly the prison cell that connected Sasakawa Ryoichi (far-right activist), Kishi Nobusuke (future Prime Minister), and Kodama Yoshio (yakuza fixer). Taoka Kazuo, leader of the would-be biggest yakuza groups in Japan, also spent time in prison, where he became acquainted with far-right ideologues. Therefore, while most yakuza members suspended their criminal career during the war years, some key figures were still able to exploit this period to make connections, thereby allowing yakuza groups to quickly regroup after the war.

The war years raise questions about the yakuza's role in the 'comfort station' system—yet that role was, perhaps surprisingly, limited. Systems that were important to the national military effort—such as forced labour and sexual enslavement—were 'forged domestically in peacetime, and then developed in wartime in Japan's colonies' (Norma, 2016: 9). The sexual exploitation and trafficking of women had indeed started both in Japan and in the colonies well before the system of 'comfort stations' was established by the military (Tanaka, 2002). In this sense, civilian prostitution and military sexual slavery are strongly interconnected. Yet, there is no record of yakuza groups being involved with the provision of women into the system of military sexual slavery in the colonies during the war: while Japanese women were trafficked into 'comfort stations' from domestic brothels (to which they had often been sold by destitute families), women from the colonies were either rounded up by expeditionary forces or recruited against their own will through deception and coercion by private agents appointed by the army (Norma, 2016). Generally, a director or private agent was appointed with the task of finding women to be sent to these facilities. The army in the field would assist in the rounding up and transporting of women, attesting to the fact that the Japanese army and the state were directly involved in the establishment of these 'comfort stations'. In Japan, women sent to the stations had to be registered as prostitutes and over the age of 21, although these restrictions were easily circumvented. In Korea, women were often deceived by the agents appointed to recruit women, forcefully rounded up, or sold by their parents (Yoshimi, 2000). Also in China, the Japanese army did not draft the women directly, nor did they randomly kidnap them: they systematically used local brothel owners, labour brokers, and the local puppet administrations (Qiu, Zhiliang, and Lifei, 2013). In Taiwan, women are reported to have been forcibly collected or recruited by deception, while a minority went willingly (Suzuki, 2011).

Once the war was over, and the yakuza at the front reunited with those who stayed at home, they immediately took advantage of the new opportunities offered by the postwar turmoil. As reported by Tanaka (2002), some leaders of fascist organisations, who were deeply interconnected with the yakuza, procured women and organised such facilities in Japan for the occupation troops. For example, the aforementioned Sasakawa Ryōichi set up a company in Osaka called the 'American Club', which was in fact a 'comfort station'. Considering how difficult it was to procure women for foreign troops, the implication is that fascist organisations and entrepreneurs worked with yakuza groups to hunt, deceive, and force women into the industry. Their involvement in setting up 'comfort stations' for the American troops during the occupation period testifies to their increased ability to control markets.

The immediate postwar period: policing the black market

The US occupation of Japan officially began on 2 September 1945. The lack of food, combined with the demobilisation of Japan's huge army and its paralysed industrial system, facilitated the rapid growth of the black market. As the governing elites were disempowered and the occupation forces tried to restore basic infrastructure, the regulation of street-level trade fell into the hands of local yakuza groups, and in particular of the *tekiya*, specialists in the organisation of markets. Black markets appeared across all the major Japanese cities by early September 1945: large cities like Tokyo and Osaka immediately started to count tens of thousands of stalls in their midst. Since these spaces needed regulating, gangs stepped in to organise the market spaces and supplies of energy and water, all with the complete support of the local police (Dower, 1999). The control that the yakuza had over the territory was further strengthened by the fact that the occupation forces delegated the management of black markets to them, in a strategic move that echoed their invasion of Sicily and occupation of Italy (Armao, 2015). The Tokyo Street Vendor Association was formed by gathering *tekiya* in Tokyo. By July 1946, Tokyo counted up to 200,000 street vendors, including part-time sellers. The Association managed licensing for street stall permits, and affiliates would collect the licensing fees daily. Anyone who wanted to operate a street stall in Tokyo had to become a member of the Association and pay a fee to the local *tekiya* group. The head of the Tokyo Street Vendor Association was Ozu Kinosuke, the head of the Kantō Ozu-gumi. In February 1946, regulations were introduced to impose stricter control on the market, starting from the prohibition on opening new stalls, and then restrictions on goods that could be sold, making it illegal to sell vegetables and seafood at street stalls. Ozu responded quickly. As soon as the restrictions came into force, he negotiated with the Tokyo Metropolitan government and the Metropolitan police department to secure permission to sell fresh fish. His strategy was to sell in markets if street stalls were no longer allowed. Ozu secured a channel for fresh seafood to arrive to Tokyo, and established 'exception markets' (*reigai ichiba*) in Ginza, Asakusa, Kanda, and Ikebukuro (JJ01/2018).

Without an authority able to effectively police the streets, two things happened simultaneously: on the one hand, the newly liberated Asian minorities, the so-called *sankokujin* ('people of the three countries', namely China, Korea, and Taiwan), rose up and organised themselves into groups controlling several black markets around the country; on the other hand, a new type of gangs emerged, known as *gurentai* (hoodlums, armed hooligans) and different from traditional yakuza groups. Recruiting from the population of jobless, hungry, young men, they used violence and the threat thereof to strong arm control over the black markets and labour forces (Kaplan and Dubro, 2003). The black market was supposed to be a place only for the Japanese (the Americans did not and could not interfere with it) and it was perpetually violent, which provided the perfect battleground for old and new yakuza groups who were either trying to survive or trying to assert themselves.

For instance, violent conflicts erupted between the Matsuda-gumi and a group of Taiwanese who had requested permission to set up stalls in the Shinbashi black market, which was under Matsuda-gumi control. The group refused, prompting the Taiwanese to attack their office and fatally beat one of their members. A month later, the Matsuda-gumi retaliated with katanas and firearms, injuring two Taiwanese and two police officers who tried to intervene. Fearing escalation, Tokyo police arrested twenty-eight Taiwanese pre-emptively, sparking protests and clashes. As tensions rose, the *tekiya* federation mobilised over 2,500 men to strategic positions in and around Shinbashi. When several hundred Taiwanese approached in trucks, the Matsuda-gumi, armed with rooftop machine guns, opened fire. Outgunned, the Taiwanese retreated, relinquishing control over the profitable market (Kaplan and Dubro, 2003). Similarly, in Kobe, the police were unable to control either the population or the *sankokujin* immigrants. Tensions over control of the black market erupted on multiple occasions. In February 1946, the Yamaguchi-gumi conducted a raid in the market around Sannomiya station, which involved the use of two trucks, handguns, swords, and grenades, and caused many casualties. Through such violence, the Yamaguchi-gumi claimed and easily obtained the informal role of a self-defence force (Miyazaki, 2008). Yakuza groups adopted the role of an alternative police force during a clear power vacuum, with the full support of the weakened local police, which could do nothing other than endorse the yakuza's violence and tacitly legitimate the order they imposed on the population.

As a yakuza boss recounted during our interview:

> That's another reason why the yakuza still exists: after the war the guns were confiscated, and there were *sankokujin* people taking advantage of the population, raping and so on. Japan did a lot [of bad things] but also a lot of bad things were done to Japan, the guns were taken away and policemen were disarmed. The yakuza were doing the police's job, it was necessary for the population and people still remember it. (C2)

Consequently, the yakuza were the only sources of governance in certain sectors of society, where the state could not enter. In 1947, under American pressure, the Diet passed a new Police Law that decentralised the force and divested the police of a number of their duties and powers. The reorganised police force did not adapt well to society and incurred immediate problems: the highly localised structure of the police meant that they came under the direct influence of local bosses and struggled to maintain law and order within their communities. By the time the 1954 Police Law—which created the more centralised police organisation that remains in place today—was passed, the yakuza had already expanded their influence within black markets and communities across Japan (Ames, 1981).

The vulnerable state of the police in the years after the immediate postwar is confirmed by a well-known anecdote that epitomises the degree to which the state was at times wholly dependent on the yakuza. When, in 1960, US

President Eisenhower planned to visit Japan (a visit that was subsequently cancelled), political fixer Kodama Yoshio used his influence to gather members of the *bakuto*, *tekiya*, and ultranationalist groups to ensure Eisenhower's safety from protestors (Hill, 2014; Kaplan and Dubro, 2003; Siniawer, 2008). Nakamura Koji's account from 1971 provides some idea of the size of the paramilitary force that was assembled for this task: 18,000 yakuza, 10,000 *tekiya*, and 10,000 *uyoku* (far-right) members, who had at their disposal 800 million yen, along with helicopters, trucks, cars, food, and various other pieces of equipment (Nakamura, 1971, in Kaplan and Dubro, 2003; Ino, 2000). By way of comparison, in 1960, there were fewer than 130,000 Japanese police officers, of which the vast majority were prefectural police (NPA, 2004b). This shows how the protection services offered by the yakuza were popular even amongst governmental groups, which were unable to rely solely on the state's power to enforce its own laws.

The yakuza used key figures like Kodama Yoshio, the political fixer who helped organise Eisenhower's visit, and Sasakawa Ryōichi, the self-described 'world's wealthiest fascist' (*Time*, 26/08/1974) to cultivate connections with conservative politicians. As outlined above, prior to the war, the yakuza had woven an extended and strong network of connections with the state. In some cases, the overlap between far-right militants and yakuza groups meant that the yakuza formed part of the local or even national government. While a new form of government could have signalled the end of these intimate connections between the yakuza and the state, most of the bureaucratic class remained intact, while most of the elite political positions were still held by prewar conservatives with moderate tendencies (Allison, 1994). The persistence of the prewar political climate soon became evident: conservative politicians regrouped following defeat and began to organise a web of connections that entangled political fixers, the yakuza, entrepreneurs, and even foreign (notably American) officials, who found common ground in their hatred for communism (Siniawer, 2008). The legitimation of the yakuza's power by the victors of the war, who would soon become the leaders of the Western bloc in the Cold War, was a significant moment in the history of the yakuza. Indeed, the occupation forces became ever more preoccupied with the communist threat and implemented forms of secret censorship and thought control under the blatant guise of free speech, distorting the neocolonial slogan 'revolution from above' in order to democratise Japan from the beginning (Dower, 1999).

While the structure of governance was different, the people remained the same: the yakuza already had important connections, as the shared value systems of conservatives and the yakuza remained virtually unchanged. Significantly, one of the first attempts at reconnecting the yakuza and politicians came from inside the government, when, in 1952, the Minister of Justice Kimura Tokutarō (who was sentenced as a war criminal during the Tokyo trials) reached out to organise an anti-communist group, before then attempting to organise a nationwide alliance of yakuza and rightists. The Liberal Democratic Party, which has practically ruled Japan without interruption since 1955, was founded by merging the Liberal Party with the Democratic Party, under the leadership of Kishi Nobusuke with Kodama Yoshio serving as a central political fixer behind the scenes—both of whom were class-A war criminals who met in Sugamo prison. These are just some examples that demonstrate how connections between the yakuza and the political elites were not only tolerated by the government but actively encouraged by them. This 'behind the scenes' way of doing politics is known as *kuromaku* (black mist), which is a term that ordinarily applies to the nexus between the legitimate world of politicians, businessmen, the yakuza and the ultranationalists (Kaplan and Dubro, 2003).

The formation of the oligopoly

When the turmoil of the immediate postwar subsided, yakuza groups were finally able to secure their power and expand their sphere of influence. Three groups emerged in this period, and are still the oligopoly of the yakuza world today. The first group is the Yamaguchi-gumi which, under the leadership of their third leader Taoka Kazuo, positioned themselves as a surrogate police force in the power vacuum of the immediate postwar context (Miyazaki, 2008). Taoka had inherited activities in the entertainment business and construction, but he had his eye on the Kobe harbour, particularly the organisation of the dock workers. The outbreak of the Korean War in 1950 opened new opportunities for the Yamaguchi-gumi. Taoka moved quickly to capitalize, establishing a transport company while simultaneously expanding in the entertainment business. As the Yamaguchi-gumi expanded its operation across the nation, so did the costs of mobilising their members—trials, imprisonment, support during incarceration demanded a strong financial base. Taoka's response was to run the yakuza group primarily on the basis of economic efficiency (JJ09/2018). Alongside monopolising the cargo loading business at Kobe port, boss Taoka issued the rule that his underlings were to avoid businesses that involved drugs and decided that the group should always have legal businesses alongside their illegal activities. He followed through on this decree by entering the entertainment and sports sector at a high level, as demonstrated by the fact that his agency represented the well-known singer Misora Hibari. At the same time, he expanded his own influence and, by 1963, his organisation included 424 groups with a total of 8,000 members—a remarkable expansion from his initial thirty-three members (Yanagi, 2017).

The second largest yakuza group, the Sumiyoshi-kai, emerged under the leadership of the boss Hori Masao, who established the policy of non-interference in the internal affairs of other groups. He obtained his first position as a leader when he became the fourth secretary general (*sōchō*) of the Sumiyoshi-kai affiliated Nakazato-ikka, and became involved with the world of entertainment, including theatre, pro-wrestling, and enka music. In 1967, he was then chosen to be the leader of the Sumiyoshi-ikka, a larger group that included the Nakazato-ikka. Through a strong internal system of honorary and permanent counsellors and vice-leaders, Hori was able to mediate significant internal crises and enhance the influence of the Sumiyoshi-kai (Bessatsu Takarajima Henshūbu, 2017).

The prosperity of the third largest yakuza group, the Inagawa-kai, is largely attributable to its first boss, Inagawa Seijō, who from the second half of the 1940s onwards, and as a result of his recruitment of young people through the paramilitary group Yokohama Gurentai, managed to expand the territorial sphere of influence of his group from their initial base in Atami (Shizuoka prefecture). By the beginning of the 1950s, the Inagawa-kai territories included Yokohama in the East, Mishima (Shizuoka prefecture) in the West, and Yamanashi in the North: nevertheless, Inagawa's ultimate goal was to reach Tokyo. To access the capital, in 1959, the Inagawa-kai founded the 'Inagawa Kōgyō' (Inagawa industries, which was later renamed 'Kinseikai' in 1963) and opened an office in Tokyo. Having stepped into the territory of other organisations, the Inagawa-kai mediated conflicts and in 1963 established the 'Kantō-kai', an association that united the *bakuto* bosses in the Kantō area. In order to strengthen their relationship with the Yamaguchi-gumi, in 1972, Inagawa Seijō exchanged sake cups in the traditional ritual of *sakazuki* with bosses of the rival group (Bessatsu Takarajima Henshūbu, 2017).

The consolidation of the yakuza world into three dominant syndicates marked a qualitative shift in the nature of yakuza governance: territorial competition became increasingly regulated through inter-group agreements, shared norms, and recognised hierarchies—the same mechanisms that had governed local territories were now operating at a national scale. By the 1980s, the three largest syndicates had continued to grow, while smaller groups had either disbanded or swallowed one another up (MoJ, 1989). As the older generation of postwar bosses began to die off and yakuza membership declined, the syndicates faced internal pressure to find new sources of revenue and authority. The economic boom of the late 1980s would provide exactly that opportunity, drawing the yakuza deeper into legitimate business, real estate, and financial markets than ever before (Mizoguchi, 2011).

Bubble economy and political scandals

The bubble economy created immense opportunities for wealth accumulation, and the yakuza were quick to enter into real estate and stock market speculation. In this period, the intertwining of yakuza businesses and legitimate businesses became ever more advanced. Taoka Kazuo, the third boss of the Yamaguchi-gumi from 1946 to 1981, had introduced the practice—which was subsequently adopted by most yakuza groups—of having at least one legitimate business to fall back on. However, the economic boom incentivised them to become even more involved with profitable legitimate businesses, particularly in the construction and finance sectors (Mizoguchi, 2012). The yakuza thus managed to diversify, expand, and modernise their activities. The modern syndicates added an international dimension to their business, through illegal channels (importing firearms, drugs, women for prostitution rackets), legal investments, and semi-legal arrangements (by organising tours abroad for Japanese businessmen whose real destinations were brothels and gambling dens). At the same time, the yakuza increasingly took part in drug markets, specifically the amphetamine trade, whose revenues allegedly financed the expansion of the three large yakuza groups (Hill, 2003).

While in the 1970s and 1980s the yakuza's relationships with businesses were running smoothly, a series of scandals had undermined their political connections. In 1976, the Lockheed scandal led to the unveiling of a web of connections linking actors in Japanese and American politics, industry, and even the yakuza (Kaplan and Dubro, 2003). Just over a year before, in November 1974, another scandal had revealed the gargantuan sums of money that were administered through Prime Minister Tanaka's political networks and dummy companies. When he was questioned about this by foreign journalists, the scandal broke and he was subsequently forced to resign. When the media revealed that 12.6 million dollars had streamed into

Japan in an attempt to convince All Nippon Airways to buy one billion dollars' worth of Lockheed aircrafts, the Japanese political sphere found itself in a deeply unstable position. Although the political fixer Kodama Yoshio was the principal recipient of this payoff money, the list of bribed officials included Prime Minister Tanaka Kakuei, the Ministers of Industry and Transportation, the Vice Minister of Transportation, and the chairman of the Liberal Democratic Party Special Committee on Aviation, along with the president of All Nippon Airways (ibid.). These scandals testify to the longstanding connection between the yakuza and politics. Kodama Yoshio was a key figure in the *kuromaku* of postwar politics: a figure who combined underworld connections, intelligence ties, ultranationalist politics, and political brokerage. It was Kodama who organised the historic alliance between the Yamaguchi-gumi and the Inagawa-kai, and worked as an intermediary between high-level politicians, business elites, and the yakuza. This provided the yakuza with a direct channel to the political elites, although his legacy continued long after his death in 1984. The political climate he helped to create meant that questionable payments and political connections with the yakuza persisted but became more secretive.

The symbiosis between authorities and the yakuza casts light on the larger problem of structural corruption that exists in Japan, despite the widespread perception of Japan as a low-crime and law-abiding society. It was within this climate of structural corruption that the yakuza built their fortune in the 1980s. Bolstered by the boom in their illicit revenues from gambling, prostitution, and retail sales, the yakuza were sufficiently skilled in knowing where to invest their money. Besides their traditional businesses (construction and entertainment), they sought the advice of professionals to expand their lawful portfolio. Through stock speculator groups, property development—and other less lawful activities such as *sokaiya* (disruption of shareholders' meetings) and bankruptcy management—the yakuza entered the world of corporate Japan. However, the 1980s also signalled a clear deterioration in the yakuza's social acceptance. Taoka Kazuo, boss of the Yamaguchi-gumi, died in 1981, but his role was not filled until 1984, when Takenaka Masahisa took his post. This enraged another potential successor, Yamamoto Hiroshi, who formed a rival organisation, the Ichiwa-kai. The turf battle triggered by this internal split caused the death of the new boss and led to a five-year gang war with casualties in the police and the population (Yanagi, 2017). At the same time, the increase in violent yakuza interventions in civil disputes and business conflicts eroded the public goodwill the syndicates had cultivated through their postwar role as legitimate providers of protection and informal order. At the turn of the decade, the yakuza's relationships with the state and society at large were approaching a tipping point that would soon prompt the state to act, as Chapter 4 examines.

Acts of generosity and community building

An important factor in the yakuza's postwar emergence and consolidation as providers of alternative, rather than purely criminal, governance was their legitimation through adherence to shared social norms centred on cooperation and assistance to the local population. This built upon their mythologised image as protectors of the weak. The role of the yakuza as dispute arbitrators and local providers of governance is not unique. The local *mafioso* can help common citizens resolve disputes and recover stolen goods (Gambetta, 1993), or in violent areas they provide security for the neighbourhood (see Arias, 2017; Blattman et al., 2025; Lessing, 2020). Even in the United Kingdom, a state hardly known for mafia presence, criminal groups able to provide illegal governance are also known to perform generous acts for the community they govern. In Salford, Paul Massey's criminal group controlled and intimidated the community but at the same time he was also seen as a benevolent figure who would help people in the neighbourhood. Indeed, at his grand funeral, hundreds of members of the community gathered and paid their respects, wearing white t-shirts and jeans as requested by Massey's family (Campana and Varese, 2018; Pidd, 2015).

In the case of Japan, the yakuza have constructed their popular image by organising social events for local neighbourhoods and by helping in times of extreme need. Indeed, as Gambetta posits, 'acts of generosity are among the preferred means of advertising' (1993: 47). For instance, in the aftermath of the earthquakes in Kobe (1995), Tohoku (2011), and Kumamoto (2016), news of the relief work performed by yakuza groups was reported by both the newspapers (Jones, 25/03/2011; Rankin, 2012) and the yakuza themselves (Yakuzanet, 2016; Ninkyō suishin iinkai, 2015). There are many reported cases of local yakuza groups either financing village festivals or distributing food and other goods to the less fortunate. A yakuza boss of a large group in Tokyo saw these kinds of social activities as being at the core of yakuza values.

> If you walk the street in front of our office, 100 metres on each side, you will see it's sparkling clean because my staff cleans it every morning.

> You won't even see a cigarette butt. This is how much we care about our territory.... I became *sōchō* [secretary-general] in 2016, the boss before me didn't care that much but I think we should do it for the neighbourhood. It snowed recently, didn't it? We cleaned the whole street: our neighbour here is an 89-year-old woman; on the other side, there's a hotel with a lot of female staff, it's hard for them to shovel the snow, but we have stamina so we help them. We have to go back to the starting point, the *bushidō* spirit, the yakuza spirit: from there you can't make any mistake. (C2)

In a similar vein to the Italian mafia's, the yakuza associate themselves with traditional cultural codes (Sciarrone and Storti, 2014). The yakuza claim to embody both the ideals of rebellion against society, as well as the most traditional of Japanese values, which is reflected in the complementary and oppositional duo of *giri* (duty, obligation) and *ninjō* (humanity, compassion) (Mizoguchi, 2011). While officially they are shut out from mainstream society, their links to political and economic elites have demonstrably been strong (Henshall, 1999). The yakuza's ability to hold an ambivalent position at the margins of society, while, simultaneously, operating to some extent at the core of it due to their embodiment of a nostalgic tradition, is a determining factor in the level of social acceptance that they have long enjoyed. Sciarrone and Storti (2014) highlight how the mafia's power is based on the exploitation of social relationships and traditional cultural norms, as well as on violence, which allows the *mafioso* to accumulate social capital. This is clear in the way in which the Yamaguchi-gumi talked about contemporary society in the introduction to their website (which has been since taken down).

> The number of vicious crimes has increased in this country; people generally are devastated. No one notices if an elderly person from his or her neighbourhood has passed because there is no communication, not even greetings exchanged any more. No one is interested or cares enough about what is going on around them except about his or herself. Unfortunately, this sensation has become normal in today's generation. If the idea of Japan becoming a country without sentiments for others worries you, it is important to learn the ancient paths of this nation to figure out what is needed to regain the importance of Japanese spirit from its tradition. (Ninkyōdō, 2016)

The Yamaguchi-gumi refer to a set of values that emphasise the sense of the collective, community spirit, and harmony within society. Miyazaki Manabu, a journalist and writer who specialises in the yakuza, argues that while the yakuza do commit crimes, they are perceived to have been protecting the civic order of the cities and as such, Japanese people have learnt to accept them (S16). In other words, they have been tolerated because they contribute in some way to the social order, by controlling the underworld and imposing strict codes of conduct upon rebellious elements. Unlike groups whose internal cohesion comes at the expense of outsiders (see, e.g., the Italian mafia or the Ku Klux Klan; Fukuyama, 2001) the yakuza promote a system of norms that fosters cooperation within the community. The yakuza have been accepted, or at least tolerated, by the population because of their relatively scarce public displays of violence (Breuer and Baradel, 2025), which, combined with their territorial control, political connections, and community embeddedness, allowed them to be perceived not as criminals but as a legitimate, if extra-legal, source of authority.

Conclusion

The emergence and persistence of the yakuza reveal how criminal actors have, at specific historical junctures, been integral to processes of governance, state formation, and social regulation. The yakuza's power did not emerge in a vacuum, but in the context of weak or uneven state presence, fragmented legal authority, and high demand for informal protection and mediation. As such, their trajectory parallels the broader arguments advanced by Gambetta (1993) and Varese (2001, 2011), who have shown how mafia-type groups emerge in contexts of institutional voids, and flourish when they are able to monopolise the supply of extra-legal protection. Like the Sicilian mafia or the Russian vory, the yakuza developed as a response to systemic failures in the provision of order, but unlike their counterparts, they did so in an environment that permitted visibility, semi-legality, and often tacit state collaboration.

Yet the yakuza cannot be reduced to protection rackets. As this chapter has illustrated, their role across history was not simply to enforce contracts or deter violence, but to regulate markets, manage informal economies, mediate disputes, and at times substitute or supplement the functions of the state itself. In this sense, their activity aligns with a broader understanding of hybrid criminal governance (see Koonings and Kruijt, 2004; Lessing, 2020; Pimenta, Suarez, and Ferreira, 2021; Villa, Braga, and Ferreira, 2021) which sees the state, civil society, and criminal groups as sharing authority and legitimacy. Governance by criminal groups can be highly institutionalised, drawing on legitimacy, service provision, and reciprocal obligations, not unlike the political institutions they compete, or collude, with (Moncada, 2021). The yakuza, particularly in the postwar period, exemplify such a model: they collected taxes (or their equivalent), managed public goods (such as black-market order or festival grounds), enforced rules, and legitimised their authority through the performance of traditional norms and nationalistic myths. The myths themselves, while clearly serving ideological purposes, also had functional roles in legitimising the yakuza's governance, whether by facilitating market organisation or mediating disputes, and should not be dismissed as merely symbolic.

The yakuza have long relied on visibility as a central tool of legitimation, using their own origin story to justify their existence. Their positive mythology frames them as contributors to national development and guardians of 'Japaneseness'. This self-image, rooted in historical continuity and nationalist sentiment, closely parallels the rhetoric of right-wing groups such as the Gen'yōsha, who similarly positioned themselves as defenders of tradition and informal agents of state formation. Unlike other mafias or criminal organisations, the yakuza have never adopted a subversive stance towards the state. Their political interventions and relationships with elites have consistently aimed to preserve the status quo. Rather than challenging institutional legitimacy, they have acted as informal extensions of state authority, reinforcing social order, suppressing unrest, and managing regulatory grey zones. Their alignment with state interests, and their ability to provide services and enforce norms, helps to explain the visibility and tolerance they enjoyed for much of the postwar period. In return, state institutions often tolerated the yakuza's illicit enterprises in exchange for support during periods of instability or institutional weakness. This created a mutual dependency: the yakuza relied on informal recognition to sustain their position, while the state turned to them to manage disorder and compensate for institutional shortfalls.

If we understand governance not as a fixed property of states, but as a function performed by various actors across institutional contexts, then the yakuza must be recognised as historically embedded agents of governance which have been, at times, indispensable. Their trajectory shows the many ways in which order has been built and negotiated also by extra-legal actors. Yet the conditions sustaining the yakuza were not permanent. Before examining their erosion, the following chapter turns to the internal architecture that held the organisation together: the rules, rituals, and hierarchies through which yakuza authority was reproduced and legitimacy maintained.

3

Reputation through structure, rules, and rituals

Introduction

While yakuza groups enjoy semi-legal status and high visibility, they cannot rely on state institutions and legal mechanisms. As a result, they have developed internal rules and mechanisms—such as codes of conduct, conflict resolution practices, and hierarchical enforcement structures—similar to those found in other mafias, in order to maintain order, regulate behaviour, and preserve organisational cohesion (Reuter, 1983; Gambetta, 1993). Since the yakuza as an association is not criminalised, there is a wealth of available information on them. For instance, it is known who the yakuza bosses are and where their offices are located. The police keep lists of active members in each prefecture and are notified when someone quits. Similarly, their rituals are well-documented, with the yakuza even circulating videos of some ceremonies in VHS, DVDs, and recently, online platforms such as YouTube. Across Japan, from big syndicates to local groups, they share rules and foundation myths. These shared practices are more than organisational conventions: they draw directly on Shintō liturgy and Japanese ritual tradition, borrowing the legitimating resources of the sacred to present the yakuza as custodians of an authentically Japanese moral order. This chapter reconstructs the internal architecture and the cultural tropes that made the yakuza legible both to their members and to the wider public. The carefully curated claims to 'tradition' were instruments of visibility that enabled the groups to present themselves as stable, bounded, and governable entities. That visibility underpinned their capacity to embed themselves in specific markets and territories, as predictability and recognisable authority made coordination possible.

21st Century Yakuza. Martina Baradel, Oxford University Press. © Martina Baradel 2026.
DOI: 10.1093/9780191987755.003.0004

Internal and external structure

The central structure of the yakuza is based on the relationship between *oyabun* (father role, the boss) and *kobun* (son role, the affiliate). The fictional family extends to brother–brother, uncle–nephew, as well as grandfather–grandson relationships. The relationship can be vertical (as in the case of father and son), horizontal (for brothers at the same level), or oblique (for older brothers and younger brothers). The single group is called *gumi* (group) or *ikka* (family), reinforcing the concept of yakuza as a family. At the top of the family stands the *kumichō* (group head) or *oyabun*, who has advisers and affiliates. His second in command are the *wakagashira* (lieutenant) or *saikō kanbu* (top executives), and below there are the members (*kumi'in*). When a high-ranking member earns enough to start his own group, he will take on a dual role: he will still be a member of his boss's group, but he will also play the role of boss of his own smaller group (See Figure 3.1).

While this is by far the most widespread organisational model, it is important to note that some groups may deviate slightly from this structure. For example, yakuza groups in Okinawa tend to adopt a more egalitarian internal hierarchy, with affiliates maintaining closer and more direct relationships with their lieutenants and bosses. Members and bosses in Okinawa are often keen to emphasise this distinction (C16). The relationship between boss and affiliates is one of absolute subordination and is similar to those of the feudal master and servant. Reflecting the timeless concern of every generation that the following one lacks discipline and respect for authority, Iwai (1963) reported members of the yakuza saying that, in the past, an affiliate would not even dare to respond to the boss or accept a cigarette from him. However, relationships are still based on the principles of absolute authority of the boss and complete obedience of the affiliates. Obedience is the core of the organisation, and affiliates are asked to suspend their judgement and follow orders, even if those orders are misguided. These relationships carry heavy duties on both sides. Affiliates have to offer complete loyalty to their bosses, and the bosses are responsible for their affiliates: the boss educates and takes full accountability of members from their training onwards (C4). The boss and the group come before the natural family, and it is not strange for members to voice that order of preference. A lieutenant of a yakuza group once told me: 'I can only be with someone who knows that my work comes first. My boss has always precedence over my wife and my children, there is no discussion about that' (C17). The training can be done 'in-house', where the prospect members live with the boss or in the office (a system called *heyazumi*), or 'detached', where

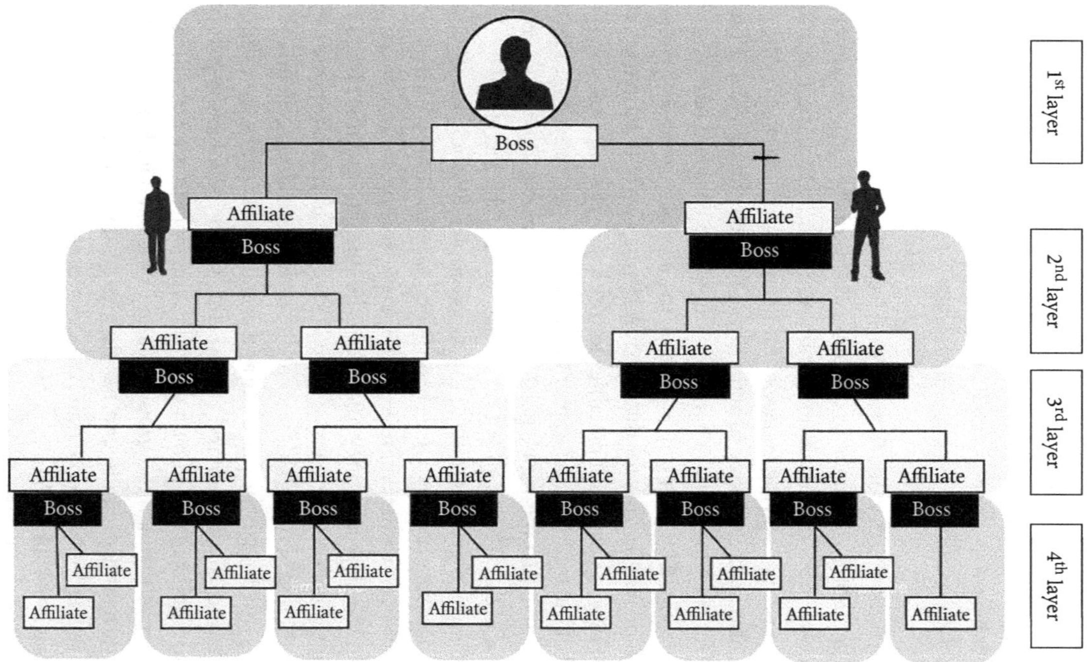

Figure 3.1 Structure of a yakuza group

they live elsewhere. Depending on the group and possibilities, the in-house training is preferred, as it marks clearly joining the new family.

> The yakuza day started at 10 a.m. Daily chores included washing dishes at the main house, cleaning the office, doing laundry for the elder sister, and walking two dogs. Our group had several young live-in members, and the office was a hangout for about ten young bikers. The office was always lively. Being a live-in member felt like being part of a true family. We all ate together, with the boss's wife calling us when meals were ready. (C14)

During the training period, recruits learn how to do standard business, such as illegal gambling, dealing with customers, and collecting protection money. They receive food and accommodation and also learn basic tasks such as cleaning, cooking, serving tea, welcoming guests, and answering the phone. They are also involved in social activities so that they bond with the boss and other members. One night, when I was out with a boss and one of his members, we dropped by their office at 2 a.m. just to wake up the 20-year-old apprentice who was on duty for the night and bring him with us to the next bar, where we played darts with penalties for the loser. The boss insisted that this was part of the training: the apprentice had to always be ready. I joked with the young man that it must be hard to have such a boss who wakes you up in the middle of the night to go out for drinks. Instead, he was elated by the situation and replied that he admired his boss completely, would do anything for him, and was very happy to have been called to spend time with him (C23).

Relationships within yakuza groups are also reflected in the financial structure. The flow of money goes from the bottom up: subordinates pay a specific monthly sum (known as *jōnōkin*) to their immediate bosses who, in turn, pay their superiors. This system allows higher-ranking members not to be directly involved in the planning and execution of crimes. In addition, this amount covers the 'trademark' (Gambetta, 1993): members pay to use the name and influence of a known group, so the *jōnōkin* is a percentage of the money earned through the group's name (V1). The *jōnōkin* amount varies by group size and strength, and has fluctuated significantly across different periods, reflecting both economic conditions and internal power struggles. In the early 1990s, in the Yamaguchi-gumi, the monthly tribute was for senior executives 1,050,000 yen and for direct affiliates 850k yen.[1] From January

[1] Exchange rates fluctuated enormously in the early 1990s, as the GBP–JPY rate went from 259 in 1991 to 135 in 1995.

1998 to 2004, the monthly tribute was reduced to respectively 700k yen and 500k yen, a decision taken due to the economic stagnation that followed the bursting of the economic bubble (Yōsensha, 2004, Suzuki, 2005). A ruling by the Osaka Supreme Court (30 October 2003 ruling, Osaka Supreme Court, Minshu Vol. 58, No. 8, p. 2166) showed that the monthly payment of the gang organisation leader in the case was 1.5 million yen (£7,950 in 2003) for the boss's direct subordinates lieutenant and above, and 650k yen (£3,500 in 2003) for a lower-level boss. At the time, the group had 15 executive members and 104 lower-level boss members, so the amount received by the gang leader in question was about 90 million yen (£477k in 2003) per month. During the heyday of the Yamaguchi-gumi, when Taoka Kazuo was the boss, the monthly membership fee was only 2,000 yen, but the regular monthly fee paid by an executive member of the Yamaguchi-gumi today is estimated to be between 850k yen (£4,400) and one million yen (£5,100). Considering that there are also extraordinary collections (e.g. for the boss's birthday), the annual total for an executive member can reach about 30 million yen (£153k) per year (Mizoguchi and Suzuki, 2021).

In periods of crisis, the amount of *jōnōkin* can cause friction within the organisation, as evidenced by the fact that the most serious recent split within a yakuza group was caused by the Yamaguchi-gumi boss's demand for high monthly sums. One faction rebelled against this demand and separated from the main group, founding the Kōbe Yamaguchi-gumi. This newly formed group set their monthly payments at 300k yen (£1,600) for executives, 200k yen (£1,080) for mid-level members, and 100k yen (£540) for young members (Nishioka et al., 2016).

Ninkyō: the code of the yakuza

Rules are an essential part of any organisation, especially mafia-type groups, which cannot rely on external authorities to enforce contracts and resolve disputes (Catino, 2019). The code of the yakuza is based both on written and unwritten rules. The unwritten code of permissible behaviour is based on an ideology known as *ninkyō*. This is centred on the central tenet of *jingi*, which is the code of honour and obligation on which yakuza practices are based. It is a concept originating from the samurai code that translates into loyalty, trust, and the importance of honour.

As it was explored in the previous chapter, the yakuza originated from two groups, the *bakuto* (gamblers) and the *tekiya* (peddlers), which were active from the seventeenth century. Nowadays, yakuza groups still claim their descendance from one of the two groups and have slightly different traditions according to this distinction.[2] Both of the groups were itinerant and were often hosted by other gamblers and peddlers on the way. Once a young man started to serve a boss, he had to adopt the strict etiquette of *jingi*. This etiquette regulated the convoluted greetings that a traveller had to make when visiting someone's house. Traveller and host met at the entrance and would both bend their knees and put their right elbow on their leg showing the palm. After a long and ceremonious back and forth, which varied according to the status of the two parties and their level of acquaintance, they would agree to break their stance and end the greeting. Rules would apply to virtually anything that a traveller might do in a host's house, including consuming food and taking a bath (Fujita, 1983).

Ninkyō embodies the ideals of protecting the weak and defeating the strong, with the ability to clearly distinguish between good and evil and to act accordingly. While its origins can be traced back to China, in Japan *ninkyō* spread among the lower social strata and criminals (Fujita, 1983).

One boss described *ninkyō* in terms that reveal both its ethical core and its social function:

> To say it in an easy way, *ninkyō* is whether you can or cannot self-sacrifice. For instance, if a senior citizen falls on the street and cars are coming, you put yourself in the middle to stop the cars. This is *ninkyō*, this courage. That's why it lasted for hundreds of years, otherwise it wouldn't have lasted for so long. I talk with foreigners, but all they care about is money. However, we have *ninkyō* at our core. That's why people still want to support us: in Japan maybe people complain about the yakuza but in the end they like us. That's why we have such a long history. (C2)

Japanese traditional tattoos, perhaps the most famous and visible marker of yakuza membership, are also an expression of yakuza values. These tattoos, known as *tebori* or *wabori*, are created using a wooden tool equipped with multiple needles that manually carves the skin, resulting in deeply embedded ink through a long and painful process. They symbolize *gaman* (endurance),

[2] Yakuza groups designated by the Public Safety Commission are mostly of *bakuto* origins, while most of *tekiya* groups are not designated.

the ability to withstand pain for prolonged periods, an essential preparation for the privations of yakuza life. Being indelible, these tattoos also represent unwavering commitment to a group on the fringes of society: they will remain forever, hindering any future social reintegration.

The rules of the yakuza are based on these concepts. The following are the rules of the Yamaguchi-gumi, drawn from a confidential document circulated within the group, that I was able to access through a source.

'The Yamaguchi-gumi aims to contribute to the prosperity of the national society in line with the spirit of *ninkyō*. Members are required to adhere to these principles:

1. To strengthen our internal circle, we must uphold the principles of harmony and unity.
2. In dealings with the outside world, maintain a sentiment of love and respect and observe proper etiquette.
3. Observe the order of seniority and always be courteous.
4. In interactions with the external world, fulfil one's duties and avoid attracting the attention of others.
5. Learn from the experiences of predecessors to improve one's character.'

Rules of other syndicates are similar to those of the Yamaguchi-gumi. In general, yakuza rules closely resemble those of other mafias such as the Sicilian mafia, the Triads, and the Russian *vory*. They mention rules of mutual support (respect the hierarchy, obey, do not betray fellow members), internal harmony, and interactions with civil society (Varese, 2018). As argued by Catino (2019), the adoption of similar rules in such diverse context suggests that mafias operate in similarly hostile environments and are subject to similar pressures. Survey data from 1993 suggest that this framing retained some public resonance even as repression intensified at the beginning of the 1990s: while the dominant public perception of yakuza members was negative—the majority viewing them as braggarts or habitual wrongdoers—a meaningful minority still associated them with values of duty and human obligation (10.8 per cent) and with the *ninkyō* tradition of protecting the weak (5.9 per cent) (Cabinet Office, 2002). This residual recognition, however limited, points to a period when the yakuza's claim to Japanese moral tradition carried greater weight—one that the regulatory transformation examined in Chapter 4 would progressively erode.

Punishment

Since rules exist, there are also sanctions for those who violate them. In gangs, the absence of a formal code of conduct means that transgressions are handled in an ad hoc manner—often through violence (Warburton, 2025). Mafias, by contrast, operate under a codified set of norms and rules, enforced through a centralised system of punishment (Catino, 2019). These include fines and expulsion from the group. There are two types of expulsion: temporary (*hamon*) and permanent (*zetsuen*). In the former case, the member is removed for a period that varies according to the severity of the transgression, but with the possibility, should no further issues arise, of being reinstated. Permanent expulsion is the most severe penalty a yakuza can receive and this eliminates any chance of future reintegration (Iwai, 1963). As I have seen in different yakuza offices, in both cases, a card is printed indicating the name of the expelled member and the terms of expulsion. The card, which reads 'We ask that you refrain from including this person in your group, as well as from engaging in work relationships or interacting with them', is sent to groups that maintain amicable relations with that of the expelled member. Yakuza offices usually keep a board on which all cards received are pinned up, so everybody knows who has been expelled. These notifications are invariably printed on paper and delivered, rather than faxed or emailed.

A further form of punishment is the *yubitsume*, a practice involving the voluntary amputation of a finger joint as an expression of apology or to take responsibility for improper behaviour, whether one's own or that of a subordinate. This practice originated in feudal times when the katana sword was widespread: without a finger joint, gripping the sword became more challenging, forcing the person to rely on the group for protection and thus demonstrating submission and dependence on the boss. *Bakuto* groups adopted this practice for serious violations not warranting death or expulsion. They were not the only ones: even prostitutes in the renowned Yoshiwara district of Edo (the ancient name for Tokyo) employed it to demonstrate loyalty to their most devoted clients. The practice later spread among *tekiya* groups. *Yubitsume* adds a gesture of genuine remorse to simple apologies, and in most cases, the individual who has behaved improperly voluntarily offers to carry it out. This can help them to avoid more severe punishments, such as temporary or permanent suspensions (Iwai, 1963). Since the errors of members are considered the responsibility of the boss, when a member commits an offence against the broader organisation (i.e. not just against his immediate boss, but against the higher-ranking superiors), the boss may offer his own finger to the higher organisation as an apology for the subordinate's error, since his affiliate was evidently not adequately trained. The *yubitsume* is a ritual that is performed either to repent for one's mistakes, or to take responsibility on behalf of a subordinate, but it is an act that should be done first of all to take responsibility with oneself rather than others (C15).

Given that this act may become necessary multiple times, in the event of further infractions, there is a specific order in which it is carried out: starting from the left little finger, followed by the right, then the second joint of the left little finger, alternating sides, progressing toward the thumb. The 'etiquette' of *yubitsume* dictates that the amputation be carried out by the individual seeking to rectify the error, using their body weight to press the knife in. Once the bone is reached, exerting further pressure becomes difficult due to both pain and the natural aversion to mutilating one's own body, often requiring multiple attempts. When continuing is impossible, a piece of cloth is tied around the finger like a tourniquet, and a second person is required to strike the knife with a hammer or mallet to cleanly sever the joint. After the amputation is complete, one must rush to hospital: there, the protruding bone is treated, and the skin is pulled upward and stitched (C14). Traditionally, the severed finger joint would be placed in a glass jar with alcohol and offered at the office altar to the boss or the group, who accepted the apology upon receiving it. Subsequently, it would be buried (Fujita, 1983). Recently, the custom of preserving severed fingertips as a macabre display has fallen out of fashion; they are simply discarded. More broadly, *yubitsume* has declined in use, with monetary penalties increasingly preferred for resolving internal disputes (C2).

Rituals

The study of rituals has been undertaken by several prominent scholars (Douglas, 1992; Durkheim, 2012; Lévi-Strauss, 1963 [1949]; van Gennep, 1960; Turner, 1969; Geertz, 1973). Rappaport defines the ritual as 'the performance of more or less invariant sequences of formal acts and utterances not entirely encoded by the performers' (1999: 24). Key features are invariance, repetition, and formality. The performance of a ritual means that something is not simply described but enacted, creating a change of disposition in participants (Bellah, 2005).

Despite their secrecy, rituals performed by criminal groups fall under the category of 'public rituals', that is, 'social practices that celebrate common knowledge' (Chwe, 2013: 4). Common knowledge is a tool of systems of authority: through public rituals, it makes sure that each member knows the message, and that all members know that everyone else has received it. Mafia groups operate in a highly dangerous environment: pressured by both the state and other illegal competitors, they must protect themselves, enforce property rights, and guarantee internal stability, while controlling conflict and concealing information on themselves and their activities. In order to guarantee stability, adaptation, and longevity, mafia groups use organisational rules. Cooperation is particularly difficult to obtain, given the lack of trust that characterises interactions in the criminal underworld. Similarly to mafia rules, mafia rituals are one of the ways in which mafias can promote cooperation within the groups, create common knowledge on the group, and expect adherence to a certain kind of behaviour (Catino, 2015).

Mafia families use rites and symbols to claim the loyalty of the associates and to create indissoluble ties amongst them. By doing so, they create and pass on a set of codes and norms that validate their existence with both their associates and the community in which they operate (Paoli, 2008). The ritual has the dual function of creating a common feeling amongst members as well as establishing before the group who is a legitimate member (Varese, 2018). Rituals are therefore instrumental in organised criminal groups in three ways: by creating common knowledge about the group's rules and codes amongst the members, by reducing asymmetric information (i.e. signalling unobservable characteristics about those who organise or participate into the ritual), and by helping the members identify with the group and therefore facilitate cooperation (Skarbek and Wang, 2015). Catino (2019) argues that mafia rituals reinforce individual and organisational identity and group solidarity, simplifying control, reducing uncertainty, reducing coordination problems and creating common knowledge, sealing nonwritten contracts and justifying punishment, and reducing cognitive dissonance by increasing the mythical and sacred aspect of the organisation.

The Russian *vory* also refer to their affiliation ceremony as 'baptism', or alternatively 'coronation'. After a scrutiny that lasts years, the initiation usually takes place during a birthday party. The senior member who vouches for the new recruit introduces him to other members, commending his actions and behaviour in the criminal world. They evaluate whether the novice possesses the characteristics that are asked of a *vor*, and ensure that he is not connected to law enforcement. Once this is established, all members pronounce an oath and the senior *vor* spells out the rules of their group. With strong similarities to the rituals of the Russian Orthodox Church, the new recruit is given a new name and starts his new life (Varese, 2018).

As a proof of their universal meaning, elements of mafia rituals can also be found in geographically distant groups, such as the Triads. Morgan (1960), in describing the initiation ritual of the Triads, reports a piece of paper on which the names of the new recruits and the oaths they swear are written. The centre of the initiation ceremony is the altar, where celebrants burn incense and bring carefully chosen offerings. On the altar, the incense burner is the core of the ritual (ter Haar, 2000). When traditional rituals were carried out in their entire form, an Incense Master was employed full time. Mass rituals would be celebrated at the group's headquarters and would last for hours, or in their complete form even days. In their traditional form, rituals involved blood to signify blood-sworn brotherhood and the recitation of oaths of loyalty to the Triad. Since these rituals require large spaces for the high number of people, and much paraphernalia, they have become increasingly rare and simplified (Chu, 2000), and are carried out secretly and using makeshift materials (Hong Kong Free Press, 29/11/2017). In the modern ceremony, the recruit is accompanied by his guarantor and, after being told the history of the Triads, he takes an oath in front of the altar. He is warned of the fate of traitors and swears his loyalty to his brothers, in some cases with his blood. Members then teach him signals and poems that will allow him to recognise other members (Chu, 2000).

Mafia initiations share four key elements: scrutiny, presence of a guarantor, recitation of the rules, and the taking of an oath. They feature a fundamental element of transformation of the self, one which cannot be reversed (Varese, 2018). Furthermore, all rituals have a connection to the sacred, giving a sacred value to the rite (Paoli, 2008). Indeed, creating important associations with the sacred, the power of the authority is reinforced (Chwe, 2013). As Durkheim posits, 'religious ceremonies . . . put the group into action; the group assembles to celebrate them. Their first effect is to bring individuals together, to multiply the relations between them and to make them more intimate with one another. By this very fact, the content of their consciousness is changed' (Durkheim, 2012: 305). When a ritual is celebrated, participants' thoughts are diverted from the everyday, they 'are centred upon their common beliefs, their common traditions, the memory of their great ancestors, the collective ideal of which they are the incarnation' (ibid.).

Initiation rituals in Italian mafias have a strong religious component. The use of religion provides legitimation of illegal behaviour, while also creating a group identity through a set of rules and codes of behaviour inspired by the Catholic tradition. In particular, during times of change and crisis, these norms help the group by maintaining consistent values and practices (Merlino, 2012). Similarly, the *vory-v-zakone* in Russia borrow traditions from the Orthodox Church. As priests and monks are renamed when they take their vows, so new members are given a new name. The images that are tattooed on the new vory are often based on the Orthodox icon paintings, featuring crucifixes and the Madonna and Child (Varese, 2018). As ter Haar (2000) argues in regard to the Chinese Triads, the sharing of a body of rituals and mythology has the very practical outcome of creating a cultural and religious identity for members, who cut ties with mainstream society in favour of a life in the criminal group. The next section explores how these common themes play out in yakuza rituals.

Yakuza rituals

Videos of yakuza ceremonies have long been available in Japan, recorded and edited by the yakuza groups that perform the ceremony. The videos are not simply a recording of the ritual, but over the years have come to feature increasingly elaborate openings. Videos usually open with views of the city in which the group is based, with a soundtrack of traditional *enka* music and the logo of the group. Before the ceremony, there is a roundup of pictures of celebrants and participants, with their names, position in the group, and role in the ceremony. These openings can last as long as fifteen minutes if the ritual involves a large number of participants.

The central ritual of the yakuza, known as *sakazukigoto*, is the ceremonial exchange of sake cups, which formalises a new relationship. As with other mafia rituals, it follows a particular sequence of gestures and actions enacted within a defined period of time, which has a tangible impact on the individual who takes part in it, and whose status is changed as an effect of the ritual itself (Catino, 2019). The background of the ceremony is invariably a room in traditional Japanese style, itself affirmative of the connection of the group with tradition. The building, the room, the altar, the words chosen for the oath, as well as the tools used and the objects in the room are all scrupulously selected. Similar to a common Shintō altar (*kamidana*), branches of *sakaki*,[3] sake, salt, and food offerings are neatly arranged on the three steps

[3] Cleyera japonica, an evergreen tree sacred in Shintoism.

of the altar. Behind the altar, a scroll reads the name of the deity to which it is dedicated[4] (Murakami, 2005a). Next to the entrance, a scroll states that seats are not assigned according to hierarchical order (*Shihō dōseki*) (Iwai, 1963; Fujita, 1983). A round mirror may be placed on the top shelf, in the middle, representing Amaterasu, the Sun Deity (Fujita, 1983; Nelson, 1996). Japanese traditional rooms are the preferred setting for the rituals: ordinary, secular spaces are turned into extraordinary, sanctified spaces to attract the attention of participants during the events, with the help of religious symbols and celebrant (van den Ende and van Marrewijk, 2018). Both large and small groups rent a hall: the office is often too small and the ritual cannot usually take place in a private house. The celebrant owns the decorations, which he takes with him to carefully prepare the room (C13).

Participants usually wear a black suit, a white shirt, a white tie, and white socks. The old boss and the soon-to-be boss sit in black and grey kimono next to the altar. The master of ceremonies (*shikai shinkō*) introduces the celebrant (*baishakunin*) and his assistants (*kaizoeyaku*). The celebrant invites everyone to face the altar, bow twice, clap twice, and bow once. Finally, the ceremony starts. Similar to Shintō rituals, the celebrant and his helpers bow twice, clap once, and bow once again. Partaking of the sake is also derived from Shintō, in which drinking ritual wine celebrates the establishment of good relationship between the god (*kami*) and the worshippers. A further resemblance with the Shintō tradition is the organisation of the ritual, which features a sequence of elegant, repeated, and highly choreographed gestures (Boyd and Williams, 1999).

The ritual is long and sophisticated but the main elements of the ceremony are as follows. The assistant walks towards the altar, his feet gliding in a semicircular movement that make his hips sway. He kneels and takes a high tray with two sake bottles in which two tall cones of paper are inserted. He returns it to the matchmaker, and glides back to the altar to take a high tray on which are placed two seabreams. Finally, he takes the high tray with the sake cups. The celebrant takes a sake cup, turns it upside down as if to check that it is empty, shows it to all those present and cleans it with a piece of paper. He proceeds to clean a pair of chopsticks and positions them back on to the

[4] In case of a group of the gambler tradition, the scrolls, right to left, may read '*Hachiman Daibosatsu*' (Great Bodhisattva Hachiman), '*Tenshō Kōtaijin*' (Amaterasu Goddess), '*Kasuga Daimyōjin*' (syncretic deity composed of five deities, each made up of a Buddhist deity and its Shintō counterpart). In the case of a group of the peddler tradition, '*Tenshō Kōtaijin*' is at the centre-bottom, on the right '*Kinjō Tennō*' (reigning emperor), on the left the saint patron '*Shinnō Kōtei*', a mythological figure known as 'Divine Farmer', of Chinese origins.

tray. The celebrant puts a piece of paper in his mouth, so that his breath does not contaminate the sake (C13). He takes the two sake bottles, shows them to everyone and takes the paper cones out. He takes a bottle and, with ceremonial gesturing, pours out the sake into a sake cup. After having offered the sake on the altar, he drinks and pats his belly twice. He pours sake from both bottles into a sake cup and, in a sequence of rhythmical gestures, he alternatively taps salt, fish, and sake. The celebrant repeats the gestures to pour the sake from the two bottles in a more emphatic fashion. These gestures are not simply for show: by moving their hand horizontally on the sake, the celebrant 'cuts the air' and the food offerings are made fresh again. He repeats the ritual with the salt, the fish, and the sake cups, and the guarantor checks again. Rituals then vary according to the relationship established by the ceremony. In a succession ritual, the old and new bosses drink from the same cup. In affiliation rituals (when one or more members become 'sons' of the boss), the sake is poured from the boss's cup into the new members' cups. In rituals where a relationship of brotherhood is established, the new brothers will drink the same sake in two different cups. The differing amounts of sake will indicate the relationship between the two brothers: two brothers at the same level will drink the same amount of sake, but if the relationship is between older and younger brothers, they will drink an amount of sake according to their seniority—usually the ratio is 6:4, or in rare cases 7:3 (Murakami, 2005a, 2005b; Stark, 1981). Throughout the ritual, sophisticated scripts are recited to clarify and ratify the actions performed.

In a succession ritual, the assistant brings to the celebrant the biggest tray from the altar, on which are placed two documents and a katana (usually fake). The celebrant reads the certificate of passage (*shōninsho*) and a catalogue (*mokuroku*). The former certificate simply recites that the old boss is leaving the new boss in charge, while the catalogue lists the objects that the old boss passes on to the new one. An example of catalogue can be taken from the succession ceremony of the fifth to the sixth boss of the Yamaguchi-gumi. The catalogue states that the new boss will receive: two pairs of fans, a sword, top-quality silk fabric, a scroll with the secret rule of the *ninkyō*, and all the rights of the group.[5] Once the celebrant puts the paper back on the tray, the assistant takes it to the centre of the room. The celebrant picks it up and places it in front of the old boss, asking him to touch it as he is going to pass it on to the new boss (C13).

[5] In the original, the list reads: *suehiro, tamashii, nerigīnu, ninkyōdō okuden, Yamaguchi-gumi ni kakawaru kenri issai.*

Succession ceremonies feature the ritual of seat-swapping at the end of the ceremony. The former boss sits on the right side of the altar, while the new boss sits on the left. Behind both of them hangs a scroll with the respective name. When the ceremony is concluded, the celebrant recites: 'Please swap your seats'.[6] The new boss and the old boss swap seats, and the scroll is torn down, revealing a new scroll with the updated name. The seat-swapping is performed even if the old boss has already passed away, with a representative acting in his place. There is record of one such case, arguably the most important of the past decades: the ceremony in which Takenaka Masahisa became fourth boss of the Yamaguchi-gumi. In 1984, Taoka Fumiko, the widow of Yamaguchi-gumi's third boss, Taoka Kazuo, took the place of her late husband, and exchanged sake cups with the new boss. It is very rare that a woman takes part in these ceremonies, as women cannot be full members of the yakuza and therefore usually all participants are men. Taoka Fumiko sat on the right side of the altar, in the same spot as an old boss would sit, although she did not sit on a cushion, but on a low chair, and the scroll behind her read her name. The rest of the ceremony was conducted normally and at the end, she swapped seats with Takenaka and the names on the scrolls were changed accordingly (Saiten, 10/01/2019).

Celebrations follow: these may consist of an elaborate lunchbox that participants consume at the table or take home, or, on more important occasions, a multiple-course menu. Companions serving food and drinks are often present at these parties, while geisha are present only in the most important ceremonies, such as those for the boss's succession.

Analysis of the ritual

Yakuza rituals have not changed much throughout time, but before the Shōwa period (1926–1989), the *sakazukigoto* was not often celebrated. Many years could go by before a prospective member would meet the boss and exchange sake cups with him (Iwai, 1963). As reported by Stark (1981), in the 1970s, a period as short as six months was deemed to be enough to allow an apprentice to join the group. In the past ten years, the situation has reverted to the pre-Shōwa era, and many years may pass before an apprentice becomes a sworn member. In a video of a recent ritual sent to me by a yakuza

[6] *Sekigawari wo onegai mōshiagemasu* or *Seki oaratemeonegaimasu.*

boss, all the new members are in their forties and fifties. Indeed, recruiting new members bears significant costs for the group: if new recruits are not entirely reliable, they might inform law enforcement about the group's illegal activities, affect the reputation of the group if they misbehave, and the group must provide them with protection and resources (Skarbek, 2008).

All passages in the ritual have a specific symbolic value. The exchanging of the sake cup symbolises blood connection, and it is used when joining a gang, and when entering the *oyabun–kobun* (parent–child) or the *gikyōdai* (brothers) connections (Kaplan and Dubro, 2003). The salt represents purification in that purity is a key concept of the Shintō tradition. Nature is understood to be the manifestation of the life-giving power (*musubi*), which is in turn associated with *kami*, the deified power that resides in nature or humans.[7] Humans may encounter some forces that obstruct the presence of positive *kami* (what we may commonly refer to as misfortune), therefore entering a state of 'pollution'. Purification is necessary then to restore the natural, positive condition of the human being (Boyd and Williams, 1999: 37–9). Almost every Shintō ceremony or festival performance features some notions of ritual purification (Uyeda, 1991: 99). The fish used are seabreams, which in Japanese are called *tai*, similar to *medetai* (congratulations), thus wishing the people involved in the ceremony well. A further reason for using the seabreams is that in the past members used to cut their forearms and mix their blood: the seabream is used to represent the smell of blood (C13). Iwai (1963) mentions that some groups also use ashes, to symbolise the lifelong subordination of the new member to the boss, until the latter has turned into ashes. Taken together, these elements—the purifying salt, the sake establishing a relationship with the kami, the mirror evoking Amaterasu—constitute a deliberate borrowing of Shintō sacred authority. The yakuza did not merely perform tradition; they performed the sacred, connecting their own hierarchies and alliances to Japan's oldest religious tradition.

The ceremonies are highly structured, and there is little variance in how they are celebrated. The greeting at the altar can be done at the very beginning, or after the initial greeting. In most cases, a mediator checks the sake before passing it on to the boss or the new member, but in some cases this

[7] The standard translation of *kami* is 'deity'. This word suggests the Western notion of a transcendental monotheistic God. However, in Shinto tradition there is no separation between divinity and humanity, and indeed *kami* are not omniscient, nor omnipotent, nor necessarily immortal (Takeshi and Goodwin, 1993).

passing on is skipped. While yakuza ceremonies allow for little variation, mafia rituals generally have a higher degree of variation and additional options (Gambetta, 1993). The celebrant recites the whole speech without fault, using a highly honorific tone.[8] As in many other rituals, the words are repeated: this reinforces the message, making it more likely that it is understood, and creating common knowledge, that is, everybody knows that everybody else is likely to have understood the message (Chwe, 2013). Also, repetition is used to direct the focus of the participants on other aspects of the objects and actions, allowing them to see them in a different light (Deacon, 1997).

As in yakuza films, in which outlaws are the most devoted defenders of social order (Igarashi, 2021), these videos portray the yakuza as the only heirs of a traditional past. These spaces and rituals are the mythical representation of the premodern world of tradition regulated by honour and honesty. They aim to represent a world which is at the antipodes of current mainstream Japanese society, characterised by ruthless neoliberalism, where individualism is taking the place of community spirit, and traditional values are disappearing. The yakuza represent an ahistorical haven in which traditional values are preserved.

A further strategic effect of yakuza rituals is the communication and sanctioning of a new leader, or a new alliance. In order to do so, a large audience is assembled and asked to participate in the rituals. Indeed, rituals of other criminal groups do not involve the number of participants that yakuza rituals usually have. The celebrant has the most prominent role, helped in the rituals by one or two assistants. The master of the ceremonies opens and closes the ritual, introducing the numerous guests. However, the ceremony may include dozens of witnesses (*mitodokenin*), recommenders (*suisennin*), mediators (*torimochinin, seiwanin, shinkōgakari*), and an audience (*tachiainin*) proportional to the size of the group and the importance of the ceremony. The filming and distribution on DVD or YouTube of the videos aim at a virtually endless expansion of the audience, further increasing the number of participants. By inviting anyone who can access YouTube to their rituals, they can gain recognition of the rites of passage from the society at large, and transform a traditionally closed ceremony into a publicly validated claim to status and legitimacy.

[8] For a script of the speeches, see Iwai (1963) and Murakami (2005a, 2005b).

Particular importance in the ritual is bestowed upon the celebrant, who can recite without hesitation long and complicated speeches. As noted by Turner (2011), the celebrants are usually authoritative representatives of the relevant community. Their special status is underlined by the special outfit worn by the celebrant and the assistants: while bosses and guarantors wear traditional male kimono (black top and grey bottoms), the celebrant usually wears a different style or a kimono in different colours, and the assistants traditionally wear white kimono. The celebrant is the only person who sits in the middle of the room, in front of the altar (even new bosses sit at one side), and almost the only person who talks. In mafia initiation rituals, a single man is usually the repository of the words that need to be recited, but the ceremony is otherwise simple (Gambetta, 1993). Yakuza rituals, on the contrary, are elaborate and long, and only very experienced members can celebrate them. Originally, celebrants were members of a *tekiya* group. This would also explain why these rituals are identical throughout Japan: as the *tekiya* were moving around the country, they brought the rituals to yakuza groups in all regions. However, nowadays, many groups (both of gambler and peddler origins), especially the bigger ones, have their own celebrant. If that is not the case, they can hire one from another group, and even from another syndicate. The ceremony features complicated gestures and speech, which are learnt by looking at other celebrants, but there is no manual from which to learn the gestures and words of rituals (C13).

The timing of the uploads of these videos on YouTube or similar platforms is also revealing: most of these videos have been recently, yet many of the ceremonies they depict date from earlier periods, when attendance was larger and the organisation appeared stronger. Thus, the yakuza's willingness to share these ceremonies (whether they directly uploaded them or allowed them to be online) needs to be contextualised within their current predicament. The yakuza have agreed to share their ceremonies online because it makes them common knowledge: not only the people there know the meaning, but they expand the audience who know virtually without limit. With the same ratio, if they were to show recent rituals, in which there are fewer participants and they are all old, they would create a different common knowledge based on the message that the yakuza is weak and declining.

The yakuza's emphasis on 'tradition' has been deliberate and strategic. 'Traditional values', such as *ninjō* and *giri* (human feelings and social obligations), were placed at the centre of the ideology the yakuza built for themselves, but the understanding that the yakuza were the defenders of these values was shared with society at large. The huge success of the yakuza films in the 1960s, an era in which many Japanese felt the immense pressure of modernising forces of rampant capitalism, is owed to the fact that viewers identified with the yakuza heroes on the screen, who represented the peace and stability of tradition, resisting the changes and greed of capitalism. The protagonist embodies tradition through gestures: traditional yakuza greetings and the elaborate etiquette of the gambling dens are signs that the hero is strictly connected to the community (Igarashi, 2021). In the same fashion, these rituals represent the yakuza as a group that is still living according to these principles.

Other rituals

While the *sakazukigoto* is the most central ritual in the life of a yakuza, there are various other ceremonies that mark the life of an affiliate.

Demukae

Being released from prison (which is ironically referred to as 'university' in yakuza jargon) is an important event in the life of a yakuza. The celebration for release from prison is called *demukae*, and it is considered to be an important rite of passage, as it demonstrates the failure of the state's attempt at re-education (Stark, 1981). Anthropologist David Stark had the opportunity to participate in a *demukae* in the late 1970s, for the release of a member who served a fifteen-year sentence for killing a member of a rival group. His action was of great significance as it led to the dissolution of the rival group and allowed the released prisoner's group to take control of a new area. Stark describes how the group started the preparation early in the morning, to be the first at the prison gates. Other groups arrived and, after the formal greetings, members positioned themselves behind their respective bosses (following the internal hierarchy where more influential affiliates are closer to their leader). The ceremony described by Stark involved 300 to 350 yakuza participants. When the prison gates opened, the boss of the released prisoner, accompanied by a couple of his associates, entered the facility and immediately pinned a badge to his chest. The badge signifies his promotion to leader, a recognition of his act that led to the group's victory over rivals and his endurance during his lengthy incarceration. It is significant that the promotion occurs within the prison walls: the affiliate emerged from prison with his new status, transitioning directly from that of an inmate to a group leader. After leaving the prison walls, the boss and the released member paused: the boss listed the names of the affiliated groups, concluding by stating that the criminal act was committed to uphold the yakuza's code. Following prolonged applause, the two went to greet the leaders of the external groups, initiating another sequence of bows, expressions of gratitude, and apologies for any inconvenience caused. After doing the same with the bosses of the internal groups, the procession of forty cars (also organised hierarchically) paraded through the city, heading to the second part of the *demukae*, which was attended only by members of the released member's main group and subgroups. In a traditional Japanese style, tatami mats were laid out with long tables: the one at the back, placed horizontally, is where the honoured guests sit (the released member and the most important members), while the other members take their seats at the long tables arranged perpendicularly. Once again, despite signs indicating that seats can be taken freely, hierarchies are respected, with more powerful affiliates seated closer to the honoured table and lower-ranking members closer to the exit. The person who was released gave his greeting speech, whilst positioned near the exit, the most humble position. Prostrated on the floor, he thanked the group for their support and apologized for any disturbance caused. His boss, remaining in his place, delivered a brief speech that concluded with a toast. In the meantime, hostesses arrived to serve drinks and keep the conversation lively: people could finally relax.

Due to the tightening of laws introduced in recent years, nowadays the *demukae* has become much simpler in order to be less conspicuous. Avoiding the great gatherings of the past, only three people are now allowed to pick up a person from prison. The *demukae* is therefore much more modest in the public eye, but celebrations can be held privately (C2).

Teuchi

In agreement with existing scholarship on conflict between criminal groups, disputes between yakuza groups arise over territory (Bichler and Norris 2024; Randle and Bichler 2016), retaliation, and threat to identity and honour of the group (Gravel et al., 2018; Hughes and Short, 2005; Lewis and Papachristos, 2020; Nakamura et al 2020; Papachristos, 2009). The rule is to avoid fighting when possible (C15), but if attacked it is imperative to retaliate (V1). To formally end a conflict, it is necessary to perform a reconciliation ceremony, known as *teuchi-shiki*, or in Kansai also referred to as *dokunagashi*, meaning 'flushing out the poison'. While the *teuchi-shiki* is a type of yakuza ceremony, it is not a celebration or an auspicious occasion. Until the rivals shake hands after the ceremony, there is no acknowledgement that the deal is made and the conflict is over.

The ceremony's order and gestures differ from other ceremonies. Key participants include an arbitrator (*chūnin*), a celebrant (*sakazukinin*), and witnesses (*tachiainin*). Additionally, a further mediator known as *honsōnin* is responsible for receiving settlement offers from both parties in the conflict. The ceremony cannot be held on either rival's turf as this could provide a geographical advantage to one party. Therefore, it is conducted in a neutral location, ideally equidistant from both parties. Traditionally, the venue, whether an inn or a hall, should have two entrances. The instigator of the conflict must enter through the side entrance. Both rivals must have a companion and no unwarranted behaviour is permitted. They are led to separate waiting rooms, where an arbitrator's representative keeps a watchful eye. In these rooms, the rivals are expected to repent and, in some cases, they may be asked to take a bath. In the middle of the ceremony hall, a folding screen is placed to prevent the rivals from seeing each other. A young person from the arbitrator's side stands on either side of the screen. The arbitrator gives a speech specifying the terms of the agreement, warning that the decision is final and that if either of the parties starts another fight for the same reason, they will become the enemy of everyone present. Upon agreement from both rivals, the folding screen is removed and the rivals share a cup of sake. During the ceremony, seabreams are used, positioned with their backs against each other. Once an agreement is reached, they are turned so their bellies touch, symbolising the resolution of the conflict. Carps can be used instead of seabreams because they co-exist peacefully in the same lake. Participants swap seats to indicate the resolution of differences. The arbitrator then makes the rivals shake hands, declares the end of the ceremony, and the participants applaud, concluding the ceremony. (Yōsensha, 2004).

Greetings

Depending on the group, seasonal meetings are held throughout the year, during which executives gather at the main office and are addressed by the boss. The most important one is the *kotohajime*, which means 'beginning of things' and is the ceremony that is usually held at the end of the year to thank everyone for their work. I watched five videos of *kotohajime* that were sent to me by a yakuza boss, who has them recorded every year. Executive members gather in the meeting room, in this case, a tatami room where they all sit on the floor. The boss enters and sits in front of everyone. First, a representative of the members makes a speech in which he thanks the boss for his hard work during the year. He confirms the loyalty that the members have for him, and asks for guidance in the next year. The boss then takes the floor. He thanks all his members for the work they are doing and then addresses the situation they are facing. Current affairs in Japan and globally are also discussed. He usually reminds everyone of their duty as a yakuza to respect their codes, respect the citizens, and act as a force for good in society. The Rokudaime Yamaguchi-gumi used to hold the *kotohajime* and other ceremonies in their headquarters in Kōbe, usually on 13 December. However, since the split of the Kōbe Yamaguchi-gumi and ensuing war, offices of the groups involved in the conflict have been closed and cannot be accessed by more than five people at the time. They are therefore held elsewhere (News Post Seven, 27/12/2022). The Yamaguchi-gumi also chooses a *shishin*, a word or motto to indicate the direction they wish to take in the following year. Since the split with the Kōbe Yamaguchi-gumi, the motto has been *washin gōichi* (friendship and unity). Previously the motto included 'Intentionally paving the way, flexibly forging paths where none exist' or 'Necessity is the mother of invention' (News PostSeven, 14/01/2024).

Other informal seasonal greetings are scattered throughout the year, depending on the boss. In one of my visits to a yakuza headquarters, I was as usual asked to wait in the common room, which is an office with desks and telephones, CCTV camera screens, television, a bulletin board, and sofas. At the entrance there are two small tables labelled 'for guests use' where guests wait until the boss is free to see them. After ten minutes, I heard a long clap coming from the boss's office, and shortly after dozens of older and young men filled the room in which I was waiting. The boss explained to me that he held a 'summer greeting' in which his executives and friendly groups (such as far-right groups) gather and he makes a speech to thank them and update them on the current situation. These meetings are another mechanism through which the yakuza enforces the set of rules and values that are at the core of their organisation. More recently, as the yakuza has become increasingly secretive, these meetings also serve to manage silence or coordinate behaviour vis-à-vis civil society.

Beyond these internal gatherings, yakuza groups have traditionally extended seasonal rituals into the public sphere as deliberate performances of community belonging. The Yamaguchi-gumi, for instance, held annual mochi-pounding ceremonies in December and public New Year shrine visits, positioning the group as a participant in the shared ceremonial life of the community. As recently as December 2025, the Yamaguchi-gumi held a mochitsuki at a subsidiary organisation's headquarters in Aichi prefecture, with nearly 200 members in attendance and boss Shinobu Tsukasa himself taking the mallet (Shūkan Asahi Geinō, 18/01/2026). While photographers and the police gathered outside, the ceremony was not open to the public as it was in the past. Similarly, the New Year shrine visit (*hatsumode*) illustrates how regulatory pressure has stripped away this public dimension. Until the designation of the Yamaguchi-gumi factional conflict as a 'specific designated conflict' in 2020, boss Shinobu Tsukasa and high-ranking officials would attend the *hatsumode* together at the Kōbe Gokoku Shrine near the Yamaguchi-gumi headquarters—a highly visible public performance of organisational unity and community belonging. Since 2020, restrictions prohibiting gatherings of five or more people within the designated conflict zone have reduced attendance to a handful of senior figures (News PostSeven, 19/01/2026). In both cases, the ritual persists, but its public dimension has been stripped.

Alliances

Alliances between groups represent an extension of the same regulatory logic that governs internal yakuza organisation. Just as rules, hierarchy, and rituals serve to manage behaviour and prevent conflict within a group, inter-group alliances formalise relationships between rival organisations, creating shared obligations and mechanisms for dispute resolution that operate at a level above the individual syndicate. Like the *kashijima/karijima* system examined in the previous chapter, they reflect the yakuza's broader capacity to institutionalise order rather than rely on violence alone. Alliances between groups were established in the 1970s and 1980s, periods of intense conflicts during which smaller groups needed to protect themselves against bigger groups. However, as the 'Big 3' (Yamaguchi-gumi, Inagawa-kai, Sumiyoshi-kai) swelled their ranks and became the oligopoly of the yakuza world, many alliances dissolved as smaller groups entered into the sphere of influence of one of these three syndicates. After the introduction of the Anti-Yakuza Law in 1991, the number of yakuza conflicts decreased, but some alliances remained active as organisations aimed at maintaining peaceful relationships amongst different families, to avoid increased police scrutiny. The three main alliances are the Kantō Shinbokukai (active in the Kantō area), the Goshakai (which includes families in the central area of Japan of Chūgoku and Shikoku), and the Yonshakai (in Kyūshū). The Shinbokukai is the successor to the Kantō Hatsukakai, an alliance that operated for forty-two years to facilitate the relationship between the groups of the Kantō region (Inagawa-kai, Sumiyoshi-kai, Matsuba-kai, Soai-kai, Toai-kai). It was not an alliance against the Yamaguchi-gumi since the Inagawa-kai has always had a good relationship with them, but there was an agreement that, to maintain the peace, the Yamaguchi-gumi would not cross into the territory of the five groups. The five groups agreed that in case of an attack on the house of one of the bosses, or if police or civilians were harmed in yakuza conflicts, the person responsible for the attack would be subjected to temporary or permanent expulsion. In 1996, they prohibited the use of guns. Due to the economic difficulties sparked by the bursting of the economic bubble, the Yamaguchi-gumi started to expand towards Tokyo, leading to a series of conflicts. The Hatsuka-kai was not able to mediate efficiently and, in some instances, the Yamaguchi-gumi resolved the conflict. The alliance was eventually dissolved and reformed under the name Kantō Shinboku-kai in 2014. In addition to the original five members, the Kokusui-kai (a group affiliated to the Yamaguchi-gumi) joined the new alliance, therefore involving also the Yamaguchi-gumi.

The Goshakai is composed of the Godaime Kyoseikai, the Yondaime Asano-gumi, the Sandaime Kyodokai, the Nidaime Shinwa-kai, and the Shichidaime Goda-ikka. The first alliance of the region was the Kansai Hatsuka-kai (founded in 1970) which had the objective of fostering good relations among its members, after a violent period of conflicts, and hindering the expansion of the Yamaguchi-gumi. In 1989 the alliance was dissolved and the new Nishi Nippon Hatsuka-kai was formed, based on the principle of 'don't interfere, don't get interfered with', and the understanding that if one group was attacked, they would all unite to fight against the aggressor. From the beginning, the alliance tried to establish a good relationship with the Yamaguchi-gumi. When it became inefficient, the alliance was dissolved and in 1996 the Goshakai was established. Executive members meet regularly, while the bosses gather to strengthen relationships between groups. The Goshakai has a strong connection with the Yamaguchi-gumi. Finally, the Yonshakai gathers the main groups of the Kyushu region. This area, despite its limited size, is home to multiple autochthonous yakuza groups and groups affiliated with the Yamaguchi-gumi. The alliance started as the

Sanshakai in 1991, comprising the Kudo-kai, the Dojin-kai, and the Taishu-kai. The non-designated yakuza group Kumamoto-kai joined in 2005, and its name changed to the Yonshakai. The executives meet once a month to discuss relevant matters. The group on duty, which is the one organising the meeting, changes every month. During these meetings, the executives gather, strengthen their relationship, and discuss how to stop the emergence of new conflicts. Everything they discuss and decide is then notified to members of their groups so that they are informed and instructed. While groups in the Yonshakai are not officially related to the Yamaguchi-gumi, relations between them are friendly (JJ2014/11).

A further point concerns the Kyokuryū-kai, the syndicate based in Okinawa. With its distinct historical trajectory and cultural identity, Okinawa was only incorporated into Japan in 1879, and its social dynamics remain markedly different from those of the mainland. According to senior executives of the group, the Kyokuryū-kai view themselves as genuinely independent from mainland organisations, even while maintaining cordial relations. As one executive explained, 'We're friends with everyone, but if someone from the mainland wants to come here and take us over . . . let them try. We'll be waiting with our weapons ready' (C16).

Alliances are sanctioned through the ceremony of the exchange of sake cups (*sakazukigoto*), in which bosses become equal brothers. Other alliances can be started separately: for instance, a boss who is in an alliance may exchange a sake cup with a boss of a group outside the alliance, therefore creating a connection to the alliance without including the new group. Good relationships are also fostered and maintained through the participation of members in other groups' ceremonies: for example, while the Yamaguchi-gumi is not part of the Goshakai, bosses of the Yamaguchi-gumi have often acted as guarantors in ceremonies of groups members of the Goshakai, thereby showing the connection between them.

Masculinity and women in the yakuza

The role of women in the mafias has been long debated. Italian mafias have a very strong sexist connotation, therefore giving little space to women (Di Maria and Lo Verso 2007). Scholarship is divided as to the role of mafia women. On one hand, a culturalist approach sees women as active participants of the mafia, although in a limited and unofficial way (Allum, 2007; Ingranscì, 2007; Siebert, 2007). In the Sicilian mafias, women have had a certain importance transmitting values and beliefs, and taking on responsibilities when their family members are arrested (Schimmenti et al., 2014). In the 'Ndrangheta, in which blood ties are central, women may play an active role and indeed, in many cases, women have been involved in the business of their relatives (Ingrascì, 2007; Siebert, 2007). On the other hand, according to a rational-choice approach, women, not being able to join the organisation, do not play an active role in it. They may have become more visible, but ultimately, they cannot formally access the group, let alone positions of power, and have no capacity for exercising violence independently (Pizzini-Gambetta, 2006). Even in the Camorra, where the role of women has been more visible, women do not start from scratch, but rather, take on roles that are afforded to them by the men around them (Pizzini-Gambetta, 2008).

Similarly to other mafias, the yakuza is an all-male organisation. Being a man is a central part of being a yakuza, and masculinity is a value in itself. A traditional yakuza song recites 'I want to become a man, I want to live like a man, I want to die like a man' (Fujita, 1983). Yakuza members often refer to the importance of masculinity and being a man to be a good yakuza. Women, therefore, cannot traditionally hold any formal roles within the organisation, but they play peripheral roles as wives and partners of members. They might support their husbands' activities by completing simple tasks or being involved in the world of night-time entertainment related to their husbands' group (C2).

Women have in the past been active members of the yakuza, although informally. Similarly to their Italian counterparts, their position of power derived from their husbands, whose role as leader they take on (Ingranscì, 2007; Massari, 2007). Matsuda Yoshiko, after her husband's death, took control of the powerful Kantō Matsuda-gumi and ran the day-to-day operation of the black market in Shinbashi, Tokyo. Most famously, Taoka Fumiko took the reins of the Yamaguchi-gumi when her husband died in 1981. The successor he had chosen died before he could take up his new position and the role was assumed by Fumiko, a silent power in the organisation. She only covered the role for an interim period but during that time she took the boss's seat at meetings and gave judgements on intra-gang disputes (Kaplan and Dubro, 2003). Usually, however, the boss's wife, known as *ane-san*, has the role of supporting new members, helping them with their transition, and mediating between them and her husband.

An exception to this strict rule is that of Nishimura Mako, who was active in a subgroup of the Sumiyoshi-kai in Gifu city. Nishimura was born into a family of government officials, in which she was strictly disciplined. In junior high school she joined biker gangs (*bōsōzoku*) which, in Japan, are a subculture for teenagers rather than adults. While *bōsōzoku* are a rare sight in Japan today, in the 1970s and 1980s they had as many as 40,000 members (MoJ, 2019), and were a recruitment hub for the yakuza: indeed, being a *bōsōzoku* after twenty years of age was considered unsuitable and those who wanted to remain in that underworld would go on to work for the yakuza in different capacities. Through the *bōsōzoku*, Nishimura met a young yakuza member who would take her with him while he ran errands, such as collecting protection money, resolving disputes, engaging in blackmail, and scouting women for prostitution. She was eventually noticed by the local yakuza groups when she helped her friend in a fight, which she turned into a bloodbath. Given her ability with violence, two different groups which were active in Gifu tried to scout her. She had been to detention centres several times during her teenage years, and had learnt the basics of the business from young yakuza that she used to accompany on his errands. She started an escort service that was co-managed with a yakuza member, hiring young women from the juvenile detention centre. She finally accepted the invitation to become a member by the boss of a group affiliated to the Sumiyoshi-kai. Nishimura recounts that she chose her boss because of his *ninkyō*-like qualities, as she saw his as someone to whom she could trust her life. She chose an older brother to follow, gave her oath, and started to live the rigorous life of a trainee. She moved into the yakuza offices with a cohort of male recruits, performing daily tasks, and eventually taking part in the group's criminal activities. Throughout her career, Nishimura was involved in all usual activities of a yakuza group, including sex trafficking, drugs, and debt collection. Her first job involved selling women to the yakuza-controlled Watarakano Island in Mie Prefecture, commonly known as 'Prostitution Island' as it hosted numerous brothels. Some establishments offered a sum in advance for a woman. Nishimura would sell women indebted to the group, collect the cash, and leave the woman there to work and repay the establishment (C14).

The case of Nishimura is an exception in the world of the yakuza. She insists that she was always treated like a man: although the only woman in the group, she underwent the same training and performed the same activities as her male counterparts. She was able, and very willing, to exert violence. Nishimura gives this as the reason she was approached by yakuza groups, and how she continued to use violence when necessary throughout her career, during which she never rose to positions of real power. But her case is unique: women who have had positions of power in the yakuza were granted leadership positions momentarily and only because of their husbands. Other women were able to have a peripheral role as entrepreneurs in markets where skills other than violence are required. Masculinity remains a core value of the organisation and ultimately makes it impossible for women to reach positions of real power, proving that a woman's ability to play an active role in the organisation is contingent on formal affiliation—that is, finding the rare boss who would accept a woman in the group—and the capacity to exercise violence independently.

Conclusion

The structures, rules, and rituals examined in this chapter reveal the depth and internal complexity of the yakuza. In a context where the state does not criminalise the organisation per se but excludes it from legal protection, yakuza groups have developed internally binding norms, codified hierarchies, and elaborate ceremonies that serve to stabilise authority and foster discipline. This level of organisational elaboration was only possible because of the yakuza's semi-legal status. Unlike other mafias that are forced into secrecy and simplicity to evade law enforcement, the yakuza could afford complexity and visibility. Internally, this clarity of hierarchy and shared ideology resolved coordination problems and gave members a stable sense of identity. Externally, it made the yakuza legible to the wider public as a recognisable social institution with its own history, codes, and relationship to Japanese tradition. The visibility that other mafias are forced to suppress became, for the yakuza, a source of authority. The relationship between boss and affiliates is strategic as much as it is personal: cemented through pedagogical practices, shared daily life, and monetary obligations, it creates bonds designed to supersede even blood ties and pre-existing loyalties. For many members, entry into the yakuza was driven not only by necessity but by a deep admiration for a respected senior, as well as the group's power, codes, and masculine identity. In a world where betrayal is an ever-present risk, this aspirational dimension can produce a rare and durable loyalty.

The rules of conduct are necessary for internal coordination, but they also have an ideological foundation grounded in *ninkyō*, a logic of masculine honour and obligation that remains central to the identity of many members. Through these rules, the yakuza position themselves not only as a legitimate group that has a well-defined internal order, but as bearers of moral authority. Rituals play a central role in sustaining these structures. The *sakazukigoto*, with its rigid choreography and roots in ritual traditions that are not exclusive to the yakuza but widespread in Japanese society, is used internally to mark affiliation or succession, but externally, it confers legitimacy upon the group in the eyes of the public. As in other mafias, the ritual's power lies in its capacity to create common knowledge: all participants witness, and know that others witness, the reassertion of hierarchy and the transmission of authority. But in the case of the yakuza, these performances are also circulated in video form, expanding the audience and extending the effect of the ritual beyond the immediate room. In a time of growing repression and declining membership, the ritual becomes both an internal reaffirmation and an external claim to continuity.

Yet this very reliance on tradition reveals the pressures of the present. As will be explored in the following chapters, the rituals increasingly feature older participants, initiation is delayed or avoided, and affiliation requires costly commitments that few are willing or able to make. As the group contracts, the symbolic burden placed on ritual increases. The sacralisation of the group, through the use of Shintō iconography, gestures of purification, and theatrical references to a lost moral order, reflects the yakuza's effort to preserve a coherent identity even as their social embeddedness erodes. As we will see in the following chapters, however, the very tools that once sustained their authority are under strain, and the meanings they carry are no longer shared with wider society.

4
Policy, policing, and punishment

Introduction

This chapter explores the government's increasing pressure on the yakuza, beginning with an overview of the three main strategies employed against the Japanese mafia: the first police campaign in 1964, the first Anti-Yakuza Law in 1991, and the Yakuza Exclusionary Ordinances (YEO) in 2010–2011. It examines the evolving police–yakuza relationship and the related level of law enforcement, before analysing sentencing patterns and the high costs that the increased law enforcement put on the yakuza. Two central assets of the yakuza's governance function were affected: first, the loss of visibility undermined their legitimacy; second, the rising cost of membership reduced their workforce, limiting their ability to govern.

According to Tilly, organised crime is different from war-making and state-making because, while they are all quintessential protection rackets, the latter have the advantage of legitimacy (Tilly, 1985: 169). To some extent, the yakuza had this advantage as well, as a group with a legal membership, which allowed syndicates to maintain a high level of visibility. The visibility, together with their ideological drive, was instrumental in their governance function, enabling them to operate openly, cultivate a strong reputation, and project an image of authority and legitimacy. Their public presence reinforced their status, attracted clients, and helped maintain their influence in both legal and illegal markets. However, this chapter shows how, as legal pressures have intensified, stricter regulations and enforcement have increasingly constrained the yakuza's ability to operate in the open. The loss of visibility has undermined their capacity to govern, as groups struggle to control their territories and maintain their traditional networks of power.

Although sentencing practices have not changed drastically, the level of enforcement has. More frequent arrests, combined with rising costs associated with yakuza membership, have made the organisation less attractive to potential recruits. At the same time, the financial burden of imprisonment has led many existing members to leave, further weakening the syndicates, and therefore further weakening their ability to govern.

21st Century Yakuza. Martina Baradel, Oxford University Press. © Martina Baradel 2026.
DOI: 10.1093/9780191987755.003.0005

Countering the yakuza in Japan: the first attempt

Until 1960 the police and the yakuza had a friendly relationship that often involved collaboration between the two groups. The first nationwide strategy against the yakuza, the 'summit strategy' (Chōjō Sakusen), was introduced in 1964 because of the pressure of public opinion, and as an attempt by the police to establish themselves as the legitimate providers of governance.

The events of 1960, 'the most politically turbulent year of Japan's post-war history' (Siniawer, 2008:161), are key to understanding the relationship between the yakuza, the police, and politicians. Indeed, the political struggle in this year saw various violent peaks: labour strikes (notably, the strike at Miike Coal Mines in Kyūshū, the longest in Japan's history), mass demonstrations against the US–Japan Security Treaty, and the assassination of Japanese Socialist Party (JSP) chairman Asanuma Inejirō (ibid.). The revision of the Security Treaty was opposed by liberals and leftists, who argued that it would permanently subordinate Japan to the United States (Igarashi, 2000). The weeks leading up to the ratification of the Treaty, scheduled for 19 June 1960, were scattered with mass protests, to which the ruling Liberal Democratic Party responded by turning to yakuza groups to suppress protesters, drawing on longstanding political connections (see Chapter 2). The political violence lasted throughout the summer, as protesters redirected their energy to the ongoing Miike strike. With the assassination of JSP Chairman Asanuma, a symbol of the anti-Treaty movement, it became clear that there was a need to put a stop to widespread violent episodes and limit the power of the yakuza. The 1964 public opinion poll on the police, which was administered by the government, reported that public opinion was showing signs of concern over the criminal groups (Seiron Chōsa—Naikakufu, 1964). Anxiety over the possible resurgence of fascism and the destruction of democracy prompted public discussions and criticism about violence. Mainstream newspapers condemned the violent episodes, while the newly elected Prime Minister Ikeda Hayato sided with the anti-violence faction. Many parties introduced bills banning violence, and by the mid-1960s, even the Liberal Democratic Party had distanced themselves from the groups they had previously hired prior to the violent events of 1960. For their part, the yakuza became less interested in using violence: the groups became wealthy and they realised that money was more efficient and less visible than using violent tactics (Siniawer, 2008).

By 1964, when the police put into effect the 'summit strategy', the yakuza had effectively already lost their favoured privileged relationship with the police. While prewar yakuza gangs comprised around fifty people each, throughout the 1950s and the early 1960s the newly emerged yakuza groups had grown to thousands of members: in 1958 yakuza syndicates counted 70,000 members, while only five years later the number rose to 184,000 (Kaplan and Dubro, 2003). Widespread public discontent, increased intra-gang violence, and the upcoming 1964 Tokyo Olympics led to the summit strategy in 1964 (Hill, 2003). Furthermore, by this time the police force and the self-defence forces had finally become organised, and, as such, needed to assert state power over the widespread influence of the yakuza that had, in the immediate postwar period, served as an alternative police force. The strategy relied on two approaches: arresting high-ranking officials rather than low-ranking members and cutting off their sources of revenue. In 1964, the police arrested 932 yakuza bosses, and 3,547 high-ranking officials. In addition, they focused law enforcement activities on ten yakuza groups which, with the exception of the Yamaguchi-gumi, subsequently had to dissolve. In the two years in which the summit strategy was deployed, 17,000 people were arrested, 20,000 weapons were confiscated, and 475 groups dissolved (Miyazaki, 2010).

The series of crackdowns had a severe impact on both small and medium-sized groups, whose income depended on the traditional crime types targeted by the 1964 strategy (i.e. gambling and extortion), while larger groups were able to remain in operation in the midst of increased law enforcement attacks (Hill, 2003). The Yamaguchi-gumi resisted these attacks by diversifying their activities domestically and abroad, while the groups that disbanded not only reformed but came back stronger and larger. This happened because during the crackdowns of the first summit strategy, small and medium-sized groups were forced to ask for protection from bigger groups, who ended up absorbing them or, alternatively, groups formed more coalitions. Therefore, the most enduring result of the summit strategies was an oligopolisation of the yakuza, that is, fewer groups which were larger and stronger (Miyazaki, 2010; Ino, 2000).

Indications of the perceived effectiveness of the summit strategy can be extrapolated from the 1971 public poll on the yakuza and the activity of the police, which showed that, in comparison to 1964 when only 22.8 per cent of the respondents thought that the police were actively repressing the yakuza, by 1971 this percentage had doubled. However, in 1978 the data once again registered a plunge in the perceived effectiveness of the anti-yakuza strategies (Seiron Chōsa—Naikakufu, 1971, 1978). Ultimately, the increased harshness of the summit strategy was not sustained within an ongoing initiative comparable to the one introduced by Japanese law enforcement in 1991 that continues to this day. The summit strategies were developed and enforced by the police and are thus better understood as an ad hoc strategy that was designed to be applied only temporarily. While their effect on the groups was also temporary, the long-term effect was the creation and expansion of big syndicates. But by forcing smaller groups to consolidate under stronger syndicates, it created a more powerful and resilient yakuza that would require a fundamentally different approach of systematic legal and administrative exclusion.

The first Anti-Yakuza Law

Japan passed the first law targeting the yakuza, the Bōryokudan Taisakuhō (hereafter Bōtaihō or Anti-Yakuza Law) in 1991. Until the 1980s, the yakuza had existed in a comfortable legislative limbo that allowed them to be prosecuted for crimes individually and not as a group. By the beginning of the 1990s, however, the situation had escalated to a critical point. A climate of economic uncertainty and concern over the increasing crime rate helps account for why polls reported that Japanese citizens felt less and less safe, despite the fact that crime rates in Japan had not increased significantly (Miyazawa, 2008). A series of factors made the population both more cognisant of, and worried about, the presence of the 90,000 or so active yakuza within the national territory (NPA, 1999), and given that the dominant Liberal Democratic Party had lost control of the upper house of the Diet in 1989, the first time this had occurred since 1955, political parties were particularly receptive towards public opinion (Midford, 2011).

The underlying reasons for adopting a more severe approach to combatting the yakuza were both domestic and foreign in nature. Domestically, a series of incidents referred to as 'violent interventions in civil affairs' (*minji kankyū bōryoku*, or *minbō*) corroded the image of the yakuza as a distant actor who did not involve civilians in their businesses. As discussed in Chapter 2, the core business of the yakuza had been private protection and dispute resolution for citizens or actors in illegal markets who could not access legal courts. However, in the 1980s, the yakuza expanded their activities to the legitimate economy, also offering their services to reluctant citizens, which was de facto extortion: however, yakuza members were able to make requests for money in a way that stopped short of constituting intimidation or extortion, for instance by handing over a business card with the group logo, or by showing their tattoos. The group's reputation for violence did the rest (Hill, 2003).

Furthermore, in the second half of the 1980s, a ferocious internal war in the Yamaguchi-gumi, the Yama-ichi war, spread violent attacks outside the circle of the yakuza. After the death of Taoka Kazuo, the legendary boss of the Yamaguchi-gumi who had led the group to become the most powerful in Japan, the two candidates to succeed him were Takenaka Masahisa and Yamamoto Hiroshi. The final decision was made by a group of high-ranking officials led by Taoka's widow, Fumiko, who supported Takenaka's candidacy. Not accepting this decision, Yamamoto split from the group and founded his own organisation, the Ichiwa-kai, in 1984. He was followed by several powerful bosses, but after initial success, many of the members who had followed Yamamoto in the breakaway returned to their original group, weakening the Ichiwa-kai. In an attempt to regain power, Yamamoto orchestrated the assassination of Takenaka in 1985. Takenaka was shot dead along with two of his top lieutenants while waiting for a lift at his mistress's home. The Yamaguchi-gumi then came under the leadership of Nakanishi Kazuo, who declared war on Yamamoto. This led to four years of violent clashes, with over 200 street shootings, resulting in the deaths of members from both factions, as well as several civilians caught in the crossfire. The conflict ended in 1989 with the Yamaguchi-gumi victory and the dissolution of the Ichiwa-kai. However, the high number of casualties, including police officers and civilians, tarnished the yakuza's reputation as a group that kept its conflicts away from the public (Nagata, 2011).

A further significant example of the yakuza's violent involvement in civil affairs was the case of the Ichiriki-ikka's office in Hamamatsu. In August 1986, the Ichiriki-ikka (affiliated to the Yamaguchi-gumi), headed by Tetsuya Aono, moved their offices to a newly constructed building in Ebitsuka, a neighbourhood in Hamamatsu City. However, the group hid the intended use of the building, denying that it would serve as a yakuza office. In response, local residents launched a campaign against the establishment of the office as part of a broader anti-yakuza movement, without the support of the police or the city council. In November, Aono filed a lawsuit at the Hamamatsu branch of the Shizuoka District Court against nine representatives of the anti-yakuza movement, demanding 10 million yen in damages for the psychological distress allegedly caused by their activities. However, the group did not only pursue the matter through legal means: on 20th June 1987, Mitsui Yoshihiro, the head lawyer representing the residents in the anti-yakuza movement, was stabbed and seriously injured by a member of Ichiriki-ikka. The courts eventually ruled against the group, prohibiting regular meetings at the building and imposing financial penalties for violations, and the Hamamatsu Central Police Station of the Shizuoka Prefectural Police, in support of the anti-yakuza campaign, set up a security outpost directly across from the yakuza office. In 1988, the Ichiriki-ikka finally settled, and agreed to remove its office from Ebitsuka, pledging not to use the building as a yakuza headquarters in the future. The group was not satisfied with the outcome, however, and three years after the settlement, one of the representatives of the anti-yakuza movement was attacked with a blade (V2, V3; Hamamatsu City, 2025; Yamadaira, 1988).

Cases like this, in which residents and their legal representatives faced retaliation simply for organising against yakuza presence, made clear that civil society alone could not address the problem and that a dedicated legal framework was needed. Murahashi Hiroshi is a lawyer in his eighties who was in the Committee of the Japan Federation of Bar Association (JFBA) for the creation of the first Anti-Yakuza Law (Bōtaihō), and then became the head of the Committee on Violent Intervention in Civil Affairs of the JFBA when the Law was introduced. He recounts as follows the creation of the Law:

> The police were powerless. Simply arresting yakuza affiliates was not enough. There needed to be a legal framework, a system that would allow the police to arrest yakuza as an organisation. This led to the creation of the Anti-Yakuza Law. All political parties supported it, agreeing that the yakuza had gone too far. While the Law could not outright deny the existence of the yakuza, it specifically prohibited their anti-social activities. The JFBA opposed the Law, fearing it could suppress the rights of civic groups and labour movement, within the JFBA only the Committee on Violent Intervention in Civil Affairs supported it. (V2)

In 1991, a Japanese commission visited the United States and Italy to learn about the anti-mafia laws that had been introduced in those countries. However, Japan has refrained from introducing a legal provision akin to Italy's Article 416-bis, which criminalises mere membership in a mafia organisation, due to concerns over constitutional constraints—particularly regarding Article 21 of the Japanese Constitution, which guarantees freedom of association. Prohibiting membership alone would require either amending or reinterpreting this constitutional guarantee. This would be contentious, as it could set a precedent for altering other constitutional provisions, including the much-debated Article 9, which renounces war and prohibits Japan from maintaining a standing military. Any attempt to modify fundamental constitutional rights, even in the context of organised crime, risks opening broader debates on constitutional revision, a topic that has long been politically and socially divisive (V1; V2).

The change of approach towards the yakuza resulted in the creation of an Anti-Yakuza Law, the Bōryokudan Taisaku-hō. The Bōtaihō is not a criminal or special penal law, but rather a police regulatory law designed to establish and enforce order violations (Fujinaga, 1992). It targets legal loopholes that were previously not covered by conventional criminal laws, as the initial legislative approach prioritised restraint in criminalisation. For instance, coercive demands made by yakuza members do not necessarily constitute extortion, but there is a high likelihood that they do in practice. Such actions should then be considered as both the violation of criminal laws, as well as the violations of administrative orders under the Anti-Yakuza Law (Bōryokudan Taisaku Hōsei Kenkyūkai, 1995). This law marked a shift in the hitherto tolerant political and institutional approach towards the syndicates. Through the introduction of this law, yakuza groups began to be officially referred to as *bōryokudan*, which literally means 'violent groups'. The Law aims to both control the yakuza's demands over the population (protection money, subcontracting, etc.) and prevent the damage caused by yakuza activities (Bōtaihō, Art.1-1). Public Safety Commissions were established and charged with designating as *bōryokudan* all those groups that collectively and regularly promoted violent illegal acts (Bōtaihō, Art.1-3). The Law seeks to end the yakuza's demands upon citizens or businesses (Bōtaihō, Art.2-9) and regulates the use of their offices during periods of turf struggles (Bōtaihō, Art.3-15). The Law also forced yakuza groups to take down the signs from their offices, and prohibited them from handing out business cards with the group's logo. The police interpreted the Law via a three-pillar strategy that consisted of promoting the rehabilitation of yakuza members and preventing young people from becoming involved with the yakuza; preventing acts of revenge against victims, witnesses, and people who are attempting to eliminate the yakuza; and guaranteeing the safety and security of concerned individuals (NPA, 1993). The Law has undergone multiple revisions, with the most significant being the 2004 amendment. This revision introduced the employer liability clause which established that, in cases where damage is inflicted by yakuza members during conflicts, lawsuits could be filed not only against the direct perpetrators but also against the leader of the organisation (Botaihō, Art. 31-2). A subsequent amendment in 2008 further broadened this clause to encompass all economic activities conducted by organised crime groups, thereby strengthening legal avenues for holding leadership accountable for the group's unlawful actions (Botaihō, Art. 31-3).

Yakuza syndicates opposed the Law by invoking the Constitution and their civil rights: many groups insisted that yakuza groups and criminal groups were two different things entirely, and refused to be called *bōryokudan* in light of the negative connotations associated with the name. Groups such as the Yamaguchi-gumi, the Aizu Kotetsu-kai, and the Kudō Rengō Asano-ikka filed a lawsuit to avoid being so designated, which was later dismissed. The Yamaguchi-gumi opposed the Law forcefully, arguing that it infringed upon the right of association and the principle of equality before the law (Miyazaki, 2010). According to the Bōtaihō, a group can also be designated as 'Specially Dangerous': under this classification, if members of the group unjustly demand money or goods from citizens within designated security zones, the police can arrest them immediately without first issuing a cease-and-desist order. In 2012, the Public Safety Commissions of Fukuoka and Yamaguchi became the first to apply this designation, classifying the Kudō-kai, a Kyūshū-based group notorious for its violent methods, as a Specially Designated Dangerous Organised Crime Group. In response, the Kudō-kai challenged the designation in court, arguing that it violated their constitutional rights to freedom of expression and freedom of association (Nikkei Shimbun, 19/01/2013). Furthermore, since legislators drew on foreign anti-organised crime laws such as the RICO Act, the yakuza rejected being classified alongside other mafia groups: 'The aim [of the Bōtaihō] was to destroy the "Japanese culture" symbolised by the yakuza, and make it easier for American capital to exert influence over Japan' (JJ09/2013:35). The subsequent amendments have also been commented on in yakuza magazines with the submission that the Law discriminates against the yakuza, leaving them without human rights (JJ05/2012). 'The fact that a prominent professor openly stated that "constitutional human rights are not guaranteed" to members of the yakuza is proof that the Japanese constitution is already in meltdown. It is blatantly ignoring Article 14 of the Constitution that states that all citizens are equal under the law' (JJ10/2012:24).

The policing model introduced by the Bōtaihō centres exclusively on designated yakuza groups, with the list of yakuza groups being updated annually by the Public Safety Commission. At the time of writing, twenty-five groups are designated and are therefore subjected to the restrictions introduced by the Bōtaihō; however, there are also minor yakuza groups that are not officially designated as such. Groups can avoid this designation by dissolving and reorganising under a different name and different leadership, or if they are not affiliated to one of the twenty-five designated groups. The Ninkyō Dantai Yamaguchi-gumi (now known as Kizuna-kai), which split from the Kōbe Yamaguchi-gumi forming a new group, attempted to avoid being so designated by not performing the ceremony of pledging over sake cups and avoiding the traditional parent–son relationship: the members were all equally medium-ranked, while the boss Oda Yoshinori did not hold the traditional title of boss, but rather took the title of 'representative' (Mizoguchi, 2017). Other criminal groups are not the target of anti-yakuza countermeasures since they are not listed amongst the designated groups. Within this model of policing, yakuza groups are visible, semi-legitimate, and although membership is not criminalised per se, belonging to a yakuza group can result in harsher sentences—although that is not always the case (Baradel, 2021). This strategy represents a double-edged sword for the yakuza: on the one hand, if a group is included on the list of designated yakuza groups, then it is subjected to more policing compared to a non-yakuza criminal group; on the other hand, they are attributed the status of a group that is one step above a 'disorganised' criminal group. While renouncing yakuza status might seem like a rational strategy to evade police attention, official recognition provides reputational benefits crucial for governance-oriented groups. Collective reputation enhances the group's ability to extract rents within its territory, as its name carries weight and signals reliability, proving that they are not merely a gang. As described in earlier chapters, yakuza groups are highly hierarchical and bureaucratic, they make use of strong tools of internal governance, well-defined systems of dispute resolution, and are considered the regulators of the criminal underworld. Their reputation as a semi-legitimate provider of protection rests precisely on this restraint: unlike disorganised criminal groups, they regulate violence rather than deploy it freely, and it is this quality that makes their name carry weight.

Exclusionary Ordinances

The Western part of Japan has traditionally been a centre of yakuza activity: from Kōbe, the stronghold of the Rokudaime Yamaguchi-gumi, to the Kyūshū region, home to a variety of yakuza groups operating shoulder to shoulder. In April 2018, I made a trip to a yakuza hotbed to meet an ex-high-ranking member of one of the most violent yakuza groups in Japan. During the interview, I found out that since quitting his group, he had initially struggled with being reintegrated in the society, but had eventually managed to open his own noodle shop. He invited me to visit him the next day, to try the noodles he had worked so hard to master. I gladly accepted and asked how I could find his shop in the busy shopping street. He told me, 'When you see a set of CCTV cameras, turn left'. The next morning, I walked the covered shopping street looking for the cameras, thinking that its placement was a strange coincidence. After a luscious cup of noodles, we had some time to talk. That is when I learnt that the camera was not there by chance: it had intentionally been installed by the police when he opened the shop, a visual representation of the scrutiny to which ex-yakuza members are subjected. It was indeed the only set of cameras in the whole street and it was pointing directly at his shop. Furthermore, his shop was probably the only one without insurance, because according to the Yakuza Exclusionary Ordinances, as an ex-member, prevented him from obtaining it. That meant that he would be liable if any accident, such as a fire, were to occur in his shop, and would also have to repay the neighbouring shop owners if their premises were damaged. These are real-life effects of the Yakuza Exclusionary Ordinances (Bōryokudan Haijōjōrei, hereafter YEO), the latest and possibly most effective anti-yakuza regulations. They come after twenty years from the Anti-Yakuza Law and coincide with an unprecedented crackdown of the yakuza. The Bōtaihō was part of a punitive trend that I refer to elsewhere as 'shaming paternalism': within this model, both current and former criminals are shamed and struggle to reintegrate, while the state's intrusiveness operates at various stages (Baradel, 2021).

The YEO were first introduced in 2010 in the city of Fukuoka and have subsequently been applied across the whole country. These ordinances propose a more radical and normative approach to the combatting of organised crime in Japan, and grant minor governing bodies decision-making power over anti-yakuza strategies. The main provisions of the YEO can be summed up in four points: do not fear the yakuza, do not give money to the yakuza, do not make use of the yakuza, do not have relations with the yakuza (Tokyo Metropolitan Police Department, 2022). These Ordinances are a form of third-party policy, in which, instead of directly targeting the offender, the police persuades third parties to take some responsibility for crime control and prevention (Hoshino and Kamada, 2021). The focus was moved from the police versus the yakuza, to the society versus the yakuza (NPA, 2010). The policing of the yakuza thus became a duty of individual citizens, who now have a personal responsibility, along with companies, to confront the yakuza, avoid contact with them, or cut all ties (Hirosue, 2016).

According to these ordinances, citizens and businesses are strictly forbidden from providing financial support to yakuza members or groups, including direct payments, donations, or indirect financial assistance. Financial institutions are prohibited from offering services such as loans, mortgages, or bank accounts to known yakuza members (Tokyo Metropolitan Government, 2011, hereafter TB, Art. 9). Yakuza members cannot legally sign contracts, including rental agreements, employment contracts, or business deals, and if a person is found to be affiliated with the yakuza after a contract is signed, the agreement can be nullified. It is the responsibility of landlords and businesses to ensure they do not knowingly enter contracts with yakuza-affiliated individuals (TB Art. 16). Yakuza members are banned from participating in certain business activities, public tenders, and obtaining professional licences. They cannot access public housing or other government services. Businesses that knowingly provide services to yakuza members may face legal consequences (TB Art. 24). Citizens and businesses are not allowed to cooperate with, or provide support to, yakuza groups in any capacity, including offering venues, transportation, or any form of logistical assistance (TB Art. 28). Companies found to be associating with yakuza members can face fines, licence revocation, and criminal charges. Individuals who assist yakuza activities, even unknowingly, may be subject to legal penalties (TB Art. 35).

These Ordinances, therefore, aim to sever the relationship between yakuza and non-yakuza individuals or companies, in order to weaken the yakuza's economy and cut revenue streams. Non-yakuza individuals or companies that do not abide by these rules are subjected to sanctions. In other words, the YEO increase the cost of being part of the yakuza, while at the same time increasing the incentives to defect (Hoshino and Kamada, 2021). Furthermore, there is a series of restrictions as to where a yakuza office can be established and operate: yakuza headquarters cannot be located within 200 metres from schools, family courts, children's welfare institutions or counselling centres, juvenile training schools, pre-disposition assessment facilities for minors, community centres, libraries, museums, and probations offices. In addition to those premises just specified, the list includes facilities that need to preserve a good environment to promote the healthy development of the youth in the surrounding area, as specified by the Public Safety Commission (TB Ch. 4 Art. 22). This makes the establishment of new offices in cities like Tokyo virtually impossible. The Ordinances also allow members of the police to enter the premises if they need to conduct a search, inspect documents, books, and other property, or question members of the group

(TB Ch. 5 Art. 26), and minors cannot enter the premises without a valid reason (TB Ch. 4 Art. 23).

Several journalists argue that the YEO were enacted as local Ordinances rather than a national law due to concerns over their constitutionality (J5). Specifically, restrictions preventing yakuza members from renting housing, obtaining mobile phone contracts, leasing vehicles, staying in hotels, or accessing public housing raise potential conflicts with the constitutional guarantee of equality under the law for all citizens. Given these constitutional considerations, implementing such measures through Ordinances allowed for regional enforcement while avoiding direct legal challenges at the national level. The yakuza reacted fiercely to the introduction of the new Ordinances. Their criticisms were voiced in yakuza magazines: 'Yakuza members cannot enter contracts, cannot open bank accounts. This shows that there is a discrimination based on status, and that the yakuza have no human rights'(JJ09/2013:35); 'Yakuza have no human rights and are not even allowed to mourn' (JJ09/2013:38). Tsukasa Shinobu, sixth boss of the Yamaguchi-gumi, said in an exclusive interview titled 'A strange era has arrived' with the Sankei Newspaper: 'All our [yakuza members'] children are now bullied and discriminated against. I know that it is said that we [yakuza] do not have human rights, but shouldn't it be different for our families?' (Sankei Shimbun, 2011/10/01).

The impact of the YEO is evident in the sharp decline in yakuza membership following the nationwide implementation of the Ordinances (see Figure 4.1). Hoshino and Kamada (2021) demonstrate that the YEO accounts for 26 per cent of this reduction. Their findings also indicate that the effectiveness of these Ordinances may be influenced by the strategic dynamics between yakuza syndicates. When criminal organisations are in direct competition, these relationships can become a crucial factor in their struggle for dominance. As extra-legal governance groups, yakuza organisations rely on a stable and sizable membership to enforce order, regulate disputes, and maintain their authority. While trade-type groups can scale down their operations—for instance, in response to technological advancements that enhance efficiency and reduce labour needs—governance-type groups depend on maintaining a sufficient number of enforcers. In this case, a decline in membership does not indicate improved operational efficiency but rather a diminishing capacity to exert control and enforce order.

However, an important point must be considered. According to Hirosue Noboru, a leading expert on yakuza reintegration, only 2 per cent of former members who left the syndicates between 2010 and 2018 were confirmed to

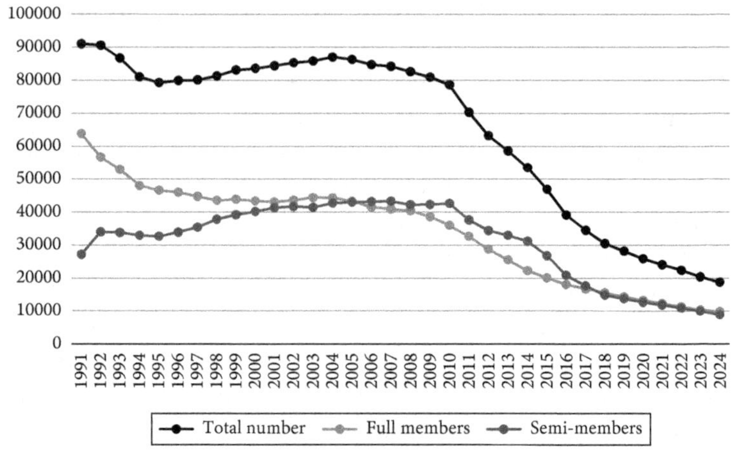

Figure 4.1 Yakuza membership
Data source: NPA, 2024

have secured legitimate employment. Yet even for this small minority, no data are available on whether they managed to retain those jobs (Hirosue, 15/03/2019). These figures suggest that while many individuals have officially left the yakuza, in practice they may continue to operate in the underworld, either informally linked to their former groups, or by joining non-designated actors such as *hangure* or *tokuryū*.

Enforcing the law

The Japanese police have been the subject of study by criminologists who have sought to explain how they managed to maintain low crime rates throughout the postwar period of industrialisation. According to Ames's seminal study on the Japanese police (1981), between the 1950s and 1980s, the police and the yakuza enjoyed a robust and cordial relationship, but from the 1960s, when the criminal syndicates began to expand considerably, the police tried to limit their influence, and this led to an increased number of crackdowns (such as the 1964 summit strategy). These repressive actions turned out to be merely a façade, as groups were often warned prior to the raid, and thus most of the arms and drugs were already removed or hidden, while arrests typically only ended in a couple of days' detention. On the other hand, Kaplan and Dubro (2003) suggest that the resilience of the yakuza can be explained by an institutionalised form of corruption with the police, revolving around personal friendships. Their complicity is also reinforced by the institutionalised role of the yakuza, namely the well-established links between conservative politicians, far-right elements, and the yakuza. However, Hill (2003) argues that the cosy relationship described by authors such as Van Wolferen (1989) ended with the summit strategy in 1964. According to him, the historical tolerance of the yakuza stemmed from the link between the yakuza and powerful conservative politicians (which discouraged the police from taking action against the criminal syndicates), the yakuza's inclination towards non-predatory crimes, and the yakuza's chivalrous ideology and masculine value system, which resonated with police culture. The yakuza operate as an alternative form of dispute resolution (Milhaupt and West, 2000): litigation rates in Japan have been traditionally low (Ramseyer and Nakazato, 1989; Ginsburg and Hoetker, 2006), and, indeed, the yakuza have regularly offered their mediation services in cases of bankruptcies, tenant disputes, and even traffic accidents (Hill, 2003). A yakuza boss reported that whenever the neighbourhood has a problem with construction sites (noise, disruption of daily activities, etc.), his group mediates with construction workers and solves the problem (C2). A traditional stance towards the yakuza is that they are a necessary evil that is tolerated insofar as they compensate for the shortcomings of the police (see Mizoguchi, 2026) for instance, the lack of foreign crime in Japan is often attributed to the pervasive presence of the yakuza within the territory (Business Journal, 01/07/2018), as well as the fact that the yakuza are unwilling to work with foreign criminal groups and are keen to preserve their monopoly (News PostSeven, 07/09/2018). According to an ex-yakuza, the reason for the lack of Chinese restaurants in Kyūshū can be attributed to the presence of the Kudō-kai (C5).

The shift from a collaborative to an antagonistic relationship between the yakuza and the police was reflected in my fieldwork. An ex-yakuza, who was in a Sumiyoshi-kai affiliated group between 2000 and 2010, recounted:

> I could do pretty much everything, and that was a time where you could also talk freely to the police. It was fun back then, we still had power in the city, but not now. If you give your name out, they'll catch you immediately, but in the past, you could go and be noisy and do what you wanted. . . . Not everybody could talk to the police, in my case we had one or two people who had the contacts. So, you get information, but you don't give it out. I mean there are some people that do so, but I've never done it. You can exchange

> information with your friends, but with police we would make them drink, have fun, treat them well and just get the information we needed. (C4)

This was confirmed by an ex-member of the Kudō-kai, a yakuza group based in Kyūshū. Although the Kudō-kai has long been famous for higher levels of violence, he noted that a shift in the population's tolerance towards the group was the result of the implementation of the new regulations. He confirmed that his group did not have formal and systematic contacts with the police, but rather an informal relationship based on personal contacts (C3).

Prior to the enforcement of anti-yakuza regulations, the relationship between the yakuza and the police used to move within the borders of the informally lawful.

> Behind the curtains the relationship with the police, of course, is going on, as with the politicians. We have something similar to a consultation: [they ask us] can you please keep your head down because Trump is coming? They come and tell us. There is that sensibility in Japan, yakuza would never refuse to do that. Soon there will be the Olympics: we know we have to be quiet, the police don't even need to tell us. (C2)

This transition is causing distress for both parties: the police, in order to prove their detachment, are targeting high-profile members to show to the public that the cosy relationship they used to entertain with the yakuza has come to an end. In 2006, Takayama Kiyoshi, leader of the Kōdō-kai and second-in-command of the Yamaguchi-gumi, was investigated for making threats against a builder who had paid 40 million yen (£275,000) to the yakuza group, and later denounced it as extortion. The builder was himself a vice-boss of a yakuza group (Nakajima Rengō-kai ōta-kai). However, Takayama was not present at the time of the threats, nor when the money was exchanged, and there are serious doubts as to whether the charges were instrumentally filed in order to issue an arrest warrant against Takayama (Mizoguchi, 2013). Indeed, Takayama had been a target of the police for a long time, as testified to by the words of the chief of the NPA, who stated in 2010: 'Without the weakening of the Kōdō-kai, there is no weakening of the Yamaguchi-gumi, and without the weakening of the Yamaguchi-gumi, there cannot be a weakening of the yakuza' (Suzuki, 2011:15). Eventually, Takayama was sentenced to eight years in prison with labour (Mizoguchi, 2013), and was released in October 2019.

Suzuki Tomohiko, the most prominent investigative journalist reporting on the yakuza, argues that sentences for yakuza members do not have a real impact on the organisation, but are used more as a nuisance to the groups:

> Now they are making a lot of arrests amongst the yakuza, but it's never for a serious crime it's always something trivial, such as something wrong with their driving licence, using a girlfriend's credit card it's considered a fraud, etc. . . . by doing so they put them in prison for one or two months, but for the police it's important just to 'arrest', doesn't matter for what or for how long. There is a bit of an impact on the organisation, but as it's a short-term arrest, it's not really that much. (J4)

The cases in which yakuza members are arrested for minor infractions are indeed numerous, including yakuza bosses arrested for going to a baseball game (Yomiuri Shimbun, 09/02/2026), for making a supermarket point card and electronic toll card without declaring their affiliation (Daily Shinchō 10/03/2023), for neglecting to clean up after their dog during a walk (yakuza893, 17/05/2023), or for having their self-amputated finger injury treated on their health insurance, claiming the injury was caused by negligence (Yomiuri Shimbun, 10/10/2024). Six expressway companies tightened regulations on organised crime, with the aim of blocking affiliates' means of using electronic toll collection and limiting its use to cash (Asahi Shimbun, 16/02/2023). Osaka District Court delivered guilty verdicts for several bosses for using a family member's device to access the motorway (14 January 2025). Some journalists argue that these arrests are a tool for law enforcement to boost arrest numbers and gain a positive image in the eyes of the population (J4). These arrests for minor infractions, facilitated by the YEO, function less as direct crime suppression and more as a strategy of attrition. By imposing frequent legal hurdles and periods of detention, authorities can unsettle the operation of yakuza groups, while signalling to potential recruits that affiliation comes with persistent legal and operational disruptions.

While in the past the police could count on the collaboration of the yakuza to maintain some sort of order at least in the criminal underworld, they are now under pressure to fight the yakuza as well as other forms of crime, but without added tools for investigations. The use of techniques such as undercover work, wiretaps, and GPS are rarely granted by the judge and have several limitations. A police chief who was trying to organise an operation against a smuggling group in his region recounted that he had asked permission to attach a GPS under the car of one of the suspects, only to be told that he could obtain authorisation only if they notified him of the installation of the device.

The increasingly invasive searches have troubled the yakuza, who are not used to such aggressive intrusions by the police in their activities and premises. In February 1998, the Kudō-kai, Taishū-kai, and Dōjin-kai released an eight-point document prescribing behaviour during searches and arrests: for example, the document orders members not to talk to the police, not to release information regarding their own group or an allied group under any circumstances, not to collaborate if they are asked for urine samples for drug tests, and to always call the executive office of their group before taking any action in cases in which the police are involved (Mizoguchi, 2013). A lieutenant of a yakuza group stated:

> I have never talked to the police and never will. I know that many yakuza do that, they have a relationship with some officer, maybe they were friends with them when they were young, from the same neighbourhood. And sometimes it can be useful because you give them some useless information and they give you some. But for me it's not worth it, because if somebody sees me with a policeman, they may talk, and a voice may spread that I talk to the police. (C17)

The yakuza are denouncing their perceived ill treatment. The chief secretary of the Kudō-kai has argued that the police are persecuting them: 'We do not think we can grapple with the police and win. But if the police try to hurt us, we shall resist. We will denounce prevarications and make fools out of them' (Mizoguchi, 2013: 122). The group uses social media as a means of communicating with the public and spreading awareness of the perceived injustices to which they are being subjected: for instance, after a car accident involving a detective in front of the Kudō-kai's boss's home, the group uploaded a video on YouTube of the altercation between the yakuza and the policemen as proof of the injustice to which they are being subjected (Takahashi Hiroki, 26/05/2015).

The Bōhaijōrei is defined and enforced at the local level: each prefectural police organisation is entrusted with applying the regulations, which are valid only in the region of competence. Conversely, yakuza groups are nationally organised and thus connected incidents may happen across different jurisdictions, but be investigated separately. This represents an advantage for the yakuza, and especially for the top three groups (Yamaguchi-gumi,

Sumiyoshi-kai, and Inagawa-kai). Bordering jurisdictions keep in touch through personal contacts, and the yakuza are able to make good use of these personal relationships. A high-ranking yakuza from the Kōbe Yamaguchi-gumi explained that in each prefectural police department there is usually a spy, who does not leak information or facts about their own jurisdiction but is willing and able to give information about investigations by other prefectural police forces. Also, there are cases in which detectives have resorted to leaking police information in order to quickly gather intelligence for their office, which was reported by a member of the Yamaguchi-gumi (News Post Seven, 16/03/2016).

The police need to maintain a certain degree of contact with the yakuza because of the information they can provide, but this relationship is now strictly utilitarian (J4). Since the police cannot effectively communicate with disorganised forms of crime, personal contacts with the yakuza remain a valuable source of information for the police (V1). Whereas in the past the police managed to receive pieces of information directly from the yakuza, the growing distance between the yakuza and the police means that they now resort to informants, such as owners of bars where yakuza often hang out, managers of semi-legal brothels, drug dealers, and prostitutes. For a one-hour chat with a policeman, an informant can earn about 20k–30k yen (£130–£200). However, since there were cases in which informants gave false information and split the cooperation fee with the policeman, this practice was strongly criticised and subsequently changed to a scenario in which an information fee is only provided for valuable information, rather than for every meeting (Suzuki, 2011).

A yakuza boss was confident that if the yakuza were to disappear, the police would be the most affected (C2). Mr Yamanouchi, ex-lawyer of the Yamaguchi-gumi, is also doubtful of the police's commitment to fighting the yakuza, since the yakuza are providers of services that are in considerable demand by the population (V1). An ex-yakuza echoed this sentiment:

> If we decide that the yakuza are bad, then it's ok to cut ties with the society, but this is only an appearance, it's not a long-term plan. I don't think it's a good plan either, because now there is weirder crime. Society wants some services (drugs, etc.), and in the case of Japan they knew who provided them, and stopped them sometimes, but it is just to look good. I don't think the police are trying to understand what goes on in the dark where the yakuza are not working. (C3)

The continued negotiation between the yakuza and the NPA, through a multitude of personal small connections, allowed for a flow of information and requests that favoured the yakuza, insofar as they avoided harsh repressions if they behaved in accordance with police expectations. In turn, the police benefitted from the collaboration as the yakuza assisted them in ruling and policing disorganised and foreign criminality, while, simultaneously, taking sole credit for the low levels of street (i.e. visible) crimes.

Yakuza members in court

Let us now turn to the way in which anti-yakuza legislation has been enforced in court. The Japanese judiciary is well-known for its extremely high rate of convictions, stemming from the fact that Japanese prosecutors only bring their strongest cases to trial. Acquittals can have a negative impact on the career of the judge who administers them, in that they are likely to serve for longer in branch offices. On the contrary, a reversed conviction is not met with significant penalties (Ramseyer and Rasmusen, 1998). Traditionally, defendants in Japan are not concerned with proving their innocence, but rather with reducing the severity of the sentence. This is due to the fact that over 90 per cent—and in first instance courts the rate goes up to over 99 per cent—of defendants confess to most of the offences they are charged with (Shiroshita, 2009). The extraordinarily high confession rate has raised concerns over possible forced confessions and wrongful convictions. Specifically, factors such as the use of pre-trial detention and limited access to defence counselling, use of physical and psychological violence to obtain confessions, Japanese judges' tendency to indiscriminately use confession documents, and inadequate access to pre-trial release have raised concerns about false convictions in Japanese courts (Fukurai and Kurosawa, 2010).

The *White Papers on Crime* published by the Ministry of Justice provide annual data on prosecution rates for yakuza and common offenders. As shown in Figure 4.2, in 2022 the prosecution rate for yakuza offenders stood at 46.4 per cent, compared with 40.6 per cent for common offenders. Over the past quarter-century, however, the decline in prosecutions of yakuza members has been pronounced. In 1998, more than 75 per cent of yakuza cases were prosecuted, but the rate fell steadily over the following two decades, dropping below 70 per cent after 2009, to around 60 per cent in 2012, and below 50 per cent by the early 2020s. Common offenders show a similar though gentler pattern, with rates decreasing from the low 60s in the late

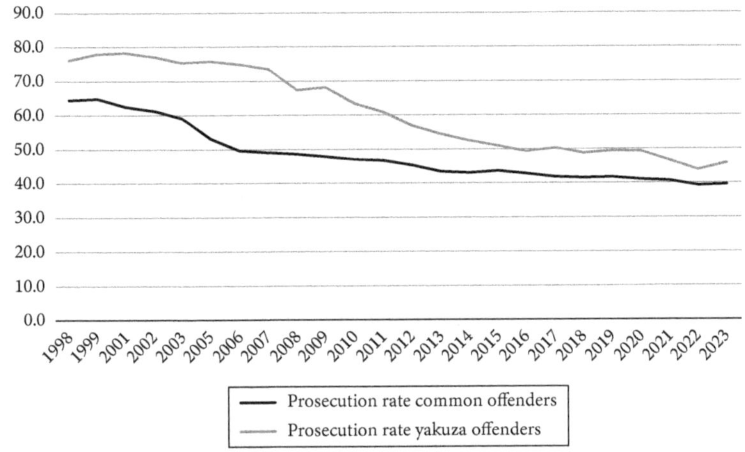

Figure 4.2 Prosecution rates of yakuza members vs common offenders
Data source: MoJ, 1991 to 2024

1990s to well under 50 per cent today. Despite recurring public commitments to crack down on organised crime, the data indicate that a shrinking number of yakuza cases now advance to prosecution.

Yet the statistical decline in prosecutions tells only part of the story. In certain cases, prosecutors have displayed extraordinary persistence in pursuing yakuza defendants through repeated trials and appeals, as in the case of Hōryū-kai boss, Takizawa Takashi. Takizawa was initially indicted for possession of a firearm, along with Tsukasa Shinobu and Kuwata Kaneyoshi (at the time both candidates for the position of lieutenant within the Yamaguchi-gumi), in a shooting incident related to an intra-gang turf war that occurred in 1997. Tsukasa and Kuwata were accused of knowing that a member of their group had a firearm, and despite the lack of material evidence, they were found guilty. Takizawa was found innocent in 2004, but the prosecution appealed, and he was tried again in the Osaka High Court in 2006, where the charges were once again dismissed. In 2009, the prosecution brought the case to the Osaka district court, where Takizawa was retried and found innocent for the third time in 2011. The prosecution appealed once more to the Osaka High Court, which again transferred the case to the district court. At the seventh hearing, twenty years after the incident, the then 79-year-old Takizawa was sentenced to seven years' imprisonment with labour (ibid.; Sankei West, 24/3/2017).

There are no official guidelines that help the judge determine the length of a sentence; however it has often been noted that the demands of prosecutors are used as a reference point to establish an appropriate punishment (Herber, 2009; Weitzdörfer, Shiroshita, and Padfield, 2018). Indeed, statutory penalties in Japan range widely, but often sentencing is influenced by factual guidelines based on precedents and prosecutorial demands, as in 70 to 80 per cent of cases prison terms are set in accordance with prosecutors' recommendations (Shiroshita, 2009). Sentencing patterns suggest that yakuza affiliation shapes judicial outcomes. Ordinary offenders are more likely to receive short sentences, while yakuza defendants tend to face longer terms of imprisonment. Few serve less than a year, and their sentences are concentrated in the two- to five-year range. Sentences exceeding five years remain uncommon overall, yet they occur almost twice as often among yakuza offenders (MoJ, 2024; see Figure 4.3).

If we look at these differences over time, the pattern becomes even clearer. Sentences imposed on yakuza members have gradually lengthened since the late 1990s. In the early years of the series, most convictions resulted in prison terms of less than three years, but from the mid-2010s onwards the balance shifted towards longer imprisonment. Four- to five-year sentences have become increasingly common, and those exceeding five years, once exceptional, now appear more regularly. The overall trend reflects a judiciary that has grown progressively stricter towards yakuza defendants, mirroring broader legislative and political efforts to curb yakuza activity (see Figure 4.4).

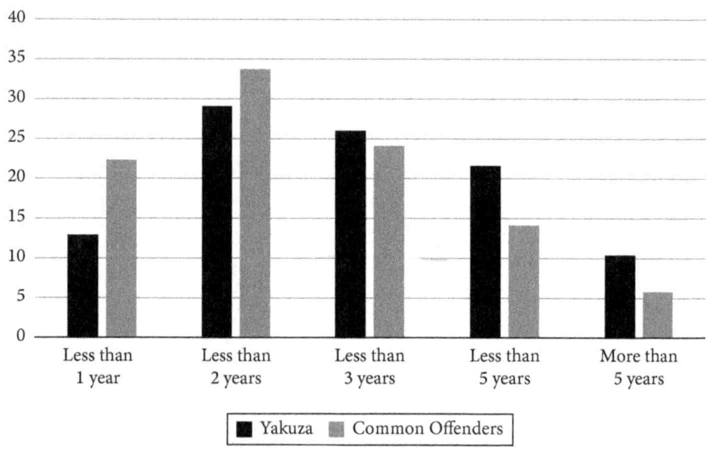

Figure 4.3 Length of sentences of yakuza vs common offenders
Source: MoJ, 2024

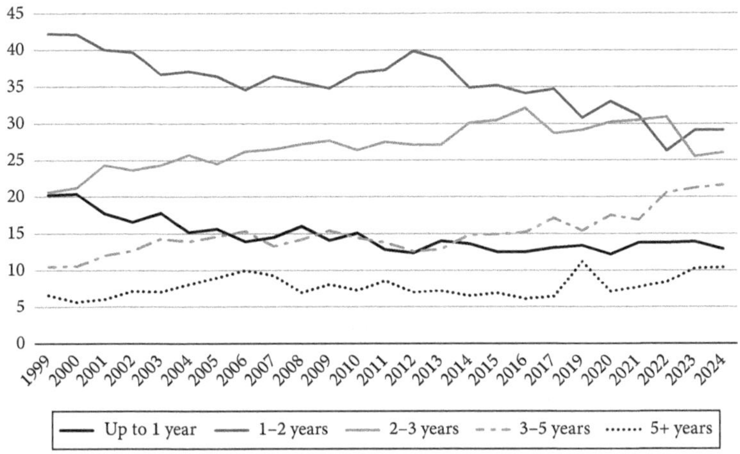

Figure 4.4 Length of sentences for yakuza members from 1999 to 2024
Source: MoJ, 1999 to 2025

The yakuza are much more likely to reoffend: only 14.7 per cent of yakuza offenders were convicted for first-time offences, while 46.5 per cent of common offenders were serving their first conviction. More than half of the yakuza offenders had been convicted four or more times previously (MoJ, 2024). Considering all this, longer sentences, higher prosecution rates, and high rates of reoffending have made incarceration an increasingly unsustainable cost for yakuza groups: legal fees, family support, and lost income accumulating across multiple convictions directly contribute to the membership decline documented above.

The Bōtaihō is substantially an administrative law that can be added to the existing penal laws. Japanese law does not have specific statutory sentence enhancements for yakuza members. However, in practice, courts often impose harsher penalties due to aggravating factors, such as organised crime involvement or systematic criminal conduct. Yakuza-related defendants are given longer sentences because their involvement suggests a systematic, ongoing criminal enterprise. Yamanouchi Yukio, former lawyer of the Yamaguchi-gumi, recollected the words of a judge regarding sentencing yakuza members: 'If a defendant belongs to a yakuza group related to the Yamaguchi-gumi, the aims and activities of the Yamaguchi-gumi itself may not be clear to him, but if, according to evidence, this person's criminal history is long, we must infer that the organisation this person works for aims at accomplishing crimes, and that he maintains this criminal behaviour in order to sustain the criminal group' (Yamanouchi, 2017: 31). In order to avoid this, people on active duty 'formally' quit the yakuza in prison. The boss writes this down and sends it to the police so that the penalty can be mitigated (C1).

Costs of prison for the yakuza

In several countries, a period in prison does not result in the prisoner being cut off from revenue streams. Other than profit collected from drug dealing behind bars, several groups are able to govern illicit markets from inside the prisons. Los Angeles dealing gangs, and in particular the Mexican mafia, are able to tax drug dealers and regulate the drug market from inside the prison (Skarbek, 2011, 2014). Brazil's Primeiro Comando da Capital has the capacity to organise attacks against the state, while imposing extra-legal governance on certain neighbourhoods through elaborate bureaucratic procedures, recordkeeping, and a punishment system (Lessing and Willis, 2019). However, yakuza members and inmates in Japanese prisons do not have the same options. Once imprisoned, a yakuza member is cut off from revenue streams such as extortion, gambling operations, and business mediation, which rely on direct interaction and enforcement mechanisms. Discipline is strict, and the walls of prisons are not porous, making time in prison completely unprofitable (Baradel, 2023). Incarceration imposes a severe economic penalty on yakuza members, effectively eliminating their capacity to generate income.

Incarceration has become increasingly costly for yakuza groups, both at the individual and organisational levels. The financial burden associated with incarceration represents a critical constraint for most groups. The ability to absorb these costs serves as a measure of a group's strength. Groups with limited resources try to avoid having their members sent to prison, as the associated expenses—legal fees, prison allowances, and financial support for the affiliate's family—can strain their operational capacity. By contrast, groups with greater financial stability are able to deploy younger members in violent confrontations, including targeted attacks on rival organisations. The decision to assign a junior member to carry out a murder is particularly revealing: it signals that the group has sufficient resources to cover the member's legal defence, maintain regular visits, provide for their needs, and compensate their family if necessary. This level of financial commitment represents a substantial investment, reinforcing the group's capacity to withstand both the immediate loss of personnel and the long-term economic burden of incarceration (J6).

An ex-yakuza member who served time in the 2010s revealed that membership in a yakuza group made his imprisonment easier, primarily due to the family support provided by the group. Despite this, rules regarding family support are increasingly variable, with some groups scaling back these allowances as their revenues decline (C4).

The group is required to support the member both financially and emotionally, as one yakuza lieutenant confirms:

> One of our members is incarcerated near Tokyo. We have a responsibility towards him, so I go visit him every month. I am afraid of flying, I really don't like to get on airplanes. But this is my job, and so every month I take a flight in the morning, I go see him, and then I take a flight back in the evening. I am afraid for the whole length of the flight, but it is my duty towards him. (C17)

Beyond the immediate financial losses, incarceration also affects an individual's long-term economic prospects and the position in the illegal market in which they operate. In the absence of a strong support system within the group, an imprisoned member may struggle to maintain social and financial stability, particularly if they are unable to rely on organisational funds for legal fees, prison expenses, and family support. Furthermore, prolonged absence from illicit markets creates opportunities for rivals—both within and outside the organisation—to take over revenue-generating activities, weakening the incarcerated member's position upon release. In economic terms, imprisonment generates both direct costs (loss of income, legal fees, and support for dependents) and opportunity costs (loss of market influence and potential future earnings). These factors contribute to a broader calculation within criminal organisations regarding the affordability of incarceration and the financial burden of maintaining imprisoned affiliates.

While yakuza members face significant limitations within the rigid structure of Japanese prisons, they do maintain some degree of influence over specific aspects of prison life. Instances of preferential treatment are reported, often due to the behaviour of prison guards or due to the strategic use of the yakuza's status. For example, certain guards might show favouritism towards yakuza members, sometimes using them for personal gain or granting them privileges not afforded to common inmates. On a broader scale, an ex-yakuza who served time in the early 2000s acknowledged that yakuza members often experience more favourable treatment within the prison system (C3). 'The places where prisoners gather, like the prison yard, don't belong to common offenders—they belong to the members of the yakuza. If a katagi [non-yakuza] does something disrespectful to a yakuza member, he will be immediately removed from the area and lose their work privileges. However, if a yakuza member only serves his own interests and behaves inappropriately, he will also lose his job in the factory. Even if you find a new job, when word spreads that you've been thrown out, you'll lose that job too. It's true that in any world, you reap what you sow... And the prison world is so small, that this rule is very evident' (C4).

Yakuza members do not establish a full control system over the entire prison population. Instead, the yakuza apply their codes of conduct within the prison, predominantly among themselves. This internal code is recognised by non-yakuza inmates, granting yakuza members some influence over the broader prison culture. However, the extent of this influence is nuanced: 'There were many yakuza among the inmates. Some would steal snacks from normal inmates, while others would go around before their release, greeting everyone politely and expressing gratitude. If you behave badly inside prison, you ruin the reputation of your group, so it is important to treat everyone with respect' (C3). Thus, while yakuza members have some degree of control within the prison environment, their power is constrained by the strict rules of the prison system. Their influence is mostly limited to interactions within their own group and to the behaviour of non-yakuza members, rather than a broader system of control over the prison population (Baradel, 2023).

Nonetheless, despite these occasional privileges, the economic burden of imprisonment remains a central concern for the yakuza. The decline in yakuza revenues, partly due to the increased pressure from law enforcement, has resulted in diminishing support for incarcerated members. The welfare packages that were once more robust are now more selective, with the group only providing support for members imprisoned as a direct consequence of their criminal activities on behalf of the organisation (C4). Being members of a criminal syndicate also means that it is not possible to be released on parole. Formally withdrawing from the yakuza is thus a straightforward and effective method to avoid additional prison time. The process is simple: if the member is already detained, he writes a 'withdrawal notification' addressed to their boss and hands it to the penitentiary police, who then have it delivered to the group's headquarters. After the boss puts his stamp on it and the letter comes back, the member is officially out of the group (Hirosue, 2017).

When yakuza membership was high, the costs of incarceration were spread across the organisation, making it a sustainable strategy for both the group and individuals. Prison sentences could serve a strategic function, as they demonstrated the group's strength by covering legal fees, providing financial support to families, and ensuring that those who made sacrifices were rewarded with higher status upon release. The organisation could also easily replace incarcerated members, ensuring continuity in the business outside of prison. However, as membership declines, the cost structure shifts. With fewer members, the financial burden on the group increases, making it harder to support imprisoned individuals. At the same time, the incentives for individuals to accept incarceration weaken, as the group's ability to compensate them diminishes. Previously, both the group and individuals benefitted from cooperation: individuals accepted prison terms knowing they would be rewarded, while the organisation maintained stability. However, as membership shrinks, the expected payoff for both parties declines: individuals now have greater incentives to defect (as officially leaving the group is rewarded with shortened prison sentences), while the group struggles to maintain its previous commitments.

Visibility

A group of men in dark suits wait in front of a four-storey building in a central Tokyo neighbourhood. One of them apologises to a driver who had to stop to let a large black car followed by a black sedan manoeuvre across the road and park in front of the building. A pedestrian, intimidated by the dark-clad guards, hesitates to pass in the middle of the scene. A man in a dark suit opens the door of the black car, from which emerges a man who clearly looks like a yakuza boss: he greets the men bowed in front of him and enters the headquarters. The bottom three floors are offices furnished with simple desks, chairs, and sofas, where the members of the group are busy talking and answering the phone. The boss's office is on the top floor and is enriched by mahogany floors and elegant furniture. A portrait of the boss in traditional Japanese clothing dominates the room and looks directly at you when you sit on the guests' sofa. Coffee, tea, and cake are served in tableware with the group's logo, along with classic pottery and silverware. When the boss needs something, he makes a call to one of the group's members, who comes running up. Members gather in the stairwells when the boss leaves the office and as he passes by each floor, they say in a loud voice while bowing '*Itterasshai*!'

(Take care!). Outside, the scene of a group of well-dressed men stopping the passersby and traffic repeats in reverse. Having had first-hand experience of these rituals in my visits to yakuza offices, I can confirm that it is impressive. But it is not an empty performance: all these manifestations of power are not superfluous, as they showcase the group's strength in the neighbourhood, and they are a reminder that they are still there.

Criminal organisations rely on reputation as a key mechanism for maintaining governance functions (Gambetta, 1993). To govern a territory, a group needs to have a workforce that in numbers and strength is able to enforce contracts, protect the rights of those who pay them rent, and are able to deliver violence if needed. A decrease in the workforce harms the ability of the group to provide these services. The ability to enforce agreements and deter defection depends on a credible threat of retaliation and a stable presence within illicit markets. When membership declines and visibility decreases, the deterrent effect weakens, making enforcement more costly and less effective (Varese, 2001). A shrinking organisation struggles to maintain its dominance over territory and regulate interactions between lawful and unlawful actors. The loss of credibility further undermines its ability to impose order, as both internal members and external actors begin to question its capacity for control.

The anti-yakuza legislation has had an impact on the visibility, and therefore also on the perceived legitimacy, of the group. Before the introduction of the Bōtaihō, yakuza offices were able to display signs with the group's name and their traditional logo, so that the offices could be recognised by the public. On the one hand, they showed the economic power of the group, with imposing buildings and luxury cars; on the other, it showed that the group had a mundane aspect to it, testifying that they were as accessible to the public as any other office. More importantly, they testified the presence of the group on the territory and showed that they had control over it. Gambetta (1993: 130) described this as the 'externality of reputation', that is, being associated with powerful symbols to enhance one's credibility. The yakuza have traditionally been involved in the organisation of festivals, as well as throwing parties for children. The Yamaguchi-gumi, until 2015, would organise the neighbourhood's annual Halloween Party for children at their headquarters (Sankei Shimbun, 16/10/2020). Even at the individual level, many of the trademarks of the yakuza were designed to advertise the notion of belonging to the group: tattoos and *yubitsume* (the ritual auto-amputation of a fingertip) are evident enough to signal one's status instantly. The dress code and style of yakuza members has also been very distinctive, with flashy outfits and recognisable hairstyles.

However, these symbols have now almost completely vanished. Cars and people still indicate the presence of the yakuza in the neighbourhood, but the trademarks have been wiped off. The disappearance from their urban headquarters of the very name of the group has caused them to lose access to the power that came with the name (Baradel and Bortolussi, 2021). Even at the individual level, while in the past it was usually obvious, it has become increasingly difficult to recognise yakuza affiliates. Based on my experience, in major cities, yakuza affiliates wear dark suits and, when seen individually, they do not attract attention, except for the fact that their attire is exceptionally elegant and they are particularly well-groomed. In more peripheral settings, they are dressed in a very common way. Many wear black sleeves to cover tattoos—although many citizens also normally wear long sleeves to avoid the sunlight. A yakuza boss I met in Okinawa had no tattoos and usually wore light-coloured suits, nothing giving away his status. His affiliates generally wore dark suits, rolling up their sleeves only in private settings. His lieutenant, the person who had the operational control of the group, would wear normal clothes with the black sleeves when the boss was not present. However, to a keen observer, a large ring bearing the group's emblem discreetly signalled his affiliation. One night, while I was having dinner with him and a friend, two young men from Osaka sat at our table and eventually asked about our jobs and why we were together. The lieutenant responded that he did many different jobs, but that he did not have a fixed occupation, and I improvised a story to corroborate his. Revealing one's affiliation to the yakuza can be risky, as it can be interpreted as a form of intimidation or coercion. For the same reasons, yakuza affiliates are no longer supposed to hand out business cards carrying the group logo—although my business-card holder contains several that prove otherwise.

State repression often forces criminal groups to adapt their structures, leading to a shift away from governance-based activities towards more transactional, profit-driven operations (Lessing, 2018). As regulatory pressure increases, the ability to extract rents through governance—such as dispute resolution and protection services—declines. Without a strong reputation for stability and authority, businesses and individuals may turn to alternative enforcers, including loosely affiliated networks that operate outside traditional hierarchical models. This fragmentation weakens the organisation's capacity to maintain monopolistic control, increasing competition among emerging criminal actors and reshaping the landscape of illicit governance.

One of the most significant consequences of anti-yakuza legislation has been the removal of the yakuza from the public sphere. Traditional trademarks of the yakuza, such as signs displaying the group's name and logo, were taken down. Even specialised media outlets, such as the magazine, *Jitsuwa Jidai*, that chronicled the yakuza world, were discontinued in an effort to further conceal their presence. Instead of outlawing the yakuza, the strategy has been to make it invisible. However, as discussed in previous chapters, the core business of the yakuza—governance—is based on reputation, which relies on visibility, or at least the visibility of some trademarks. Even the power of the secretive Sicilian mafia, which has faced much stricter legislation outlawing membership itself, is based some level of visibility of its trademarks (Gambetta, 1993). Much of the yakuza reputation was built on symbols tied to tradition and a narrative that positioned them as the legitimised guardians of a certain type of history. The combination of reduced membership and diminished visibility has had a profound impact on the yakuza's ability to sustain their core business of governance.

Conclusion

The Japanese way of policing the yakuza has been radically different from approaches largely adopted abroad. For many years, authorities allowed the yakuza to govern illegal and semi-legal markets, as well as to provide dispute resolution services to citizens. The yakuza were born and grew as a governance-type group, legitimated by the state (in the sense that they were not outlawed) and by an ideology that resonated with the community. The yakuza's ability to regulate the underworld, their legal status, and their responsiveness to police demands enabled the development of a collaborative relationship with law enforcement. This strategy was successfully adopted, in part, because of the yakuza's highly bureaucratic structure, and the many tools they have to control conflict and to limit violence (Breuer and Baradel, 2025). The yakuza, used to being treated as a legitimate enterprise, reacted negatively to the introduction of specific anti-yakuza countermeasures that designated them as criminal groups. However, their reaction did not escalate to attacks against the state: accustomed to operating as any legitimate association, yakuza groups tried (and still try) to contest these measures through the media and in court, although without significant results.

Moving away from governance-type activities is not easy, especially if the group is ideologically driven. In the yakuza, several groups doubled down on their traditional roots: 'From now on, we will study even more to conduct ourselves properly, and the Yamaguchi-gumi will continue to evolve. However, as an organisation, we do not particularly favour going underground . . . As individuals who live by the way of *ninkyō* [the chivalrous code], we will uphold human dignity with a firm sense of pride and continue to guide the younger generation with unwavering conviction, no matter how strong the headwinds may be' (JJ05/2012: 15). In one of the first interviews I conducted with a prominent yakuza boss in 2018, he was optimistic, and saw the new regulations as an opportunity to weed out affiliates that were in the yakuza just for the money:

> I think it's good they made these Ordinances: once you became a yakuza to make a lot of money, now you become a yakuza and make no money. But people who join the yakuza now they do it because they believe in *ninkyō*, they have this old thinking of how we can protect this area, they believe in *bushido* [the ethical code followed by the samurai]. People who think the yakuza is driving a nice car and living the good life quit, people who believe in the *ninkyō* spirit remain, so that's good because there were many fake yakuza. (C2)

Yet, financial pressures persist. Yakuza affiliates must still generate income to meet internal obligations—that is, the requirement to pay a percentage of their earnings to their bosses every month—and concerns about making a living have grown for the majority of yakuza members. Yakuza magazines reported on the financial pressures of yakuza members, and warned of the shift that would happen in the Japanese criminal underworld.

> The most dangerous individuals are those expelled from their groups through expulsion or severance, but the next most dangerous are those who leave their organisations and form small groups to earn money. For them, extortion is routine, and they will resort to fraud, robbery, or anything else that turns a profit. Their common refrain is, 'If we don't eat, we die.' Amid the increasing pressure from law enforcement, a new breed of delinquent gang is rising to power, exploiting the gaps left by yakuza groups that are now unable to move freely. Many of these groups are named after their leader's nickname or initials. Unlike traditional yakuza, they are not

> yet subject to the anti-organised crime Ordinances or the revised Anti-Organised Crime Law. (JJ10/2012: 28)

If law enforcement limits the ability of governance-type organised crime to exercise their primary function, they need to compensate with different activities: production, trade, or simply predatory activities. However, as will be shown in Chapter 6, when they do so, they lose all legitimacy to govern.

The rising costs of membership have weakened a second key asset of yakuza governance: their workforce. With fewer recruits and higher dropout rates, their ability to regulate the underworld has declined, further undermining their governance function. As the state discredits traditional criminal actors, it also erodes the informal regulatory functions they once provided—though it does not eliminate the demand for their services. Visibility is crucial to the social legitimacy of criminal governance, and as the yakuza's presence diminishes under Japan's legal pressures, so too does their authority. While these policies may suppress yakuza activities, they also create unintended consequences: with reduced recruitment, other groups may seize the opportunity to absorb the displaced workforce, a dynamic explored further in Chapter 6. However, anti-yakuza regulations are not the sole cause of the yakuza's decline; as the next chapter will show, the simultaneous re-regulation of the markets in which the yakuza operated removed the structural conditions that had made their governance function both necessary and profitable.

5
Regulating markets

Introduction

From the postwar period until the 1980s, the Japanese economy was booming: living standards rose steadily, exports thrived, and Japan emerged as a global leader in the technological sector. Japan was not only performing astoundingly well economically: educational achievements, low crime rates, low levels of income inequality, and other social indicators all testified to the success of 'model Japan' (Vogel, 2006). During the same period, the yakuza thrived under conditions of rapid economic growth and loose regulatory oversight. Their quasi-legal status enabled them to participate in both formal and informal sectors, extracting rent and providing protection in markets ranging from real estate and labour brokering to nightlife and gambling. This equilibrium began to shift in the early 1990s, when the collapse of the economic bubble triggered what was initially called Japan's 'lost decade'—a term now expanded to 'lost decades' as stagnation extended into the 2000s and 2010s (Funabashi and Kushner, 2015).

Until this turning point, most yakuza groups had sustained a relatively affluent lifestyle by capitalising on Japan's loosely regulated markets and their own quasi-legal status. Their embeddedness was made possible by the coexistence of formal legality and informal governance in sectors such as nightlife, entertainment, and construction. However, a combination of prolonged economic stagnation, yakuza-specific criminalisation, and state-led re-regulation of formerly grey markets has significantly weakened this position (Baradel, 2021). Japan's economy was historically characterised by a network economy, defined by *keiretsu*—a system in which 'a major assembler maintained close, trusting, and reciprocal relations with a relatively small cadre of dedicated suppliers and subcontractors' (Lincoln and Gerlach, 2004: 2). The system of informal coordination was defined by large insider boards, *keiretsu* obligations, main bank ties, tight-knit trade associations, and guidance by regulators. This allowed for flexibility and rapid decision-making but created opaque governance structures and regulatory ambiguities that fostered grey zones within multiple sectors (Lincoln and Gerlach, 2004). After the

21st Century Yakuza. Martina Baradel, Oxford University Press. © Martina Baradel 2026.
DOI: 10.1093/9780191987755.003.0006

bursting of the bubble, Japan entered a period of economic reform with a push for deregulation and liberalization to make markets more competitive and efficient. However, deregulation did not translate into a complete absence of rules: rather, in several markets it meant re-regulation, with the introduction of new, complex, and targeted rules to control the newly liberalised markets (Vogel, 1996).

Several of these former grey zones—notably construction, real estate, labour brokerage, and the entertainment industries—used to provide fertile ground for non-state actors, including the yakuza, to embed themselves within both legal and semi-legal markets through rent-seeking, informal regulation, and protection rackets. The state began reasserting control in some of the legal markets that had once been profitable for the yakuza—such as informal labour and construction—by strengthening property rights, regulating key sectors, and increasing competition through legal intermediaries.

Against this backdrop, the chapter traces how different regulatory mechanisms operated across different market types, and specifically, it distinguishes between three mechanisms of displacement: regulatory exclusion targeting yakuza participation in legal markets; institutional re-regulation of formerly ambiguous sectors; and technological transformations that erode territorial control. The Yakuza Exclusion Ordinances (YEO), explored in the previous chapter, further limited the yakuza's participation in legal markets, as they impose penalties on economic actors engaging with yakuza members. But markets that remained in a grey area, such as prostitution, night-time entertainment, and gambling, continued to be susceptible to yakuza control, and markets that are outright illegal, such as drug trafficking, remain spaces where governance functions continue to matter, and where the yakuza retain influence both as providers of order and as participants in trade, alongside other actors. However, even in this sector, new challenges have arisen, such as the emergence of digital marketplaces, which has further undercut yakuza power. The expansion of virtual markets, especially in services like online escorting or drug sales, has made it difficult for the yakuza to extract rents or maintain territorial dominance. These markets lack physical locations, depend on anonymity, and invite decentralised participation, reducing the need for coercive protection and limiting the yakuza's ability to assert control.

The Japanese case illustrates how organised crime can be undermined not only through repression, but through a broader transformation in the governance of markets. The yakuza's decline is not simply a legal story of targeted anti-yakuza regulation, but one of structural displacement. Pushed out of legal and semi-legal activities because of increased regulation, illegal markets became more profitable, leading to a displacement towards darker activities. This shift is also tied to the fact that they no longer need to uphold the reputation of a respectable group: as discussed in the previous chapter, their criminalisation as a group has stripped them of their status as trusted and legitimate actors. Without state tolerance or societal acceptance, they no longer have to behave in ways that signal legitimacy.

While the yakuza encompasses twenty-five syndicates, each composed of hundreds of local branches, analyses of the yakuza often rely on generalised accounts of their economic activity, treating them as a unified criminal organisation. In practice, the yakuza's operations vary significantly across local chapters, as they operate according to the conditions of the local economy. A group based in rural Shimane, for instance, operates under very different economic logics than one embedded in central Tokyo. Although this diversity resists simple classification, it is still possible to identify some of the recurring practices and structural features that have characterised the yakuza's embeddedness across Japan's legal, illegal, and semi-legal markets. The yakuza is known to participate in a variety of markets, including: protection, drugs, gambling, prostitution, loan-sharking, debt collection, frauds, construction, waste collection, entertainment, and hospitality (NPA, 2025; Hill, 2003; Rankin, 2012).

This chapter focuses selectively on a subset of these: namely, protection, drugs, gambling, prostitution, labour brokerage, and the fish industry. This selection is not meant to offer a comprehensive mapping of yakuza activities, but to illuminate the broader argument advanced in the chapter: that the decline of the yakuza is best understood as a consequence of structural displacement from markets historically characterised by institutional ambiguity, limited state regulation, and high demand for informal governance. These chosen markets exemplify the varying degrees of regulatory transformation, digital disruption, and territorial erosion that have reconfigured the economic environment in which the yakuza once thrived. The final two cases (labour brokerage and fish market mediation) illustrate a different mechanism of decline: here, the yakuza had operated in formally legal sectors, profiting from regulatory ambiguity and informal brokerage. In these contexts, it was not only criminalisation per se, but market reforms and institutional re-regulation that progressively eliminated the structural conditions sustaining yakuza involvement. By examining sectors where the yakuza's role was both prominent and now increasingly unstable, the chapter illustrates how different regulatory pressures and technological shifts interact to challenge legacy forms of organised criminal power. Finally, the last section shows how the loss of state tolerance and social legitimacy has reduced the need for yakuza groups to perform respectably, further accelerating their retreat from semi-public roles and pushing them towards more predatory and concealed forms of criminality.

Protection

The core business of mafia groups is supplying private protection: the group aims at protecting any transactions within the territory they control. These services are often sold to other illegal entrepreneurs, whose rights and transactions are not protected by the state. However, mafia protection is also sought by entrepreneurs in the legal market, in particular when the state is not able to offer protection, enforce rights, or solve disputes swiftly and efficiently (Gambetta, 1993; Varese, 2001, 2010). However, it is rare that criminal groups establish exclusive control, eradicating the control of the state (Reuter, 1985). In many cases, criminal groups and the state engage in a symbiotic relationship that leaves space for both agents. Moreover, criminal governance may be discontinuous, meaning that in the same territories only some domains or activities are controlled (Lessing, 2021).

Within this fragmented landscape, criminal groups may play the role of enforcer of property rights, dispute mediators, and crime controllers (Milhaupt and West, 2000). The yakuza offer services that are hardly replaceable. In a night club, when a fight breaks out, the involvement of the police is costly as it brings scrutiny to the establishment and often involves closing the business to investigate responsibilities. A yakuza group offers a more convenient type of protection, in which the troublemaker is expelled without disrupting the activity and business can continue. The expulsion can be done with force, or in a more discreet way, asking the customer to talk outside so that there is no commotion in the business (C2). The relationship between the entrepreneur and the supplier of protection is based on trust. In this case, the entrepreneur cannot trust that involving the police will be beneficial since their intervention may harm the club's reputation and disrupt business—putting both the evening's revenue and the establishment's image at risk. Police presence signals to customers and passersby that something serious or illegal may have occurred, creating the impression of a dangerous or poorly managed venue. The club may become associated with violence and regular or elite clientele may start avoiding places that appear disorderly or unsafe. Moreover, there is no guarantee that the officers dispatched will simply deal with the trouble-makers and leave; they may also scrutinise the business itself and investigate its legality. On the other hand, relationships with private protectors are rooted in the group's territorial dominance: the business operates in a space where one specific yakuza group exercises their control and the entrepreneur relies on that group alone for protection; no competing group is allowed to provide similar services there. The entrepreneur will probably have had an individual relationship with the protector and, as the customer of the protection service, they can ask that the situation is handled in a way that does not harm business (C17). One night, after having dinner with the local boss, his lieutenant, and two group members, I went for a late-night drink with the lieutenant and another affiliate. Although this group consisted mainly of young and somewhat unruly members, they always ensured a designated driver on our nights out: the yakuza, when compliance does not interfere with their earnings, are willing to follow the rules. We ended up at the bar owned by the lieutenant's brother, located in an area controlled by the group. I asked whether they were still able to collect protection money in the neighbourhood despite increased law enforcement scrutiny. The response was affirmative, though they had to be particularly cautious about violence and its implicit threat. However, this had not deterred them. Their approach was straightforward: when a new shop opened in the area, they would send someone to inform the owner that they either needed to purchase something from them monthly or pay a set amount. If the owner refused, there would be no direct threats or coercion. Instead, one or two individuals would loiter around the shop, discouraging potential customers from entering. Most people understood the message and within a few months, the business would fail.

Furthermore, paying a protection fee also serves the purpose of protecting against the damage that the yakuza group itself can inflict to those who decide not to pay:

> Then there is *mikajimeryō*. There are two meanings: one is we protect you from harassers, the other is we protect you from people like us. It works like that in the underworld, even though the police are now trying to stop it. (C4)

These demands can be made to the protectee under the guise of protection money (*mikajimeryō*) or 'bouncer fees' (*yojinbō*). Similarly, the money can be collected by selling towels, soaps, or other supplies at inflated price.

Protection services may also include violent methods of dispute resolution, such as debt-collection services.

> The most thing, 50, 60 per cent, I was doing drugs, the rest was debt collection (*toritate*). There are people who need it, when yakuza does debt collection the fee is 50 per cent: if you have one million yen debt, we collect it and we take 500k yen. It's quite a lot, but if you don't ask the yakuza then you get zero. So there are people who need the yakuza, citizen who need the yakuza, and the yakuza can't disappear. (C3)

Debt collection in Japan is exclusively processed by lawyers[1] but since, in Japan, the number of lawyers remains low, there is space for the emergence of extra-legal competition, which has traditionally been taken up by the yakuza (Hill, 2003).

Focus groups with the police (S28–C28) confirm that while the yakuza maintained strong control over entertainment districts in the 1990s and early 2000s, they have since lost much of this grip. This is reflected in governmental data, which show that extortion—the category that is most closely related to protection—has been a significant and persistent category of crime associated with yakuza groups, especially throughout the 1990s and early 2000s. During Japan's economic bubble and its immediate aftermath, extortion cases were particularly high, reflecting the yakuza's entrenched role in extracting protection fees from businesses, especially in nightlife districts, construction, and small to medium-sized enterprises. The YEO transformed the structure of the protection market by inverting the incentives of third parties: whereas previously businesses faced the yakuza alone if they refused to pay, the Ordinances made cooperation legally risky and refusal institutionally supported. Banks, landlords, and business associations now had legal reasons—and legal cover—to exclude yakuza-affiliated actors, making it harder for protection relationships to be sustained even where demand persisted. This decline suggests a shrinking scope for yakuza protection rackets, as many businesses have either disengaged or have been legally deterred from paying protection money. Nonetheless, the police claims extortion remains a visible and ongoing activity within the yakuza's criminal portfolio. The data indicate that while large-scale, high-profile extortion operations

[1] Since 1998, 'servicer' companies can also collect debts but they must have at least one lawyer on their board of directors, de facto granting the monopoly of lawyers over legal debt-collection services.

have declined, smaller-scale, localised extortion cases persist (MoJ, 1993; 2000–2024).

Mizoguchi Atsushi, a veteran of yakuza journalism, insists that, leaving aside some areas, protection money is no longer widely paid.

> In cities like Nagoya, Kitakyūshū, Fukuoka, shops are still paying. But not so much in Tokyo. Hostess clubs and illegal casinos, are easy to ask. Bars, snack, restaurants, do not pay so much. In Ginza, there are both clubs paying and not. In the end, it depends on the type of activities of that particular group. (J2)

Control of the territory for the yakuza still matters, as does the reputation of the group. On another occasion, two yakuza members took me to a newly opened snack bar. As we sat drinking with two young hostesses, one of them wore a sly smile, only half-engaged in the conversation as he scanned the room. When I asked what he was thinking, he gestured around us and said, 'This is a new place, so they're not paying us anything yet. I'm just figuring out how much we should ask them each month.'

The owner of a sushi bar who was paying protection money to the local group explained:

> I pay the yakuza to solve problems before they happen. Once a problem has already happened, I can call the police. (V5)

This remark reflects the continuing relevance of the yakuza in two main scenarios. First, in areas where yakuza presence remains strong, local shop owners, used to their historical role, continue to perceive them as a legitimate source of informal regulation and conflict resolution. In these neighbourhoods, the 'network economy' described by Lincoln and Gerlach (2004) does not apply solely to large conglomerates; rather, even small businesses operate within tightly knit relational networks where mutual exchange is the norm. Bar and restaurant owners, for example, often frequent each other's establishments, maintaining a flow of resources and reinforcing bonds of reciprocity within the community. Second, yakuza protection remains valued by those operating in legal grey zones or in sectors where police involvement is unwelcome. In such contexts, the presence of a group capable of enforcing informal rules and deterring disorder without attracting state scrutiny is perceived as beneficial. These areas of activity are particularly resistant to state penetration: as long as certain markets remain only partially regulated, they remain vulnerable to the influence of alternative governance providers.

Drugs

In the postwar context, the first epidemic of drug abuse—which in this particular case was stimulant drugs—began at the end of the war and ended in 1956 with the enactment of the Stimulant Control Law. The second epidemic (1957–1969) saw many stimulant drug users turning to narcotics or other depressants, and, indeed, there were outbreaks of abuse of these two categories of drugs registered in different areas. The third period, that started in 1970, was marked by a rapid increase in arrests for stimulant drug abuse (Tamura, 1992). Given that the East Asian methamphetamine trade is one of the biggest and most profitable in the world (Kaplan and Dubro, 2003), it comes as no surprise that the yakuza wanted to have their share. In the 1990s, the yakuza became the main player in the importation and distribution of methamphetamines for a number of reasons: their coordinated structure, the high profitability of this market, the opportunity this market provided to absorb other (rival) criminal groups, and the fact that many yakuza members were users themselves (Tamura, 1992).

The end of the 1980s and the early 1990s saw an increase in the yakuza's connections with other countries in Asia. The 1991 *White Paper of the Police* (Keisatsu Hakusho) featured for the first time a whole section on the drug problem in Japan, making clear that the problem of drugs, and especially methamphetamines, had been spreading across the country. While the yakuza were reported as being consistently involved in the phenomenon, the police were also worried about the possible entry of the Colombian cartels into Japan, a threat that never materialised. According to this White Paper, there is no organisation involved in all phases from production, to middle-men, and finally to retail: rather, a group buys tens or hundreds of kilos from abroad—mainly from South East Asia, but also from Korea and China—and then sells it to the middle-men, who then move the load to different parts of Japan and sell it to the retailers. The local retailers are, therefore, usually yakuza groups with many members who are able to make a much higher profit than in other countries (NPA, 1991).

Officially, the yakuza, and particularly the Yamaguchi-gumi, have always taken a stance against drugs. Taoka Kazuo, the third boss of the Yamaguchi-gumi, was one of the founders of the *mayaku tsuihō kokudo jōka dōmei* (alliance for the banishment of drugs and clean-up of the country), a group founded in April 1963 as part of a peace agreement between conflicting yakuza groups. The current boss of the Rodu-daime Yamaguchi-gumi, Tsukasa Shinobu, shares this position. High-ranking members of the yakuza tend to share this position, as a yakuza boss confirmed: 'You need regulation, also for drugs, you can't let drugs come in too easily from say China. Of course the yakuza has a connection with China: but also we say don't bring in more than this much, because it'll be too much trouble if we have a lot of addicts' (C2). Although there are valid reasons as to why the yakuza would not want to be associated with drugs—drug-related crimes are punished more severely than other serious crimes, such as prostitution, and the organisations that conduct these types of business are invariably despised and repudiated by society—the police have continuously highlighted the yakuza's participation in drug trafficking (Hill, 2003).

Japan's drugs market is predominantly centred on methamphetamine, which accounted for 82 per cent of all drug seizures in 2023 (1,978 out of 2,406 kg) (Brewster, 2018; Nakamura, 2016; NPA, 2023; MoF, 2024). Methamphetamine is typically trafficked into the country in relatively small quantities, as indicated by an average seizure size of 6.5 kilograms (MoF, 2024). Entry routes include both air and maritime channels: drugs are brought in via air cargo, international mail, or passenger luggage, as well as through sea cargo or small-scale maritime smuggling (ibid.).

Existing research has identified only limited involvement by the yakuza in high-level drug smuggling and importation. While certain yakuza groups and individual members participate in domestic wholesale and retail drug distribution, their activities are concentrated on methamphetamine and other stimulants, with a relative avoidance of substances such as cannabis and cocaine (Baradel, 2021; Hill, 2003); where involvement occurs, it is typically by individuals acting as independent entrepreneurs (Baradel and Breuer, 2024).

According to police sources, individuals involved in drug distribution who are affiliated with yakuza groups must still obtain explicit permission from the organisation to operate. This often entails paying a portion of their profits to the group. They are also expected to shield their immediate superiors from legal exposure in the event of arrest. Because of the high cost of purchasing even a single kilogram of product, which can be sold for 60 million yen (400k dollars)/kilo (Baradel and Breuer, 2024), it is common practice for individuals to form small consortia to buy in bulk and subsequently resell. Nonetheless, law enforcement reports that a considerable number of actors continue to operate independently (P10–17).

Despite the yakuza's ongoing presence in distribution, several barriers constrain their involvement in production. According to a yakuza member, production is difficult due to the need for an isolated location to cook the substance (typically in wooded areas) which are increasingly hard to find. Moreover, repeated use of the same site degrades the surrounding environment, with nearby trees often dying off. Each batch also yields less than the previous one. Regarding marijuana, he noted that while seeds can be purchased from the United States, cultivation is resource-intensive as it requires a significant amount of energy (C10). Information from a former dealer further illustrates the evolving structure of the market. He had limited interactions with his superior, who was a yakuza; as he explained, it is the responsibility of the yakuza groups to control the flow of information downwards and non-affiliated individuals are rarely entrusted with details that could later be disclosed to the police. During his trial, he provided little testimony, claiming he genuinely lacked knowledge about the broader operation. While serving his sentence, he received regular monthly transfers, intended to ensure his silence (C8).

Territorial variation further complicates the picture. Yakuza influence remains strong in areas like Saitama and Chiba, where drugs markets tend to be territorially structured—that is, each group have their well-defined territory and exclusively operate within it. In contrast, Tokyo lacks a clearly defined territorial market, meaning that success depends more on the quality of service and the ability to build trust with clients (C6, C8). In the case of stimulants (mainly methamphetamines), transactions are based on established personal connections rather than open street-level sales (C7). In rural or semi-urban regions territorial control is more visible, with dealers operating within defined physical spaces. However, discretion is still necessary: it is generally considered unwise to sell drugs in close proximity to a yakuza office (C8).

Indirect operations are increasingly common. Rather than relying solely on registered members, yakuza groups often work with non-affiliated individuals who conduct sales on their behalf. This strategy reduces the risk of liability for senior figures and minimises exposure in the event of arrest. As a former dealer explained:

> I worked freelance for the yakuza, but I was never officially registered as a member, it's too dangerous. I just handled sales for other people, including some online. A friend of mine who's good with computers helped me set up the business and we used platforms like Telegram to communicate with clients. You don't need that many customers; if you've got five regulars, that's

> enough to live off for a month. . . . You have to be careful, though. If you sell bad stuff even once, you lose the customer. That kind of trust is everything. (C8)

This shift is exacerbated by technological innovation. The control of the drugs market is becoming more difficult for the yakuza, as drugs have been increasingly sold online. A former yakuza boss with experience in drug dealing confirmed that encrypted sites and fake accounts are used to transfer money, with drugs sent via post and payment received upfront. These transactions bypass the territorial networks through which yakuza groups once exercised control (C10).

Recent arrest data underscore these shifts. The number of persons arrested for drug offences has remained virtually unchanged in recent years. Around half of the arrests for methamphetamines involve yakuza members. The most prominent category throughout the period remains drug-related offences, especially violations of the Stimulant Drug Control Act. These offences consistently account for the largest number of arrests, though figures show a gradual decline from 2013 to 2022. This is likely to reflect both enhanced enforcement and changing distribution networks less reliant on traditional syndicate structures. By contrast, the marijuana market tells a different story. The number of arrests for marijuana offences has continued to increase since 2014, mainly among young people under 30 years of age, with 5,482 arrests (of which only 789 were yakuza members) in 2021, exceeding the previous year's record high. Yakuza arrests for marijuana thus constitute only a small fraction of the total (MoJ, 2014–2022).

While traditional syndicates maintain a strong presence, especially in stimulant distribution and territorially structured markets, their influence is increasingly challenged by freelance dealers, encrypted online platforms, and shifting drug preferences. Territorial control remains a key source of power in some regions but is less relevant in urban centres. Marijuana markets, in particular, appear to be dominated by younger, non-affiliated actors (P1, P10–17). As a result, the yakuza's role is transforming: from monopolistic control towards a more discreet and adaptive role within an increasingly plural market.

Gambling

Most forms of gambling are illegal in Japan. Exceptions include betting on public races (such as horse races, motorboat racing, bicycle racing, and Auto

Race[2]), lotteries, and pachinko.[3] According to Article 185 of the penal code, gamblers can either receive a fine of up to 500k yen (simple gambling crime; *Keihō*, 185*jō*) or imprisonment with labour for up to three years (repeated gambling crime; *Keihō* 185*jō* para. 1), whilst the sentence for the operator of the gambling parlour is imprisonment with labour, with a minimum sentence of between three months and five years (*Keihō* 185*jō* para. 2). The yakuza are involved in a variety of gambling activities: cards, dice, and roulette games, illegal book-making, and pachinko (Hill, 2003; NPA, 2025). Recently, illegal casinos[4] have gained in popularity. Located either in a room in a mansion building or in a multi-tenant building, these casinos have no outward signs and, indeed, customers can only access them if they are approached and escorted by a *kyacchi* (a street-level tout who approaches passers-by to bring them into bars or clubs). These illegal casinos can be found in big cities and their growing popularity is attested to by the fact that gambling cases involving celebrities are often featured in the news. In 2016, the badminton player Nishimoto Kenta saw his inclusion in the national team revoked after news broke that he had frequented an illegal casino on two separate occasions (*The Huffington Post Japan*, 19/04/2016), while, in 2017, the actors Endō Kaname and Shimizu Ryōtarō were both placed under house arrest for committing the same crime (Sankei Shimbun, 11/02/2017). The yakuza have historically managed the gambling market, and thus have the expertise to continue their involvement in this activity. At the same time, the ongoing campaign to expel the yakuza from the legal parts of the market means that they continue to infiltrate the emerging illegal part of this sector.

During the fieldwork, gambling emerged as an important activity. Yakuza groups organize 'tournaments', for example including games such as the popular mahjong, in their offices if they have space. Each player is required to bet a minimum amount of money (for instance 10,000 yen), and the groups gets a percentage of each table. If a player loses immediately, they are given additional money to continue betting; otherwise, the game would not be enjoyable. Revenues come not only from the organisation of the tournaments, which includes a percentage cut from each table and mandatory entry

[2] Ōto Rēsu, a flat-track motorbike race held on an asphalt course which originated in Japan.

[3] A kind of magnetic slot machine, pachinko occupies a distinct legal position: although effectively a form of gambling, it operates through a three-stage prize exchange system—players win tokens, exchange them for prizes, and then exchange those prizes for cash at separate booths—which technically circumvents the prohibition and has been tolerated by authorities as a grey-zone activity.

[4] Known as *yamikajino* (dark casinos), *urakajino* (underground casinos), or *inkaji*.

fees, but also from the debts that players incur while participating. When players lose and are given additional funds to continue betting, these are recorded as debts which the group later collects with interest or through other means (C17).

Prostitution

Japan did not have a law on prostitution until it introduced the 1956 Prostitution Prevention Law. This Law was steeped in moral rhetoric, describing prostitution as harmful to human dignity and public morals, but imposed no penalties on those directly engaging in sex work. While it prohibited both selling and buying sex, it criminalised only third-party involvement, such as solicitation, brokering, and coercion. Women who engaged in prostitution were subject to state intervention and potential prosecution for solicitation, but not for the act of sex itself. Prostitution was legally defined as 'intercourse with unspecified persons for compensation', interpreted by authorities to mean exclusively penile–vaginal sex (Koch, 2021). With the enactment of the Law, all brothels were closed down. But entrepreneurs in this sector soon found a new opportunity: providing services that verged on sexual intercourse but did not include it.

The yakuza involvement in the sex industry is of dual nature. While individual yakuza members operate businesses such as date clubs and escort services, their ability to function depends on the broader governance capacity of the group: reputation, territorial control, and the credible threat of violence. These protection and enforcement services are also extended to lawful entrepreneurs operating in the night-time economy, who pay for territorial security and dispute resolution. Date clubs can be set up in an office space where operators take calls from customers. A driver will escort the woman to the customer who will be waiting in a love hotel. The work of the driver consists in transporting the women, ensuring their safety, monitoring their schedules, and collecting or delivering payments (C20). Nishimura Mako, who operated a date club in Gifu during the 1990s, described how the business functioned. She would place advertisements in public payphones, prompting male clients to call the listed number. After asking about their preferences, the operator would instruct them to check into a hotel and call back, at which point a women would be dispatched. The fee was a flat 20,000 yen, a rate fixed by a local agreement among the yakuza operating in Gifu at the time. The standard profit split was 40 per cent to the shop and 60 per cent to the women, meaning the shop earned 8,000 yen per dispatch. Business was brisk and there were times when there were not enough women to meet demand. In such cases, she would borrow workers from other clubs and share the 8,000 yen profit equally, with each shop taking 4,000 yen (C14).

Women were sometimes sold to brothels for a profit, exploiting a system of debts. On one occasion, Nishimura gave housing and sold drugs to a woman who had previously worked in her date club. After developing a methamphetamine dependency, the woman was allowed to accumulate a debt for drugs, food, accommodation, and other living expenses which were calculated unilaterally and inflated by Nishimura. When the woman attempted to escape, she was located through Nishimura's contacts in the yakuza, forcibly returned, and made to acknowledge the full amount of her debt. A contact introduced Nishimura to the yakuza that controlled Wakatanojima, an island off the coast of Mie famous for the concentration of brothels. Through his mediation, she was able to sell the indebted woman to the owner of a shop in exchange for an advance payment of 3.5 million yen that would cover the woman's debt. Fixed shares were distributed to intermediaries who helped capture the woman while Nishimura retained the bulk of the proceeds (C14).

A system of debt is also what usually keeps street and foreign prostitutes working for the yakuza. Many women have entered the country illegally or overstayed their visa, and have incurred debts with the brokers that arranged their arrival into the country. Typically passed to a second broker (often a yakuza), their debt increases and they are forced to repay it by working as prostitutes either in clubs or on the streets (Hill, 2003).

The 'water trade' (*mizu-shōbai*), as the night-time entertainment sector is known, includes a list of activities that range from simple bars up to brothels. Hostess bars feature hostesses at a counter or sitting down at customers' tables serving them drinks all night, while chatting, singing, and sometimes flirting. Customers are usually men and specifically, male co-workers: hostess clubs are often used as a space in which work relationships can become more relaxed and a sense of community can be fostered across company hierarchies. At the same time, hostess clubs are also a business space, where deals can be cemented and business partners get to know each other in a more personal way (Allison, 1994). These bars include the most elegant Ginza *kyabakura* to the countryside karaoke bar run by a woman in her eighties. In normal *kyabakura*, touching is not permitted, however there are particular types of *kyabakura* (*pinku-kyaba* or *seku-kyaba*) where it is possible to caress the women (and possibly proceed to engage in intercourse although this is illegal). Nevertheless, it is not uncommon that after a few drinks customers try to touch the hostess: if this happens, the women usually kindly ask the customer to stop or report this to staff.

All these premises are regulated by the 1948 Business Affecting Public Morals Regulation Law (*Fūzoku-eigyō nado no kisei oyogi gyōmu tekiseika nadoni kansuru hōritsu*, 2017), which was created to regulate *kyabakura*, bars, dance halls, as well as more sexually explicit businesses such as soaplands[5] and love hotels. Although some of these bars are owned by the yakuza, they do not necessarily have ties with the local family. In a small to medium-sized town (40,000 inhabitants) with an important company that employs thousands (which means there are men living temporarily in the town with no family around), there may be dozens of hostess bars of different types. The *sunakku*[6] are run independently by owners (usually women) and have varying levels of connection to the local yakuza. The *kyabakura* have a closer relationship: the venue may be owned by the local family who employ associates to run it. For instance, a contact in the Shizuoka prefecture reported that he managed a *kyabakura* that was owned by the local yakuza group but was adamant that the management and business were conducted legally. Similarly, the floor manager, who is also a personal acquaintance, was not formally affiliated to the yakuza group but reported that he had always worked for them.

Although there are no official data on the level of yakuza infiltration within these sectors, some general data on the entertainment business can be extracted from the 'Report on the Entertainment Business and Control of Related Crimes' (2022).[7] A recent police estimate from 2022 counts 78,934 entertainment establishments (these include bars, mah-jong, and pachinko parlours) in Japan, a number that has been in constant decline from the 94,769 activities estimated in 2014. During the past five years, the number of businesses connected with the sex industry has slowly but steadily increased: in 2022, around 33,000 businesses nationwide offer 'delivery fashion health' (dispatch escort service), pornography, adult video stores, bars for

[5] A soapland is an establishment where men pay to be washed. They pay an entry fee to use the bathing facility and a separate fee to the masseuse who is supposed to wash them. They exploit a legal loophole insofar as soapland operators claim that the customer and the masseuse perform sexual acts as a couple, having grown fond of each other over the course of the massage (Hongo, 27/05/2008).

[6] A *sunakku* is a small-scale drinking establishment characterised by a warm, informal atmosphere where customers can enjoy drinks and light snacks, engage with hostesses or bartenders, and often sing karaoke songs.

[7] *Reiwa 4 nenhan ni okeru fūzoku eigyō nado no genjō to fūzoku kankei jihan no torishimari jōkyō nado ni tsuite.*

encounters, and similar activities (NPA, 2022). The sector is driven by the special sex industry business based on non-store operations,[8] which is commonly referred to as *deriheru* (dispatch escort service) business and does not require a physical shop (NPA, 2015b): these companies have steadily increased in the past five years, while businesses based in physical shops are declining (NPA, 2022). The *Bōhaijōrei* have limited the yakuza's ability to rent physical spaces to run their business, causing them to move towards this type of activity (Baradel and Bortolussi, 2021). As this business is not based around an office, it can ignore regulations that prohibit sex-related commercial activities from being near schools, hospitals, or other buildings used by children and the community.

From the perspective of the yakuza, this shift represents a critical challenge. The traditional yakuza model relies heavily on territorial control to exact protection fees from operators within their domains. Virtual or delivery-based sex services, by their decentralised and ephemeral nature, effectively evade this system of rent extraction. Without a physical storefront to monitor or threaten, yakuza syndicates are unable to enforce payment of rents, thereby losing a substantial—and historically stable—source of income. This erosion of territorial rent extraction destabilises the yakuza's economic base, forcing them to adapt by seeking new illicit revenue. Concurrently, industry resistance has intensified: for instance, in Osaka, brothel owners have formed associations explicitly aimed at barring yakuza infiltration of the prostitution market. These associations coordinate with law enforcement to close down illicit 'massage parlours' established by yakuza affiliates, further driving organised crime activity underground (Yamanouchi, 2016).

The grey area in which the night-time entertainment sector has operated provides the yakuza with ample opportunities, ranging from legal 'girls' bars' to a plethora of sex services. The increased regulations and controls on this sector are pushing the yakuza out of the neighbourhoods where these services are usually provided, towards more undetectable forms of business.

The police have been focusing on eradicating private protection services offered by the yakuza, particularly in night-time entertainment districts such as Kabukichō (Tokyo). Since paying a monthly fee to a yakuza group can now lead to prosecution for the owner of the establishment, and since it can be reported as extortion and punished accordingly, the number of shops paying protection money has decreased considerably. However, these regulations

[8] *Mutenpogata seifuzoku tokushuu eigyou.*

are introduced at the prefectural level, they are not applied homogeneously across Japan. In the night-time entertainment area of Nakasu in Fukuoka, for example, the influence of the yakuza remains considerable, although it has been weakened by the increased police scrutiny. This has left space for the emergence of non-traditional forms of crime such as *hangure* and Chinese-led gangs, which are not subjected to the same restrictions as the yakuza. After the introduction of the Ordinances, the number of shops connected to Chinese-gangs and non-yakuza criminal groups increased (Baradel and Bortolussi, 2021).

These days, collecting protection money in Tokyo is not as common as it once was. Businesses like host clubs, illegal casinos, and online gambling operations are still commonly targeted, whereas more ordinary establishments—bars, snack bars, and diners—are less frequently asked to pay. The persistence of *mikajimeryō* depends both on the region and on the type of activity practised by a particular group. Notably, in areas like Fukushima, reconstruction projects have also provided opportunities for such practices to continue (ibid.).

The same logic of control and exploitation extends, in its most predatory form, to minors. '*Enjō kōsai*',[9] a term that literally means 'mutually beneficial relationship', has since the 1990s has been used to refer to a form of compensated dating that involves a man and either junior or senior female high school students. Although the State Department (2018) raised concerns that dating services connecting adult men with underage girls are linked to the sexual exploitation of children in prostitution, '*enjō kōsai*' remains common in Japan. An informant who was once involved in criminal activities and served twenty years in prison, now runs a halfway house for ex-prisoners. He reported that the yakuza are often involved in managing girls.

> If you go to Akihabara there are many girls who are dressed like high school girls or maids: around there they surely have a lookout. If something gets weird, they can call him. When it's dangerous the lookouts come out. There is a system like this. And they get a share, let's say 40–60 per cent. The girl gets 40 per cent and the lookout 6 per cent and then part of that goes to the yakuza. In this way they can't catch the yakuza, because they don't do it

[9] This term encompasses activities that range from a date in a café with an adult man motivated by a sexual interest in girls' bodies, to the sexual exploitation of children. Given its widespread use in the media, I use it here for convenience, but since in most cases '*enjō kōsai*' is merely a euphemism for prostitution amongst teenage girls and the sexual exploitation of children (see Fifield, 16/05/2017; Ueno, 2003), I place it in quotation marks.

> directly, they are not there on the spot.... If you sell junior high school girls, well you can make 100 or 200k yen [700–1,400 GBP]. There are men who would spend that much money for a junior high school girl. (C1)

He added that such scenarios present a double opportunity to make money, insofar as the yakuza are also to blackmail the man who paid for '*enjō kōsai*' by threatening to reveal details of his encounters with underage girls. Underage girls are also exploited in girls' bars and *kyabakura* managed by yakuza groups, where they are employed despite age restrictions and often without proper documentation, making them particularly vulnerable to abuse and coercive control.

Market regulation

For most illegal enterprises, diversification translates into a multiplication of exposure to different law enforcement agencies and is, therefore, avoided (Reuter, 1985). However, due to their semi-legal status, which allowed for stable, long-standing leadership and reduced law enforcement pressure, the yakuza could branch out into different sectors and diversify their business. Beyond illegal markets such as prostitution, drugs, gambling, loan sharking, and debt collection, the yakuza also accrued revenues from legitimate business. In particular, the yakuza have traditionally infiltrated legal markets such as public works, construction, temporary staff recruitment, industrial waste business, entertainment, sports entertainment, clubs, bars, and the food business (Yamanouchi, 2016). Many mafia-type associations are involved with legal activities (Milhaupt and West, 2000) but in the case of the yakuza, such activities represented a major share of their revenues. According to Suzuki, a yakuza journalist, approximately two-thirds of the yakuza's businesses were legal (J4).

The organisational structure of yakuza-owned companies illustrates how the group embedded itself within the formal economy. Yamanouchi Yukio, former legal adviser of the Yamaguchi-gumi, explains this with the example of the companies he helped to manage. He gives an example of two companies owned by the Yamaguchi-gumi, the Tōyō Shinyō Jitsugyō (established in 1975) and the Yamaki (established in 1991). They are both located in a building near the Yamaguchi-gumi headquarters in Kobe. The companies own and manage Yamaguchi-gumi real estate: this is particularly convenient because under anti-yakuza legislation, bosses may be held responsible for the members' unlawful behaviour. While in the past it was the norm for bosses to hold property in their name, it is now avoided because it might be seized in case of trial. The companies are run by the Yamaguchi-gumi board which employs bosses and executives as board members and CEOs. Employees are members of the Yamaguchi-gumi who effectively help to run the company. However, while both companies raise money from members and groups to buy real estate, they are managed differently. The Tōyō Shinyō Jitsugyō owns a club, called the 'Orient Club': Yamaguchi-gumi members who join the club pay a membership fee (200k yen) and the collected capital is invested through the Tōyō Shinyō Jitsugyō. The Yamaki has more capital, therefore shares can be bought in the company, and money is collected and invested that way. Furthermore, having a legal activity is useful to process a whole range of payments. For instance, Yamanouchi would receive a fixed sum of 100k yen from each company for his work, instead of receiving it directly from the Yamaguchi-gumi (V1). By interposing legal entities between the organisation and its assets, the Yamaguchi-gumi was able to maintain continued participation in regulated sectors despite the increasing scrutiny of the 1991 Anti-Yakuza Law. However, the introduction of the YEO significantly altered this environment by formalising exclusion clauses and restricting access to contracts, finance, and property transactions, thereby making such corporate embedding strategies increasingly difficult to sustain.

While such structures allowed the yakuza to embed themselves in the formal economy and shield their assets behind corporate fronts, this strategy became increasingly untenable in certain sectors as regulatory reforms altered the conditions that had previously enabled their participation. In particular, efforts to formalise labour brokerage and wholesale market transactions, though not explicitly targeting organised crime, introduced clearer rules, licensing requirements, and institutional oversight that left less room for informal brokers and non-compliant actors. The following two cases, casual labour markets and the fish market, illustrate how regulatory intervention in specific sectors disrupted the environments in which the yakuza had long operated, ultimately pushing them out.

Labour brokers

Japan has traditionally had a large casual labour sector with deep roots in Japanese social organisation. This system was based on the labour markets (physical spaces in the city known as *yoseba*), where day labourers gather to be picked up by the labour-brokers who receive a fee taken from the labourers' wages. The employment chain involving one or more middle-men can often be found in the construction sector, starting from before the industrial revolution of the Meiji period (1868–1912), when employers would receive requests from a company for specific jobs and hire the necessary number of people to carry out such jobs. After the Second World War, the government tried to regulate the casual labour market, with the not so secondary intention of limiting the yakuza's intervention in it (Gill, 2001). However, because of how this market was structured, it was prone to irregularities and in constant need of a casual workforce, and thus favoured the emergence and persistence of local criminal groups regulating its dynamics.

The extreme economic growth of the 1960s and 1970s saw an increased demand for casual labour, a demand which continued to grow throughout the 1980s. In the 1990s, the burst of the bubble economy gave way to a long economic recession. Instability and unemployment led to a precarisation of the labour market that affected the construction sector in particular, which was subsidised by the state and thus in need of manual labourers. Construction firms saved money by keeping as many workers as possible off the payroll: they used a system of subcontracting and (informal) labour brokers to obtain the necessary men for each project without having to hire them full-time. By doing so, fluctuations in the business cycle could be easily absorbed, by hiring workers only when necessary (Fowler, 1996). Working on short-term subcontracts, these casual labourers gathered in the so-called *yoseba*, low-income urban centres where it was possible to spend the night in cheap accommodation, and where labour brokers went to pick workers for the day (Stevens, 1995).

The yakuza used to control the labour market in many *yoseba*. Stevens, who spent a year in Kotobuki, the *yoseba* in Yokohama, stated that the yakuza held 'a monopoly on criminal activity in town' (Stevens, 1995: 239), although Gill (2001) a few years later posits that most labour brokers were independent operators paying a fee to the local yakuza group. San'ya (Tokyo) was populated by different yakuza groups, but the Kanamachi-ikka had the monopoly on the area. The yakuza controlled how the men earned their wages as well as how they spent them, providing entertainment for the workers through gambling joints and prostitution. According to Fowler's interviewees, the police often collaborated with the yakuza to keep the unions under control. As well as organising the labour market, the yakuza also sold insurance stamps for unemployment compensation on the black market (Fowler, 1996). In San'ya, the yakuza would also settle disputes between salarymen and workers since the workers could not ask the police for protection, as their relationship with the labourers was strained (V4). The casual labour market lent itself to the control of the yakuza: it was legal but it was formally monopolised by the state, and public agencies lacked the capacity to service the highly casualised construction sector. The yakuza then acted as labour brokers: they matched workers and recruiters, organised recruitment chains, settled disputes, enforced informal norms, and extracted fees from both sides of the transaction.

However, if one visits San'ya, Kotobuki, or Kamagasaki today, little of the *yoseba* of the 1990s is left. The population of labourers has transformed into a population of old men without families or homes. In 1999, the government amended the Employment Security Law and Worker's Dispatching Law, liberalising restrictions on private employment placement services and removing the monopoly of governmental agencies. This allowed private employment agencies to enter the market of casual labour (Tsuneki and Matsunaka, 2011). The 1999 revision of the Worker Dispatching Law radically liberalised the scope of dispatchable work by replacing the restrictive 'positive list' of twenty-six permissible occupations with a 'negative list' system under which dispatch was generally permitted except in designated sectors. More fundamentally, the parallel revision of the Employment Security Law marked a shift from the principle of state monopoly in employment placement to a co-existence model in which private fee-charging agencies were recognised as legitimate actors alongside public employment security offices (Araki, 1999). Labour intermediation was thus relocated from a predominantly bureaucratic domain into a regulated competitive market for supply–demand adjustment. In a context where public placement had limited reach in certain segments of the labour market, informal and relational brokers—including yakuza-affiliated intermediaries—had previously occupied this space. The institutionalisation of licensed private competitors reduced the structural demand for such extra-legal brokerage.

At the same time, liberalisation was accompanied by consolidation of a permit-based regulatory regime. Registration-type dispatch agencies were required to obtain authorisation from the Minister of Labour, comply with codified administrative procedures, and satisfy newly articulated disqualifying criteria, including exclusion of individuals convicted of violent offences within the previous five years. The reform imposed strict temporal limits on dispatch relationships, prohibiting client firms from receiving workers in the same post for more than one year, empowering the Labour Minister to issue corrective guidance, and authorising fines and public naming for non-compliance. Dispatch agencies were subject to reporting and disclosure obligations, while client companies were required to coordinate contractually to prevent unlawful continuation of placements (Araki, 1999). Labour brokerage thus became a licensed, inspectable, and sanctionable activity embedded within continuous administrative oversight rather than a loosely mediated labour supply practice. The regularisation of labour brokerage reduced the structural demand for extra-legal intermediation: mafia-type organisations are most competitive in markets where rights are weakly defined and regulatory oversight leaves room for discretionary intermediation.

The yakuza have not been completely expelled from labour brokerage, however. Several groups operate a labour-dispatch businesses, recruiting and dispatching workers to construction sites. Although the numbers are declining overall, the majority of violations of the Workers Dispatchment Act in recent years have been committed by yakuza members (see Table 5.1).

Yet, regulatory exclusion prove fragile under emergency conditions, when urgency and labour scarcity temporarily restore demand for informal intermediaries. In one famous incident, the yakuza were involved in the aftermath of the 2011 Tōhoku earthquake and tsunami, which provided the yakuza with both business and publicity. Despite the fact that under the new regulations the yakuza should be excluded, Fukushima district and TEPCO (the company managing the Fukushima Daiichi power plant) only began to implement the regulations a few months after the disaster, which left enough time for yakuza members to infiltrate the labour-brokering market. Moreover, the desperate situation at the Fukushima power plant meant that TEPCO and its subcontractors needed as many men as possible to clear up the nuclear debris and simply could not afford to turn anyone away. The labourers brought in by yakuza labour brokers were unskilled and, in many cases, picked up from the streets and sent to the most dangerous spots (Rankin, 2012). In some cases, homeless men were recruited and either used as part of the workforce, or, alternatively, were forced to apply for emergency financial aid in different

Table 5.1 Violations of the Workers Dispatchment Act

	2012	2013	2014	2015	2016	2017	2018	2019	2020	2021
Total	31	32	34	23	7	6	12	23	15	12
Yakuza	13	15	18	3	2	2	1	5	4	6
% Yakuza	73.8%	86.5%	87.2%	62.2%	21.9%	42.9%	48%	69.7%	55.6%	92.3%

(Source: NPA, 2021)

locations (Suzuki, 2014). Recently, given the scarcity of manual labour, the yakuza have been collaborating with foreign groups supplying illegal immigrants to carry out work related to the construction sector, such as demolition and waste disposal (NPA, 2022).

From poaching boats to the biggest fish market in the world

On a cloudy afternoon in January 2023, after a talk in a café in Ginza, Suzuki Tomohiko took me to what remains of Tsukiji, Tokyo's old fish market. The market itself moved to Toyosu in 2018, leaving behind empty shops and a rundown commercial area. But Suzuki was not interested in the remnants of the market—he led me to a wooden house nearby and told me it belonged to the boss of the Tsukumasa-ikka, the yakuza family that had controlled Tsukiji for generations. The group's founder, Kaneko Masakichi (1857–1934), had started out selling clams before becoming, by his twenties, the leader of the yakuza group whose function was to impose order on Tsukiji's chaotic trading environment. They enforced rules, arbitrated disputes, and mediated conflicts between competing interests. In 1887, when fish market workers clashed for three days and nights with stockbrokers over a proposed market relocation in what became known as the Matsubara Incident, it was Kaneko who mediated the resolution (Kawaguchi, 1985).

Tsukiji was the world's largest fish market and the yakuza have been a long-established presence since Kaneko's time. Yakuza members have since worked as intermediaries or brokers navigating the market's complex price fluctuations on behalf of fishmongers and restaurant owners. High-end sushi restaurants in particular relied on brokers who could identify the best product at the best price each day—the market price system that defined Tokyo's premium seafood trade depended on intermediaries with deep market knowledge and the authority to enforce informal standards. The profit margin ranged from 10 to 30 per cent. For instance, a fisherman sells a salmon for 700 yen. The broker will then sell it for 770 yen to the retailer, who will sell it to the final customer at 1,000 yen. The market had its own informal regulatory codes—fish dealers used specific marks to identify themselves and their product—and the yakuza broker's role was to guarantee that these codes were respected and that transactions between competing parties were conducted without cheating (Suzuki, 2018).

The market also attracted a workforce of people with few other options: workers recruited through job ads with no background checks, paid cash daily, starting work at 3am. This grey zone employment, unregulated but essential to the market's functioning, was the kind of environment in which the yakuza had historically embedded themselves (ibid.). But on 1 April 2012, prompted by the anti-yakuza regulations, the market declared the severance of all relationships with the yakuza. According to these regulations, nobody can engage in business with, or pass money to, members of the yakuza. The declaration changed the official status of these relationships but not immediately their substance: brokers continued operating through informal arrangements and front companies, their presence made less visible rather than eliminated. The move to Toyosu in 2018, and the Tokyo Metropolitan Central Wholesale Market Ordinance Enforcement Regulations,[10] amended in 2020, proved the more decisive transformation. The ordinance states that members of the yakuza, and individuals with ties to organised crime groups, cannot take part in market transactions. Furthermore, only those with a licence for intermediate wholesale dealing can buy fish from the authorised consignee companies. Buyers do not need a licence to buy from the brokers, but they must buy by the kilo, which makes the transactions less convenient. The new market's stricter licensing requirements, formal transaction systems, and internationalisation (with foreign buyers now lining up in their hundreds for tuna auctions) replaced the informal governance environment in which the Tsukumasa-ikka had operated for over a century with one the state could regulate directly. Direct sales from producer to final buyer have since increased, bypassing the intermediary role entirely (Suzuki, 2018).

However, if we look up the supply chain, there are sections of the market where the yakuza is still active. Abalones are marine gastropods which are considered a luxury seafood, particularly in the Asian market. To meet the demand for this expensive product, abalones are both farmed and wild harvested (Hoshino et al., 2015). Although wild harvesting of abalones is permitted in certain areas, the Ministry of Agriculture, Forestry and Fishery (MAFF) has reported an increase in illegal poaching of sea cucumbers and abalones. Poaching by non-fishermen has been increasing and now constitutes the majority of cases (MAFF, 2022). According to Taya (2007), poached abalones account for 45 per cent (906 tons) of all abalones traded in Japan. Since abalone is valued at 4,000 yen per kg, the scale of the abalone poaching market alone reaches around four billion yen. This figure increases to ten billion yen if we include the poaching of other expensive seafoods (sea

[10] *Tōkyōto Chūō Oroshiurishijō Jōrei Shikō Kisoku.*

cucumbers, sea urchins, and so forth). Official data confirm the organised crime dimension: the Japan Coast Guard reported that yakuza-affiliated actors used diving equipment to strip abalone, sea snails, and sea cucumbers from areas cultivated by local fishermen. The predatory character of this activity was particularly visible in the aftermath of the 2011 Great East Japan Earthquake: while local fishermen struggled to rebuild, yakuza-affiliated actors carried out large-scale abalone poaching operations in the same devastated coastal areas (Japan Coast Guard, 2013).

Poaching operations in the Sanriku region take two forms. The first involves inflatable boat gangs travelling from outside the region, who pay local yakuza groups for logistical support (e.g. hotels, cars with local licence plates, and sales channels) while remaining organisationally distinct from them. The second involves local yakuza groups conducting poaching directly, using modified boats with seven or eight people on board, driving at high speed between fishing grounds and unloading points. Furthermore, there is a distinction between direct yakuza operatives and affiliated groups: in Iwate, poaching gangs are not formal yakuza members but use the name of local groups, paying a fee in exchange for the right to operate under that name. Different yakuza groups can collaborate: members from different yakuza families share the same boat. The most dangerous moment for any poaching operation is unloading, because that is when goods, people, and equipment are briefly in the same place. To minimise this window, gangs coordinate land-based lookouts, multiple transport vehicles, and precise timing to scatter the catch before any checkpoint can be established (Suzuki, 2018).

Poached abalones enter the legitimate supply chain by being mixed with farmed abalones and sold through regular dealers to markets and restaurants. Farmed abalones can be identified by a green mark on their shells, but this is insufficient to prove origin with certainty, and buyers may purchase poached product at a discount while dealers sell it on as legitimate. The key intermediaries are not yakuza but people within the fisheries industry itself: dealers with access to wholesale markets who can absorb and redistribute illegal catches without attracting scrutiny. In 2008, the Miyagi Prefectural Police and the Japan Coast Guard raided Tsukiji Market and Sapporo Central Wholesale Market, leading to the indictment of two employees of a Tokyo Stock Exchange-listed company for knowingly selling poached abalone. The case was unusual in exposing how far up the legitimate supply chain the poaching network reached (Suzuki, 2018; Japan Coast Guard, 2013).

The abalone case illustrates a broader principle: where resources are limited, the environment ungovernable, and legal frameworks unable to reach, the yakuza retain their role as informal regulators. The open sea cannot be policed in the way a physical market can, and the scarcity of abalones creates conditions for black market governance that the state cannot replicate. The Tsukiji market, by contrast, represents the opposite case: a fixed, visible, and commercially significant institution where the state had both the capacity and the incentive to intervene—and where, over time, it did.

Conclusion

During a visit to a yakuza office, as I was waiting in a room with members of the group fretting through their daily activities, my gaze landed on the bulletin board. One of the notes said, in big characters: 'Senior members, keep an eye on young members so that they do not engage in frauds – it is prohibited!'. While the indication from the management is clear, at the end of the month the membership fee needs to be paid: it is up to lower members to come up with ways to earn enough money to pay up and to make a living at the same time. The involvement of the yakuza in frauds seems to have decreased in the past five years, but as informants confirm, there is the increased suspicion of the use of actors not officially affiliated to the yakuza to carry out fraud in order to reduce the risk of arrests.

Many yakuza members lament that because of the harshening of laws, they have to find alternative ways of earning money: for instance, a member of a group under the Yamaguchi-gumi umbrella explained how he has to make his livelihood through frauds on *Mercari* (a selling platform similar to eBay) by selling empty iPhone boxes. Despite joining the yakuza because of the prospect of earning good money, he now reported earns barely 200k yen a month (roughly 1,200 GBP), which evidently does not allow for a very glamorous lifestyle (Nikkan SPA, 23/05/2017). Furthermore, the introduction of the new anti-yakuza laws, which attempt to stop citizens from paying protection money or conducting business with yakuza-related activities, also served to reduce the income of many yakuza members, who were left with little choice but to turn to fraud. Originally, fraud, stealing, and robberies were banned under the yakuza code of honour, but now they are engaging in them to compensate for lost protection money (Rankin, 2012). An ex-yakuza states:

> Recently there have also been frauds on senior citizens . . . in the past there was a pride, we could put the sign out and say we are yakuza, we are cool,

> this is our city, come to us if you need trouble. Now we can't put our sign out, we have to hide so our image is not as cool as before. (C4)

The prolonged economic downturn, which began at the same time as the introduction of increasingly restrictive regulations, had the effect of eliminating the grey area that had ensured the existence of the yakuza up until the 1990s. After being evicted from this in-between area, the yakuza have responded by infiltrating more deeply both the illegal market—through their constant presence in drugs, gambling, and prostitution—and legal markets, due to the employment of partners and increased invisibility. Official data from the White Papers on Crime confirm this long-term trend: the yakuza are no longer primarily enforcers of physical violence but increasingly discreet actors operating in fraud and drugs, with residual control over grey zones such as gambling and nightlife (MoJ, 2000–2024). The figures reflect both strategic adaptation and structural decline, aligned with broader legal, technological, and economic transformations in Japanese society.

Far from being eradicated through repression alone, the yakuza's diminishing presence reflects a broader reconfiguration of the institutional and economic spaces in which organised crime historically embedded itself. When they were able to exploit the institutional opacity of Japan's coordinated market economy, the yakuza occupied key niches in labour, construction, entertainment, and semi-legal markets by leveraging their quasi-legal status and provision of informal governance. These arrangements were made possible by the co-existence of formal legality and tolerated—but controlled—illegality. The post-bubble era, however, brought about a dual pressure: the repression of the yakuza as a criminal group, with the consequent loss of visibility and legitimacy, and the regulation of certain grey zones in which the yakuza were active. Even within a single sector, the pattern is visible: at Tsukiji and Toyosu, market re-regulation and relocation expelled the yakuza from a fixed, visible institution, while in the open sea off Sanriku, where the state cannot reach, poaching networks under yakuza influence continue to operate.

The result is a fragmented criminal landscape that will be further explored in the next chapter. While elite yakuza members try to preserve influence through legal front companies and complex partnerships, lower-ranking affiliates have been pushed into precarious, often petty forms of illegality—from fraud to online scams—that violate traditional codes of conduct and signal the erosion of the yakuza's internal rules. Digital technologies have accelerated this fragmentation: markets such as drug distribution and prostitution, once embedded in neighbourhoods and reliant on physical control, have increasingly migrated online, reducing the demand for coercive protection and rendering traditional forms of rent extraction obsolete. As market governance becomes more formalised and criminal economies shift from physical to digital terrains, more decentralised and digitally embedded actors gain ground—while the yakuza's hierarchical structure, tested by these transformations, is in many cases found wanting.

6
Post yakuza

Introduction

In recent years, headlines in Japanese newspapers have declared the yakuza's downfall and the rise of alternative groups in increasingly alarming terms: 'The upstart gangs filling the yakuza power vacuum' (Nippon, 12/12/2017); 'The decline of the yakuza and the secretive *hangure*' (Sankei News, 08/08/2023); 'The Chinese Dragons: feared even by the yakuza . . .' (FNN, 17/10/2022); 'Anticipating what comes after the yakuza's collapse: from syndicates to *tokuryū*' (SPN Journal, 09/09/2024). Alongside these proclamations, new criminal figures have periodically emerged in the media and police reports, each more elusive, disorganised, and threatening than its predecessor. In the 2010s, the focus was on the *hangure*, loosely organised and violence-prone gangs operating outside traditional hierarchies. Later, attention shifted to Chinese gangs and transnational fraud rings. Today, the spotlight is on *tokuryū*, an abbreviation of *tokumei ryūdōgata hanzai gurūpu*: anonymous, fluid criminal formations recruiting through encrypted apps and black-market job ads. This evolving media narrative raises a crucial question: is the decline of the yakuza—reflected in falling membership numbers, diminished territorial control, and financial constraints—leaving behind a vacuum that is now being filled by new forms of organised crime? And if so, what characterises these emergent actors, and how do they differ from the yakuza they supposedly replace?

This chapter will show that, contrary to popular portrayals, these emerging formations are not replacing the yakuza in any direct or functional sense. The yakuza's central role from its emergence has been governance, particularly within specific territories and economic sectors. By contrast, groups like the *hangure*, transnational scam rings, or *tokuryū* networks operate with entirely different aims and organisational logics. They are less interested in regulating markets or managing disputes than in extracting profit through predatory, often one-off, criminal acts, such as frauds, burglaries, or short-term schemes with low entry costs and minimal accountability. Rather

21st Century Yakuza. Martina Baradel, Oxford University Press. © Martina Baradel 2026.
DOI: 10.1093/9780191987755.003.0007

than competing, the yakuza and these groups often occupy parallel criminal economies that sometimes overlap. In fact, under increasing regulatory and public pressure, yakuza syndicates have found it strategically advantageous to outsource labour-intensive or high-risk operations to such loosely affiliated groups. This allows them to retain influence and income while distancing themselves from liability. As was shown in the case of domestic drugs markets, where yakuza members outsource dealing to non-yakuza actors (see Chapter 5), this tactic is not entirely new, but one that has become more pronounced as formal yakuza structures are hollowed out.

As Hill (2005) has observed, non-yakuza groups lack the informational and logistical infrastructures the yakuza once commanded, including connections with legitimate businesses and local institutions. This asymmetry does not necessarily lead to conflict; instead, it creates conditions for mutually beneficial collaboration, where each side compensates for the other's deficits. What defines current criminal operations is the role of technology. Social media, encrypted messaging apps, and online job platforms have enabled the formation of ephemeral, anonymised criminal networks that can plan and execute operations without ever physically meeting or sharing compromising information (Lavorgna, 2015; Moyle et al., 2019; Tung, 2021). This allows for the creation of 'action-sets', which Sullivan (2005: 175; see also Boissevain, 1971) defines as 'an aggregation of individuals cooperating together in a coordinated line of activity'. The activity does not continue over any quantified period of time, and the people involved do not need to recognise themselves as an association on a permanent basis. Some scholars have noted how the impact of technology has led to a 'hybridisation' of street offending (Roks et al., 2020), with the boundaries between physical and digital dimensions becoming increasingly blurred (Lane, 2019). Although the capacity for decentralised coordination presents new challenges for policing and regulatory control, many of these offences remain relatively rudimentary—a point underscored by Pyrooz et al. (2015)—and often retain a strong offline component, such as burglaries coordinated through digital platforms.

This chapter begins with a close look at the *hangure*, tracing their emergence, structure, and ambiguous ties to traditional syndicates. It then turns to *tokuryū* groups and the high-profile 'Luffy' case as a paradigm of fluid, tech-enabled coordination. A third section examines the recruitment and organisation of *yami-baito* (black-market jobs), with attention to labour fragmentation, technological mediation, and risk displacement. The following sections consider how the yakuza have responded to these shifts; through adaptation, strategic outsourcing, and symbolic distancing. Rather than a linear succession, from yakuza to *tokuryū*, these formations co-exist: governance-oriented, territorially embedded yakuza syndicates with organisational continuity, alongside ephemeral networks that fragment labour, mask risk, and extract profit through episodic schemes.

Emerging criminal phenomena

Hangure groups, *tokuryū* networks, and illicit part-time jobs schemes (known as *yami-baito*, literally 'dark part-time jobs') represent a broad spectrum of criminal formations. These groups engage in activities that range from limited governance-functions, to trade-based enterprises, such as drug trafficking, to more commonly predatory activities (i.e. illicit practices that generate profit through the extraction of value from unwilling victims through deception, coercion, or force) including fraud and organised robbery. These formations may also invest in physical businesses such as bars or brothels and can operate either independently or in connection with yakuza members.

Activity can determine the organisational structure of a group (Morselli et al., 2007). Trade-oriented criminal groups face low entry costs and prioritise short-term returns, leading to pressure for quick payouts and fast coordination. Governance-oriented groups, by contrast, rely on reputational capital and community control, which require higher investment and a longer-term outlook. Their network structures reflect these differences: transactional groups favour flexibility and speed, while governance groups build for stability and continuity (Breuer and Varese, 2023). *Hangure* groups mainly engage in trade-type activities, but in some cases, they embed themselves in the territory and perform governance-like functions. Compared to *tokuryū*, they tend to be more stable, with longer time horizons, more durable relationships between actors, and a degree of hierarchy. In contrast, *tokuryū* networks are action-sets more strongly rooted in online platforms. Although law enforcement often highlights their anonymity, the organisers frequently know each other offline, even if their collaboration is intermittent. Actual perpetrators are kept isolated from the broader organisational structure, assigned compartmentalised roles that prioritise secrecy, and can be discarded at any time.

Hangure

The term *hangure* comes from 'han' (half) and 'gureru' (become a delinquent), meaning half delinquent, but also harks back to 'grey', so someone who is not a common citizen nor a yakuza. It was coined by journalist Mizoguchi Atsushi in 2011. At first, they were described as groups of former motorcycle gang members who, with other acquaintances, acted together in loose networks. *Hangure* groups often include 'genuine defectors' (i.e. former criminals who failed to reintegrate into society) and 'strategic defectors' (i.e. yakuza affiliates who left the group in a calculated manner). The high proportion of former members who remain unemployed after leaving the yakuza (Hirosue, 15/03/2019) suggests that many maintain unofficial ties despite their formal exit.

A member of *hangure* described the organisation:

> It's really easy to get into *hangure* groups. In the Kantō region, they tend to be more organised; you've got groups like Kantō Rengō or Dragon with some structure. But in Kansai, it's different. There, they usually don't have a name or any clear organisation. People in Kansai also don't really use the word *hangure*, and they don't call themselves that either. The term has a negative tone, it kind of implies that they're not 'real' or 'serious' criminals. It's almost an insult. If anything, they might prefer being seen as *outlaws*, a bit rough around the edges but still professionals. The general image is that outlaws are like lone wolves or pros who operate without a big organisation, while *hangure* are seen more as small-time crooks, more chaotic and less respected. (C9)

Criminal groups are built on relationships formed in the neighbourhood, or at school, where relationships between senior (*senpai*) and younger (*kōhai*) acquaintances transition into criminal partnerships. However, these relationships are primarily profit-driven. Even in groups where profits are generated through intermediaries, a system of control remains in place, often based on local connections. As explained by a *hangure* member:

> Betraying one's *senpai*[1] is not an option, but this dynamic differs from the yakuza concept of *oyaji* [boss or paternal figure]; here, it is strictly a *senpai*

[1] While the terms *senpai* and *kōhai* are often associated with school settings, where they denote senior–junior relationships among students, they more broadly refer to hierarchical dynamics in a wide range of contexts, including workplaces, sports teams, and even organised crime groups.

> relationship. That said, control within these groups is weak, and a *senpai* is not usually particularly strict. Unlike the yakuza, where hierarchical structures such as *heyazumi* [mandatory residence in the group's headquarters] and assigned duties or shifts enforce discipline, criminal groups operate with a singular focus on financial gain. The 'boss' may claim that by working hard, one can earn as much as him, but this is misleading. Unlike in the yakuza, these relationships lack real cohesion, making it difficult to define *hangure* as an actual organisation. (C10)

Broadly, *hangure* groups are engaged in trade-type activities, as well as predatory activities such as fraud schemes and organised robberies. Compared to the yakuza, they offer looser structures, fewer formal rules, and greater flexibility, allowing members to pursue quick profits while avoiding the visibility that comes with hierarchical affiliation. As Breuer and Varese (2023) argue, the organisational form of a criminal group tends to follow the nature of its primary activity. Since *hangure* groups are primarily involved in trade-type crimes rather than territorial governance, a modular and flexible structure is more efficient from the standpoint of operation and risk management. Nonetheless, some *hangure* formations might prefer a degree of internal structure, as it offers coordination, protection, and a mechanism for managing trust (C10), and indeed some are organised in ways that closely resemble yakuza groups. For instance, the Kantō Rengō, formed in 1973 as a federation of bōsōzoku (motorcycle gangs) in the Karasuyama area of Setagaya Ward and Suginami Ward in Tokyo, were active for thirty years, having disbanded in 2003. However, key members continued operating under the name for several years. Although bōsōzoku were often seen as a stepping stone into the yakuza, few Kantō Rengō members actually joined syndicates and the group generally maintained independence from the yakuza world. Some local business owners even claimed that the Kantō Rengō was the only group in Roppongi that directly confronted the yakuza (Mizoguchi, 2011). Groups like 'Dragon', composed of second- and third-generation descendants of Chinese war orphans and Chinese nationals, can also be classified as structured *hangure* groups. Like the Kantō Rengō, some *hangure* groups maintain an internal organisation and clearly defined roles. Over time, this can enable them to embed themselves in the local social fabric and take on governance-like functions, including informal regulation and conflict resolution. In some cases, they form connections with local yakuza groups, to whom they pay a fee in exchange for permission to operate (Jiji, 04/10/2024). In practice, *hangure* groups are also used by yakuza to carry out specific tasks while the yakuza maintain distance from the action. As one *hangure* member described, yakuza groups in Tokyo would direct them to carry out 'missions' such as confronting specific individuals or intimidating targets on behalf of the group (C12). Beyond task outsourcing, the yakuza also retain enough territorial authority to extract fees from groups operating in their area—a residual governance function that persists even as their operational power declines. The yakuza name and reputation remain the basis of this authority. As several police officers noted, the yakuza are still in charge; when a group weakens, another may come in, but not with the same prevalence (P3–9).

Tokuryū

In order to describe what we mean by *tokuryū*, this section will analyse what was defined as a pioneering case, known as the 'Luffy incident'. Between 2022 and 2023, a series of robberies occurred across Japan, leaving one person dead and many injured. Over forty perpetrators were arrested, as well as four ringleaders, who were indicted. The criminal ring first emerged in 2017, when Watanabe Yuki, an individual connected to the yakuza who ran pubs and escort services in his hometown of Sapporo, established a fraud-based organisation in Thailand. The group's primary activity at this stage was special fraud, in which operatives impersonated officials or relatives to deceive victims in Japan and extract funds. Shortly thereafter, operations shifted to the Philippines, where Watanabe acquired greater control over logistics and recruitment. In the summer of 2018, Kojima Tomonobu joined the group. Recognised for his technical skills, he was tasked in early 2019 with managing recruitment. A four-person team was assembled for this purpose. Each member operated approximately five smartphones and managed around thirty Twitter (now X) accounts, which were used to advertise high-income overseas job opportunities. Interested individuals were asked to submit ID and a photograph of themselves and were interviewed via telephone. Those selected were registered on Excel spreadsheets and tracked systematically.

By this time, the organisation had significantly expanded. Watanabe purchased a defunct hotel in the Philippines for 1.2 billion yen, which was repurposed to house approximately sixty Japanese nationals acting as *kakeko* (fraud callers). From this location, large-scale fraud operations were conducted, with reported monthly proceeds exceeding 200 million yen. In November 2019, the hotel was raided by local authorities. Watanabe and

Kojima fled but were later detained in April 2021. To avoid deportation to Japan, they allegedly paid over 100 million yen in bribes to fabricate local criminal charges, thereby securing their detention within the Philippine system and avoiding repatriation. They were held in Bicutan Detention Center, where conditions allowed continued communication and coordination. Inmates reportedly paid staff approximately 50,000 yen per device to gain access to smartphones. Kojima and Watanabe lived in what was known internally as the 'VIP room', with air conditioning and access to outside food, while continuing to direct operations.

By early 2022, the group had shifted from fraud to robbery. Another detainee, Imamura Kiyoto, began using the alias 'Luffy' to coordinate robberies in Japan, while Fujita Seiya took on the name 'Kim' to serve as a secondary handler. Recruitment followed a similar model to that used during the fraud phase: social media posts advertised high-paying temporary jobs and applicants were screened remotely. Those selected were told they would participate in robbery assignments. Kojima again handled recruitment, using his smartphone from detention to post messages about 'high-paying opportunities'. Successful applicants were connected to Fujita, who relayed instructions. Between October and December 2022, multiple robberies were carried out across Japan, some of which involved extreme violence. The operation began to unravel in January 2023, following a robbery in Komae City, Tokyo, which resulted in the death of an elderly woman. Subsequent investigations led to the identification and eventual extradition of the four ringleaders from the Philippines to Japan (Yomiuri Shinbun, 17/07/2025).

Notably, the organisational structure was non-hierarchical and geographically dispersed. Unlike *hangure*, who maintain relatively stable networks with some degree of physical presence and recurring relationships among members, *tokuryū* formations typically consist of a small core of organisers, sometimes a single individual, surrounded by layers of disposable and anonymous participants who have no knowledge of each other or of the core. These formations reflect a post-organisational logic of crime, characterised by anonymity, offshore coordination, and a gig economy-style division of labour. Importantly, this form of criminality is not only more difficult to detect but also more socially corrosive as it draws in ordinary individuals, who are often young and in economically precarious circumstances, under the guise of legal or low-risk work. The use of amateurs creates the risk of sudden explosions of violence against victims, as in the case of Luffy (C9). Such incidents are rare in the case of the yakuza, where violence is an asset used with parsimony and directed mainly at other members rather than civilians (Breuer and Baradel, 2025).

These networks are coordinated by organisers who plan a variety of revenue-generating activities. As illustrated in Figure 6.1, the structure of *tokuryū* operations relies on online recruitment and decentralised coordination rather than fixed hierarchies. Organisers delegate tasks through middle-men or recruiters who use job advertisements and encrypted communication platforms to connect with potential perpetrators. Respondents (often unaware they are applying for criminal work) reply and are moved to encrypted platforms for further contact. There, the middle-men request identity documents and other personal details, creating an information asymmetry: the recruiter knows far more about the recruit than vice versa. That asymmetry becomes a source of control: middle-men can use the gathered information to coerce or threaten recruits into continuing illicit activity or to silence them if they consider speaking out. Once pressured or instructed, the recruited perpetrators carry out tasks, such as contacting victims, collecting payments, or transferring funds, while organisers and middle-men remain shielded higher in the network and reap the proceeds.

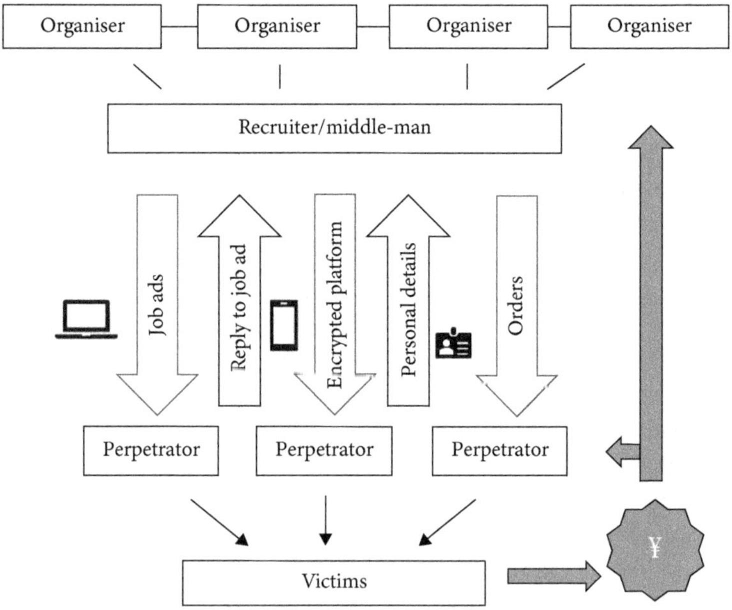

Figure. 6.1 Organisation of activities in *tokuryū* networks

Their activities cover a wide range of offences, including special fraud, organised robbery and theft, illicit recruitment for the sex industry, fraudulent home renovation services, and drug trafficking. Profits are often reinvested into new ventures, such as sex-related businesses, creating a financial loop that channels resources back to the group's core organisers. In some cases, yakuza members act as organisers themselves, while in others, they collaborate indirectly, serving as intermediaries between the yakuza and *tokuryū* networks (NPA, 2025). As one ex-yakuza explained, people outside the organisation are used to carry out operations—in a fraud group, participants do not know each other, and only the organiser knows the full picture (C21). In this way, yakuza participation in *tokuryū* operations is deliberately invisible: to law enforcement, to the other participants, and often to the yakuza organisation itself.

Yami-baito

Connected to these organisations is the use of online recruiting, known as *yami-baito*. This is a broader term describing illegal jobs (often criminal in nature) advertised online, especially to vulnerable youth (Hirosue, 2023). These schemes fragment criminal operations into small tasks, recruiting unconnected people online to perform a single action through computer- and mobile-mediated communication, while encrypted communication apps are used to securely manage the flow of information.

> They use Telegram to communicate because, unlike regular messaging apps, it's harder to trace, and people think you can't take screenshots. But that's only partially true. You can't screenshot on the same phone, but someone could still take a photo of the screen with another device, so it's not totally safe. That's why phone calls are still seen as the most secure way to talk. Usually, the boss doesn't talk to everyone directly. He gives instructions to one trusted person, and that person passes them along. (C9)

These schemes are structured to prioritise security for organisers by limiting personal interaction and relying on text-based communication. Such communication lacks social cues like tone of voice or physical presence, which are crucial for detecting risk and assessing trustworthiness (Riegelsberger, 2005; Cheshire, 2011). In interactions that happen via the web, an individual's online reputation is completely detached from their physical one and criminal actors use completely different strategies to signal their trustworthiness (Lusthaus, 2012; Evelyn and Wang, 2025). As a result, individuals recruited for these illegal part-time jobs often fail to recognise the criminal nature of the scheme as they have no direct contact with organisers and cannot verify who they are dealing with.

A fraud operation involves the following roles:

- Organisers
- Callers (*kakeko*): responsible for making fraudulent phone calls to victims following pre-written scripts to impersonate officials, lawyers, or relatives.
- Receivers/money mules (*ukeko*): physically collect cash, bank cards, or personal information from victims.
- Withdrawers (*dashiko*): withdraw money from ATMs using the victim's bank cards. Quickly transfer funds to other accounts or convert to cash. Can be the same person as *ukeko*.
- List providers (*meibōya*): Sell lists of potential victims, often the elderly, including phone numbers and personal data.
- Manual providers: people who provide fraud scripts.
- Infrastructure providers: sourcing phones, SIM cards, Wi-Fi routers, bank accounts, and office spaces.

Organisers can operate individually or in small groups. As shown in Figure 6.2, each function (calls, fraud manual, cash collection, scripts, data provision, and infrastructure) is handled by separate units, outsourced to individuals or groups with no direct knowledge of one another. In that way, organisers prioritise security. The division of labour is rigid: organisers procure contact lists, phones, fraud manuals, and office space from third parties. They then use online job ads to hire callers and money mules, who take part in the scheme either aware or unaware of its criminal nature, at least in the beginning. The callers contact victims using the manuals, money mules collect funds in person and take them to the organisers. Earnings are then distributed according to role and rank, with ringleaders collecting most of the revenue while lower-tier actors receive modest, one-off payments (C19, C21).

Beyond the classic roles of organisers, callers, and money mules, information providers constitute a crucial yet often overlooked component of fraud and robbery operations. Interviews suggest that multiple types of personal data are commodified and traded, with their value varying by specificity and risk. Information can include employment details, household composition,

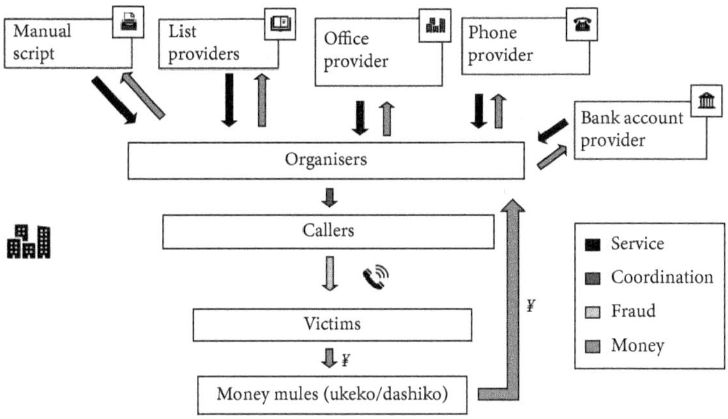

Figure. 6.2 Organisation of a fraud operation

or family networks, but particularly valuable (and expensive) is intelligence on individuals who keep large amounts of cash at home and are unlikely to report crimes, such as bar owners or tax evaders. Information providers serve as intermediaries who collect and sell data to underworld groups. Some specialise in researching cash-rich households; others are simple workers in services that are rich in information (day services, schools, workplaces) who want to make extra cash. One informant noted that younger individuals are increasingly involved in stealing data, attracted by the ease of access and high profits: 'Money is guarded, but PCs are not.' These stolen datasets are not only sold to fraud groups but also trafficked on the dark web, alongside drugs and cryptocurrency (C9).

Fraud groups operate through a deliberately fragmented structure in which participants are kept isolated from one another. However, the offline dimension should not be ignored, as noted by Lusthaus and Varese (2021) in their research on cybercrime in Romania, where cybercriminals operated from the same town and had strong connections with each other. In the case of Luffy, the organisers were all from Hokkaidō and had met in their youth while working in the Susukino entertainment district of Sapporo (Diamond Online, 22/04/2024). But those carrying out specific tasks might also get to know people working in the same space (e.g. call centres), and typically not know who else is involved at other stages of the organisation. This compartmentalisation is strategic: if a member is arrested, they are unable to disclose information about others, limiting exposure across the network. In cases where yakuza members are involved, they often conceal their participation from their own organisation. Engaging in special fraud can be grounds for expulsion from a designated yakuza group, prompting affiliated individuals to operate covertly and avoid drawing attention to their involvement (C19, C21). The yakuza may no longer carry out the scams themselves, but they manage them from above (P3–9).

Different schemes require different people to be recruited.

> For burglaries, you actually need some skills—like how to pick locks or disable alarms. Robberies are more straightforward. But for fraud, you've got to be clever and know how to manipulate people. (C10)

These dynamics reveal how fraud groups have adapted to contemporary conditions by outsourcing risk, fragmenting labour, and exploiting digital platforms to recruit disposable workers. The emergence of *yami-baito* has enabled a flexible and scalable criminal infrastructure that minimises traceability while maximising reach. In this system, even those connected to traditional organisations such as the yakuza often operate covertly, distancing themselves from both their groups and their collaborators.

Coexistence and delegation

In November 2024, at the entrance of the headquarters of the Tokyo-based Inagawa-kai's Himonya-ikka, a new notice was put up on the bulletin board, framed in acrylic next to the entrance.

> Recently, black-market jobs, frauds, and burglaries have been occurring frequently, but if people or groups that engage in such activities enter our territory (Shinagawa Ward, Ōta Ward, parts of Setagaya Ward, parts of Meguro Ward), our group will take care of them harshly. We strive to create a community where everyone can feel secure and at ease.

The economic power of a yakuza group correlates with the scale of the economy in their base area. Ensuring residents can live safely within their turf is ultimately beneficial for the yakuza too (Suzuki, 17/5/2025). While yakuza members have been found to have close connections with *hangure* or *tokuryū* networks involved in predatory crimes, yakuza groups denounce the 'less noble' criminal groups. This distancing serves both reputational and strategic purposes: by contrasting themselves with actors who exploit rather than regulate, they attempt to preserve a sense of legitimacy and maintain their embeddedness in local economies. In a context where formal oversight is intensifying and social tolerance waning, such symbolic boundary-setting is a tool for survival. The main syndicates have released internal communications in which they order members to avoid engaging in frauds. In May 2020, the headquarters of the Inagawa-kai released a notice that ordered members 'not to get involved in special frauds such as bank transfer frauds'. The Yamaguchi-gumi has strictly prohibited special frauds as well. A senior member of the group testified: 'Our group has been notified many times not to commit (special) frauds. But even if we're told not to do this or that, it doesn't mean we'll just say, Yes, we'll do that.' (Bunshun Online, 23/05/2020). While notices to newspapers served to publicly distance syndicates from special frauds, these directives were also disseminated internally. During visits to yakuza offices, I observed bulletins instructing members to monitor their subordinates and ensure they were not involved in fraud, indicating that these prohibitions were meant not only as symbolic gestures but also as operational guidelines within the organisation.

As shown in the previous chapter, the governance dimension of the yakuza remains central and, depending on the group's strength, rent extraction continues to be a profitable activity. Reputation is essential for mafias, and it rests not only on the ability to use violence or offer protection, but also on stability and the capacity to guarantee the group's long-term survival, even as illegal competitors emerge and vanish (Gambetta, 2009; Sberna and Vannucci, 2019). One night, a yakuza lieutenant took me to a small, dusty bar that stayed open late into the night. Before we left, the owner, an elderly woman who ran the place alone, tried to give him a small amount of money, like one would to a grandson. He laughed loudly and told her she did not need to pay him, but her small, wrinkled hand insisted, forcefully pressing the notes into his much larger one. She told me she had known him since he was a child: he had always been loud, but gentle, and as he grew older, he had looked after her. In the end, he persuaded her to keep the money, promising he would be back soon. These are the kinds of relationships that allow the yakuza to sustain their core business of protection. Social embeddedness and local connections are increasingly difficult to maintain but they remain among the most important assets of yakuza groups. When asked whether the yakuza were bound to disappear, one boss replied:

> I think the groups like us, the groups that are connected to the territory, will stay. (C2)

Yakuza groups have been cultivating stable relationships with lawful entrepreneurs that, in the pre-2010 framework, allowed them to invest heavily in the legal economy. Yakuza groups have developed a strong tendency to operate as almost-legitimate businesses, both in terms of the type of activities and the bureaucratic structure. Rooted in their communities, they have long been considered a legitimate alternative by lawful business partners.

Because of their success and resilience in the legal economy, yakuza groups face high costs when attempting to expand into new sectors, particularly in illegal or emerging markets. Their visibility makes them vulnerable to police detection and their rigid structure poses coordination challenges. Moreover, they often lack the technical expertise or flexibility needed to operate effectively in unfamiliar domains. In other words, the very features that made the yakuza effective as governance providers—visibility, bureaucratic structure, community embeddedness—become liabilities in markets that reward anonymity and flexibility. As a result, yakuza groups frequently rely on *hangure* and other unaffiliated actors as disposable intermediaries in the illegal underworld, allowing them to limit risk while maintaining influence at a distance, as confirmed by both the police (P18–19, C32, C33; see also NPA, 2025) and criminal actors (C8, C10, C11, C12).

While the core structure remains unchanged and the group internal connections are solid, yakuza members can have connections with other actors for single business ventures, that can be cut at any moment to avoid police detection (P18–19, see Figure 6.3). The porous boundary between the yakuza and *hangure* formations is further reinforced by the fact that most individuals who leave the yakuza are not reintegrated into the legal labour market. As a result, many continue to operate in the underworld, drawing on their

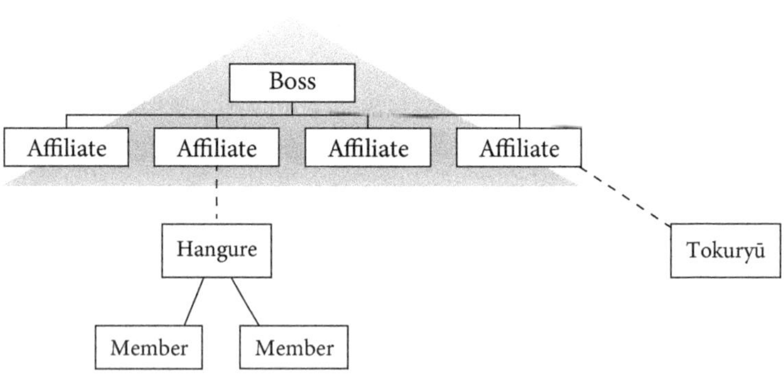

Figure. 6.3 Connection between yakuza, *hangure*, and *tokuryū* networks

existing networks and exploiting residual ties to maintain access to illicit opportunities. In some cases, especially with bōsōzoku-style youth gangs, members are allowed to operate freely, sometimes using the yakuza name informally. For these younger affiliates, membership fee can be as low as 5,000 yen per person, though it can rise to several tens of thousands depending on the group. Sometimes, multiple small groups pool their payments. In the past, fees hovered around 20,000 and 30,000 yen per head, but today there are cheaper 'plans' available. Often, it's a front company that covers the cost, with the company's representative linked to a yakuza syndicate. This setup makes it increasingly difficult to trace which group is really behind a given operation (P3–9). The cheapening of membership fees is analytically significant: it signals that the yakuza name retains enough value to be worth paying for, but that the organisation can no longer command the prices it once did.

Stationary bandits in retreat

The yakuza is not in direct competition with *hangure* groups and *tokuryū* networks: the latter engage in trade or predatory activities and do not have the capacity or ambition to take control of segments of the market. As an organisation, the yakuza, although weakened, focus primarily on governance functions, that is, managing disputes, regulating markets, and controlling territory, rather than purely predatory or transactional crimes. Their role persists because they act as competitors of the state, in the sense proposed by Tilly (1985): they provide forms of protection and regulation in spaces where state authority is weak, absent, or distrusted. Even in efficient states, there are 'pockets of low state presence, but ones that generally states can penetrate at will' (Lessing, 2021: 2). In the case of Japan, these are illegal or semi-legal markets where the state cannot intervene to regulate transactions and disputes. In contrast, most *hangure* groups and *tokuryū* networks operate opportunistically, engaging in fraud, robbery, and other short-term illicit activities without offering any sustained governance. In other words, following the classification proposed by Varese (2025; see also Breuer and Varese, 2023), the yakuza's core activity is governance, while *hangure* groups focus on trade. This distinction is not absolute. Some yakuza actors, in order to profit, may also engage in trade, often independently. Because the very structure of the yakuza dictates that a member is also an individual entrepreneur, this encourages solo business ventures (Baradel and Breuer, 2024). *Hangure* groups, when stable and socially embedded, might also provide governance services, as in the case of the Kantō Rengō or Chinese Dragons (Sankei News, 21/12/2014). As for *tokuryū*, they generally engage in predatory activities.

This distinction between the yakuza's governance orientation and the *hangure* and *tokuryū*'s opportunism can be further illuminated by drawing on the theory of 'stationary' versus 'nomadic' bandits. While Olson (1993) originally proposed this distinction to describe the emergence of states, later scholars have applied the framework to the study of criminal governance (see Lessing, 2021; Skarbek, 2011; 2024; Sanchez De La Sierra, 2020). According to Olson (1993), stationary bandits differ from roving ones because they remain in one area and therefore have a long-term interest in its prosperity. Rather than pillaging and moving on, they maximise returns by protecting producers, stimulating economic activity, and enforcing order. Having a stable monopoly on violence allows them to make credible commitments to extract taxes, becoming partial residual claimants of local economic output. In this way, they perform state-like functions such as war-making, protection, and revenue generation. Taxation of production, stationary bandits, and protection are thus closely related (Sanchez De La Sierra, 2020). The essential functions of a state are eliminating external rivals and oppressing internal opponents, repressing threats to the property of the governed, and designing the means to finance these activities (Tilly, 1985). Mafias, being on the same continuum as the state, have similar ambitions, although on a smaller scale (Varese, 2010). Stationary bandits increase revenue if they create more value added through the effect of their protection on investment than they destroy through the disincentives induced by their taxes (Sanchez De La Sierra, 2020). Therefore, stationary bandits that cannot provide enough protection—because the workforce is too old, too scarce, and too weak—will increasingly collect less taxes. Even less if the competing power (the state) gives taxpayers incentives to stop paying taxes to stationary bandits. Nomadic bandits, by contrast, have no incentive to invest in long-term relationships. They pillage, move on, and do not expect to return. Because their interaction with the population is non-repeated, they have no reason to provide security, enforce rules, or promote local growth. Their interest lies in immediate gains rather than ongoing governance.

In this sense, the yakuza resemble Olson's stationary bandits: they have settled in the same place for generations and have incentives to foster local economic growth, maintain order, and provide public goods such as protection and security in order to maximise long-term extraction. However, as territorial control erodes, this model is increasingly under strain. The collapse of traditional yakuza authority has not left an empty map: some groups still retain control over specific areas, while elsewhere a new map is emerging, reconfigured by digital networks, volatile connections, and online transactions. If the yakuza were defined by their embeddedness in local space, controlling districts, running offices, and policing nightlife, the new criminal formations that have emerged operate across radically different spatial registers. Fraud groups, robbery rings, and *hangure* networks are not grounded in place but in circulation. Their operations are often coordinated from offshore locations, such as detention centres in the Philippines (as in the Luffy case), and carried out by individuals recruited online who travel across prefectures to commit crimes in unfamiliar areas. The logic is deliberately deterritorialised: by avoiding familiar ground, they minimise detection by local police and bypass the informal rules or retaliation mechanisms enforced by traditional groups. In other words, there are no turf wars because there is no turf.

The distinction is not only between rooted and mobile, but also between public and invisible, as argued in the previous chapter. The yakuza's presence, once visible in the nameplates on their offices, participation in local festivals, and policing of nightlife areas, served both a symbolic and regulatory function. Their control over space was functional as well as performative: it signalled authority, deterred rivals, and cultivated legitimacy. In contrast, the emerging criminal groups are structurally invisible. They do not mark territory nor do they aim to control it. Their operations are designed to be short-lived, partly online, and difficult to trace.

Yet, spatial relationships still matter. While criminal actors may be nomadic in operation, their recruitment and cohesion remain partially rooted in local networks; former school ties, *senpai–kōhai* relationships, or shared neighbourhood affiliations. In this sense, criminal economies are not entirely placeless; rather, they mobilise pre-existing social geographies to populate temporary criminal projects. Technology plays a key role in enabling the shift from territorial control to transitory, compartmentalised operations. Messaging apps like Telegram and platforms like X (formerly Twitter) allow recruiters to span prefectural and national boundaries, while cryptocurrencies and offshore exchanges decouple financial flows from geography. These technologies facilitate a form of criminality that moves not through contested zones of influence, but through transitory vectors, courier routes, anonymous bank accounts, and digital wallets. Unlike yakuza syndicates, which built legitimacy through visible and repeated contact with communities, these emerging networks thrive on invisibility and disposability.

Emerging criminal groups in Japan are shaped by fragmentation, anonymity, and modularity. Their organisational model is leaner and more flexible than the yakuza's, built not on loyalty or cohesion but on expediency and compartmentalisation. Organisers rarely have direct contact with the individuals who carry out operations, instead delegating communication to a trusted intermediary, who instructs other members via encrypted apps—a chain that limits exposure even if one participant is arrested. Labour is fragmented into modular tasks, with each actor performing a single action: delivering a package, opening a bank account, transporting cash, recruiting others. Recruited online, most participants carry out one or two tasks before being cut off, mirroring gig economy dynamics in which anonymity and disposability are structural features, not bugs, minimising organisers' liability and negating the need for enforcement mechanisms or loyalty structures.

While effective in the short term, this model of organisation does not build reputations, cultivate networks, or establish governance. Instead, it borrows tools of efficiency from legitimate labour markets and applies them to illicit ends. The result is a criminal formation that is fluid, ad hoc, and precisely the opposite of the model once embodied by the yakuza. This distinction between stationary and nomadic not only describes the current criminal landscape but explains why the yakuza's decline does not produce a functional replacement: nomadic actors have no incentive to govern, and governance cannot be improvised.

The erosion of stability

The progressive weakening of the yakuza does not affect only the organisations themselves. It has an impact across the social, economic, and criminal fabric of contemporary Japan. As anti-yakuza legislation tightens and public tolerance wanes, members find it increasingly difficult to operate openly, secure income, or exit the underworld. Recruiting and officially affiliating new members has become increasingly difficult for the yakuza. One boss complained:

> We have young guys coming in, but I can't just make them members, this is not the right time because the police would get angry. It's important to know how to use them and move them. Also, the way I educate them is different: before there was like a dorm and new people woke up early, cleaned,

> and so on, but not now. They used to stay here and if there was some trouble in a bar they would go and settle it, throw out the troublemaker. But now we can't do it anymore. Now the police say they'll do it, but they don't. (C2)

Although this boss has a relatively high number of young men in his orbit, he waits several years before officially affiliating them into the group. Formal affiliation is no longer automatic after a few months (see Stark, 1981), nor is it desirable. The risks outweigh the benefits: youths who are not experienced enough may attract police scrutiny and the group's ability to offer them a stable role has diminished. The yakuza has traditionally had a role in employing marginalised young men. An ex-yakuza in his early thirties, for example, described how he joined the syndicate after ageing out of a bōsōzoku gang: 'the yakuza were the only ones who offered to take care of me' (C24). Personal networks have historically played a crucial role in yakuza recruitment. Many men entered the organisation not through formal channels, but by following the path of a trusted *senpai*—an older peer or mentor figure. These relationships created a snowball effect: once a young man joined, others from his social circle often followed. Loyalty and the promise of belonging were central to these early bonds. As several members recalled, they joined simply because their friend was already in the group and encouraged them to come along. In such cases, recruitment was not the result of active scouting or strategic calculation, but of proximity and familiarity within pre-existing youth networks.

This mode of organic recruitment was particularly effective when the yakuza had strong ties to local bōsōzoku gangs, construction crews, and nightlife venues, spaces where hierarchy, masculine identity, and peer loyalty were already embedded. But as legal pressure has increased and yakuza presence in these environments has diminished, these informal pipelines have begun to dry up. The weakening of social ties, combined with the risk of surveillance and arrest, has made it increasingly difficult to sustain the relational infrastructure that once ensured a steady stream of recruits. The ageing of the yakuza population is now a central concern for the police and the syndicates alike. As data from the National Police Agency (NPA) show, members in their twenties and thirties are steadily decreasing, while older members continue to make up a growing proportion of the organisation (NPA, 2020–2025).

Police officers note that the ageing of yakuza membership has made recruiting younger members increasingly difficult, while *hangure* groups, with their lower barriers to entry and immediate financial rewards, have a distinct advantage in attracting youth. The financial structure of the affiliation has also changed: the traditional monthly payment have largely disappeared, replaced by modest membership fee. Further, those who cannot afford to pay can operate independently. Yet, the *kanban*—the yakuza name and reputation—retains symbolic and organisational weight that *hangure* cannot replicate. Occasionally, when one syndicate begins to weaken, another steps in. But *hangure* and other loosely affiliated groups have not fully replaced the yakuza at the top of the criminal hierarchy (P3–9).

It is difficult to join the yakuza, but it is also difficult to stay and to leave. Active yakuza members and members that have left the organisation for less than five years (who are still considered to have a connection to the yakuza) have difficulties finding legitimate jobs and are forced instead into temporary or part-time employment. For instance, a yakuza member who had not formally left the organisation reported that he had started working at a friend's construction company, but when his name came out in an unrelated investigation and the police searched the company where he was employed, he was let go. Unable to find another occupation, he was forced to accept a temporary job with a daily pay of 5,000 yen (35 GBP) (Livedoor News, 25/01/2019). Declaring one's current or former membership of the yakuza automatically rules out the chances of being hired, but hiding it may lead to an accusation of fraud, as happened to one yakuza member who was accused of fraud and arrested for not disclosing his membership when applying for a part-time job at the Post Office (Okita, 05/02/2019). Wider socio-economic issues also impact upon the yakuza as cases of yakuza members getting caught committing petty crimes are becoming increasingly common. The phenomenon of the 'poor' yakuza is indeed becoming increasingly widespread and leading to a wide range of minor crimes (*NHK*, 28/05/2018). For instance, in the region of Hokkaido, there have been repeated instances of yakuza trespassing on salmon hatcheries in order to steal salmon, while in Tokyo there have been cases of yakuza members pawning their firearms (ibid.). In June 2017, a yakuza member of a group affiliated to the Kobe Yamaguchi-gumi was prosecuted for stealing rice and daily necessities in a supermarket at the request of his *kumichō* (*Asahi Shinbun Digital*, 23/05/2017). Yakuza members are also reported to be taking on part-time jobs to compensate for the loss in earnings. They can usually find employment in industries that are connected with the yakuza, such as bars, restaurants, markets, and the construction industry (Suzuki and Mizoguchi, 2019).

In research conducted between 1967 and 1973, one-third of the 433 yakuza who left the organisation were able to find employment and be socially reintegrated (Hoshino, 1974) while, of the 4,170 members who left between

2010 and 2017, only 108 (2.6 per cent) are currently employed (Hirosue, 15/03/2019). The several cases that see ex-yakuza members involved in a *hangure* group, or the persistence of members of Kantō Rengō in using their group's name for a decade following the official disbandment of the group indicate that the majority of the yakuza are still operating in the criminal underworld, both in an unofficial capacity for the same group or with less structured groups. The harsh anti-yakuza regulations that continue to be applied to yakuza members even after leaving the organisation severely undermine their reintegration into society. As (ex-)members often lack the expertise to engage in more sophisticated crimes, they cannot leave the syndicates and are thus forced to commit petty crimes to meet their basic needs.

Therefore, new recruits are scarce and long-term members are forced to leave. Once the yakuza can no longer perform their traditional role, because they are too weak, too old, or too persecuted, internal dynamics collapse. Weakened yakuza groups cannot shield their actors and their customers from violence or extortion at the hand of other criminal actors. As customers do not want to pay taxes to a group that cannot enforce their rule, revenues decline. Overall, disorder grows in the criminal ecosystem as no one has the authority to control markets, to mediate, or regulate transactions. The actors that find space to emerge are usually predatory and unable or unwilling to build stable economies, they simply extract what they can and move on quickly. Thus, the collapse of the stationary bandit is not just a problem for the organisation, but for the governance ecosystem: the economic rationale for their existence disappears, and no other actor has the same incentive to govern the underworld.

Conclusion

Shinobu Tsukasa, leader of the Yamaguchi-gumi, in an exclusive interview with the mainstream national newspaper, *Sankei West* (2015), stated:

> If the Yamaguchi-gumi dissolved now, public order would deteriorate greatly.... Young people will run astray on the streets, and in the end, they will join another yakuza group, or they will become a gang of their own. So, it makes no sense to dissolve our group. It is not a nice thing to say, but when the wind blows dust and dirt away, and it all gathers in the corner, similarly in this world there are people who are outcasts: people who are left behind, people who do not adapt into society, there are also these kinds

> of people in this world. Our organisation is the place upon which those people can rely. But if they are not under our control, they will have no rules and no boundaries, nobody will punish them, and they will do as they please. And that is anything that provides an income. Hideous crimes such as theft and robbery will increase.

This is a common narrative used by the yakuza, claiming that, while unlawful, they impose internal regulation and provide social containment for otherwise unruly elements of the underworld. If the yakuza is a regulatory force, channelling deviance into a bounded system of rules and punishments, its depletion will cause the emergence of new forms of crime, which is what seems to be happening. In other words, the state weakened a governance-oriented organisation, but inadvertently created space for actors with no interest in regulation and no territorial commitment producing a criminal ecosystem characterised by volatility and predation.

This paradox reflects a broader transformation in the structure and meaning of organised crime in Japan. As regulatory pressures intensify and public tolerance diminishes, the ideal yakuza figure is no longer the stoic enforcer or the flamboyant outlaw, but someone able to navigate legal grey zones, maintain low visibility, and broker informal deals without attracting attention.

The recruitment strategies of new criminal groups seem to mirror the broader precarisation of labour in contemporary Japan. As companies reduce the number of full-time employees and outsource non-regular workers to overcome difficult economic junctures, the yakuza keeps a core of members, and, when needed, relies on non-officially affiliated external actors. Where the yakuza once relied on symbolic authority, ritual, and community ties to attract members, non-yakuza networks target individuals with no long-term aspirations, offering quick financial rewards in exchange for low-commitment participation. There are no rituals, no ideology, and no awareness of the larger scheme, just single transactions orchestrated by actors that sporadically cooperate. Orchestrators of the schemes often know each other personally, while recruitment of other actors occurs online. Recruited members can work together for a single mission, as in the case of organised burglaries, however tasks that require some training, such as more complex frauds, require cooperation and members can meet in person or work from the same office. Fraud groups and robbery rings post ads on media platforms, advertising 'high-income jobs' with minimal effort and no prior experience required. These recruitment practices are characterised by a profound information asymmetry between organisers and applicants. Individuals are typically asked to submit identification documents and photographs of themselves, often under the pretence of a background check, and are given only essential details about the tasks. This deliberate withholding of information minimises the risk for organisers while maximising control over participants.

The motivation is almost exclusively economic. One investigator described it as a 'disposable workforce of the desperate': people who enter not out of loyalty or belief but because they have run out of options. Unlike yakuza affiliation, which historically carried obligations, rituals, and the promise of belonging, participation here is a single transaction, and often not recognised as criminal at all.

The strategic outsourcing of labour-intensive or high-risk tasks to loosely affiliated actors allows yakuza groups to reduce exposure while retaining partial control over revenue streams. However, this shift comes at a cost: criminal organisations face a problem of internal governance. They set rules to ensure coordination and cooperation among members, to settle dispute and manage violence, and to maintain secrecy (Catino, 2019). However, rules do not apply to external, temporary collaborators who have no long-term stake in the organisation's reputation or survival. While yakuza members undergo rituals, accept long-term affiliation, and dense networks of reciprocal obligation, outsourced actors are transactional rather than embedded, often anonymous, and replaceable. This makes them harder to monitor and incentivises short-term gains over long-term alignment. Yet yakuza groups appear willing to accept these risks. The outsourcing model, while fragile, allows them to exploit cheap, expendable labour without the burdens of governance and, if information is managed in the right way, without risks from law enforcement. It offloads the monitoring problem onto new intermediaries, such as digital platforms, recruiters, or even informal hierarchies within black-market networks. But the result is a general system in which discipline is limited to yakuza groups, violence is more erratic, and overall organisational coherence is gradually eroded. In effect, what is gained in flexibility is lost in control. In this environment, classical *mafioso*-style monitoring becomes increasingly difficult.

Importantly, the official decline in registered yakuza membership may also mask a shift in behaviour. Many yakuza members now believe that their unregistered status gives them greater latitude to engage in predatory crime without immediate detection (C10). The boundary between formal membership and external criminality is increasingly porous, further complicating the analysis of decline and replacement.

A post-yakuza order

When a mafia dies

This book began with a question: What happens when a mafia begins to die? Over the previous chapters, I have shown that the answer is far from straightforward. The yakuza's decline was not an abrupt dismantling, nor did it resemble the dramatic collapses often associated with criminal organisations undone by state repression or internecine war. Rather, what has unfolded in Japan over the last three decades is a slow and complex process of transformation, in which a historically tolerated and deeply embedded mafia-type group became the target of legal, economic, and symbolic exclusion. But while their visibility diminished and their market share contracted, the yakuza did not vanish. Instead, they underwent a strategic retreat that reconfigured their presence, function, and authority within the underworld and the upperworld. In this chapter, I will bring together the book's core findings and reflect on their broader implications, tracing the transformation of the yakuza from a quasi-legitimate organisation to a semi-invisible structure. I also consider how the Japanese case sheds light on the evolution of organised crime under conditions of legal and market saturation. Finally, I outline potential trajectories for the post-yakuza underworld.

Japan presents a paradox. Unlike Italy or the United States, where the fight against organised crime has often centred on high-profile prosecutions and leadership-targetting strategies, Japan's approach has been one of quiet administrative suffocation. Through a layered system of laws, regulations, and prefectural ordinances, the Japanese state has constrained the capacity of yakuza groups to hold offices, access financial services, rent property, and operate openly, as shown in Chapter 4. These measures have been effective: group membership has plummeted from around 90,000 in the early 1990s to under 18,800 by 2025 (NPA, 2025); their visibility has diminished, and their capacity to govern informal markets has contracted accordingly. But beneath the surface of these numbers lies a more complex process in which criminal actors

21st Century Yakuza. Martina Baradel, Oxford University Press. © Martina Baradel 2026.
DOI: 10.1093/9780191987755.003.0008

adapt, reconfigure, and persist in altered forms. This quiet repression strategy, while effective in dismantling yakuza infrastructure, has also contributed to the creation of a vacuum in underworld governance, and the subsequent reconfiguration of the power dynamics that sustain criminal order.

The yakuza are no longer what they once were: they no longer dominate entertainment districts, run protection rackets in the open, or sponsor *matsuri* and local welfare schemes (Baradel and Bortolussi, 2021). At the same time, they have not vanished. Instead, they have retreated into a corner of the underworld, still striving to control certain markets and transactions and refusing to shift entirely to trade-type or predatory activities. I have argued that this transformation is best understood through three interlinked arguments. First, regulatory saturation can dismantle criminal organisations: formal affiliation to a yakuza group has become increasingly economically and socially untenable, as shown in Chapter 4, but this comes at the cost of reconfiguring underworld power dynamics. Second, mafias can survive institutional decline by retaining certain governance functions even as their operational structures shrink. Third, the demise of a mafia does not automatically produce a successor. The erosion of yakuza governance has not prompted a contest for control, but a shift to fragmented criminal markets.

This book is not only about how a mafia ends, but about what it leaves behind. As a member who served as a celebrant of yakuza rituals explained, 'For us, everything is based on *ninkyō*' (C13). This ideological core has been central to the yakuza's organisational model. Internally, this common belief reduced the costs of criminal cooperation by solving problems of trust and loyalty, and externally, it granted the yakuza a reputation not as common criminals, but as actors who operated according to recognisable Japanese values of honour and obligation. As Gambetta observes, 'If mafia maintains the reputation of a dangerous entity, to be able to claim "We are the true mafia" carries a powerful, effective economic value' (2009: 214). The yakuza's symbolic trademarks functioned as valuable economic assets precisely because they were believed by both members and society. Yet this reputational capital is eroding. While *ninkyō* continues to hold the remaining yakuza together, externally their trademarks carry weight only in specific circles. The criminal field is now populated by actors who are opportunistic rather than embedded, transactional rather than ideological, as shown in Chapter 6. In contrast to the yakuza's enduring symbols and ritual coherence, these new actors eschew permanence and public identity. This is also a book about the role of the state and repression in reshaping the underworld. Japan's case offers a distinctive vantage point from which to rethink theories of mafia persistence and decline. The book identifies broader patterns in how mafias govern illegal markets, maintain authority, and adapt—or fail to adapt—to regulatory change. Theoretically, the book shows how criminal authority can endure through decline, migrating from visible offices and rituals to symbolic capital, residual loyalties, and the gaps left by the state. The yakuza may no longer hold the monopoly they once claimed, but the systems they shaped—and the voids they have left—continue to define the contours of Japan's underworld. Their transformation is a lens through which to reconsider the future of criminal governance itself.

Regulatory saturation

One of the central arguments of this book is that the decline of the yakuza was not primarily caused by internal collapse, but by the convergence of two forces: the escalating legal and social costs of affiliation, which made membership increasingly untenable for both existing members and potential recruits; and the re-regulation of the markets in which they operated, which dismantled the structural conditions sustaining their governance functions.

As shown in Chapter 4, the legal environment was reshaped to discourage yakuza affiliation. The shift was not abrupt: throughout the postwar period, state responses moved from negotiated containment to administrative exclusion. The 1991 Bōtaihō was a turning point, but it was the 2010–2011 Yakuza Exclusion Ordinances (YEO) that profoundly altered the everyday conditions of membership. These prefectural measures prohibited any social or economic transaction with known affiliates. Through third-party liability, landlords can now be fined for renting to yakuza, banks refuse access to basic financial services, mobile contracts are denied, and legal business owners are pressured to stop serving known members. Affiliation no longer provides a source of recognition or protection, but rather triggers exclusion from welfare, employment, insurance, housing, and banking. These changes also affected the internal functioning of the groups. While some groups continue to attract young people, formal affiliation is now postponed for years to avoid drawing police scrutiny. As a result, recruits are often mobilised without being officially affiliated since the legal and social costs of membership have become too high. Incarceration, once a manageable cost distributed across the group, has become economically unsustainable. Once a source of authority and legitimacy, visibility—embodied in norms, rituals, and offices—underpinned the yakuza's credibility and deterrent capacity.

As repression intensified, this visibility was curtailed: names were removed from doorplates, rituals like the *sakazuki* were concealed, and practices such as in-house training were abandoned. This loss was not merely symbolic; it impaired recruitment, eroded reputational capital, and undermined the groups' ability to stabilise illicit markets. With fewer members, declining revenues, and diminishing ability to support imprisoned affiliates, many groups faced a contraction in both their workforce and operational capacity.

At the same time, as detailed in Chapter 5, these legal constraints were compounded by a reorganisation of the markets in which the yakuza had historically operated. The introduction of tighter regulatory controls in sectors such as labour dispatching, wholesale markets such as the fish trade, and nightlife entertainment reduced the structural demand for alternative dispute resolution, a traditional role of the yakuza. Police scrutiny of entertainment districts made it difficult for yakuza groups to manage clubs, settle disputes, or collect fees. Labour markets, especially those involving precarious workers, were re-regulated with the introduction of competition that effectively pushed the yakuza out or forced them to operate informally, without the ability to stabilise transactions or claim authority. In the fish wholesale market, the relocation of Tsukiji to Toyosu and the introduction of strict licensing requirements replaced the informal environment in which yakuza brokers had operated for over a century.

The legal exclusion and market re-regulation did not just reduce yakuza membership. They undermined the infrastructural base that had made yakuza governance possible. The erosion of public recognition, the dismantling of brokerage positions, and the increasing invisibility of the yakuza all contributed to a transformation that left the groups operationally diminished and symbolically residual.

Surviving through residual authority

The second argument of this book is that yakuza groups have continued to exercise forms of authority despite institutional decline, drawing on accrued reputation. As shown in Chapters 2 and 3, symbolic and reputational mechanisms still support the organisation internally and uphold its image externally. The group has undergone significant structural downsizing: in some cases, members operate semi-officially or under a different guise, while the group's name retains currency in certain circuits of the underworld. As shown in Chapter 6, unaffiliated actors sometimes invoke the yakuza label to secure respect or intimidate others, even without formal ties. This suggests that reputation continues to shape perceptions of power, even without institutional visibility.

The governing capacity of the yakuza has diminished, particularly in nightlife regulation, debt collection, and dispute resolution. Nonetheless, some relational structures remain intact: hierarchical ties, obligations of loyalty, and the strategic invocation of group identity. Here, rituals, ideology, and normative discourse gain renewed importance. As Chapter 3 demonstrates, ceremonies such as the *sakazukigoto*, the observance of hierarchical codes, and the use of *ninkyō* rhetoric have traditionally helped preserve internal cohesion—and do so even more now that revenues have declined. These elements do not restore lost power but they do help to sustain the group under restrictive conditions. For some members, participation remains meaningful even without financial benefit. While predatory actors such as hangure and tokuryū have entered the criminal landscape, they offer little in the way of stability, order, or recognisable norms. By contrast, even in decline, the yakuza provide a sense of proper role and identity, grounded in shared codes of honour, obligation, and historical continuity, not only to members, but even to the communities they inhabit. Their legitimacy now rests less on enforcement and more on recognition. Their ability to function as a governance-type mafia depended on public visibility which made them appear trustworthy. Embedded in local economies, connected to political actors, and active in managing both legal and illegal markets, they cultivated a legitimacy that set them apart from other criminal actors.

That visibility, however, came at a cost. It made them vulnerable to shifting state priorities and exposed them to public scrutiny. As regulation intensified—with the YEO, financial restrictions, and criminal liability for associations—the very visibility that once ensured their survival became a liability. In response, yakuza groups began to withdraw from the public sphere. This retreat was neither uniform nor immediate, but what emerged in place of overt presence was a condition of strategic invisibility. Yakuza groups became more selective and insulated, and rather than maintaining broad hierarchies, they are now moving towards the preservation of a tight executive core, while operational tasks are outsourced to unaffiliated or loosely connected actors. This reorganisation begins to resemble the structure of the *vory v zakone*, where only a small elite of recognised figures are formally affiliated (Varese, 2001). The result is not the death of the yakuza but their reconstitution: no longer public institutions of semi-legitimate order, but nodes of residual authority operating in a more fragmented and unstable criminal ecosystem.

Recruitment

When I was working in the Japanese countryside between 2013 and 2015, I would often go to a decrepit karaoke bar that did not close until the very last customer had stumbled out—sometimes not until morning. Strewn with remnants of the Shōwa era, the place felt suspended in the 1980s: dark floral wallpaper, red velvet sofas covered in cigarette burns, yellowing posters of the Twin Towers, and ageing TV monitors scrolling song lyrics in bold font and fuzzy resolution. One night, I ended up at a table with some guys who looked like thugs and a couple of young women who had just finished their shift at a hostess bar. At one point, S., who was sitting with us, was accidentally bumped by one of the men from the other group on his way to the bathroom. S. responded by glaring at them with growing intensity. The rest of us kept chatting and singing, and just as my song finally came up, and I launched into another embarrassingly off-key performance, a fight broke out between the two tables. K., seated beside me, began yelling at them, shielding his face with his hand in a way that prominently displayed his bent little finger, as if to show it was missing. The groups eventually came to blows, until the bar owner and other customers intervened and forced everyone outside. But the fight continued in the parking lot and only stopped when S. threatened to call the local yakuza boss. It was then that I realised K.'s gesture was meant to show *yubitsume*, and that he was trying to signal a yakuza affiliation. The next day, a bar-owner friend told me she had banned both S. and K. from her place because of their rude behaviour. As for S., who had claimed to be the manager of a hostess bar, the actual manager (who was indeed affiliated to the local group) later told me that S. was just a driver, the group would never have let someone like him manage a club. When I asked other bar owners whether S. and K. really had ties to the local group, the most common reaction was laughter. A respectable group, they said, would never hire hotheaded, good-for-nothings like them. I ran into them again for drinks a couple of times, our nights sometimes ending early when they had to leave to join some friends in a fight. Both had tried working at the local power plant, only to be fired. Both were socially marginalised, cantankerous young men who had been pushed to the fringes: too aggressive to hold down a job and too undisciplined to rise through the ranks of the yakuza.

Encounters like these reflect a broader reality: the young men who in the past would have been ideal recruits—unfit for the formal labour market because too violent, impulsive, unschooled, and in need of belonging—are not wanted anymore, as the group cannot absorb the risk they present. As one member put it bluntly: 'Nowadays, you cannot be a yakuza if you are diligent, but also if you are not' (C10). At the same time, with the yakuza's loss of public authority, market control, and financial security, the organisation no longer attracts the calibre of candidates it once did. With dwindling power, visibility, and revenues, the yakuza can no longer afford to take risks with unreliable members. Candidates are now subjected to much closer internal scrutiny: those who are too aggressive, unpredictable, or conspicuous are turned away as their behaviour could attract unwanted police attention or damage the group's fragile standing. But from the outside, the yakuza have also lost their appeal. For potential recruits, the benefits no longer outweigh the risks. Why pledge loyalty to a declining syndicate and assume the stigma and legal liability of affiliation, when operating independently offers more flexibility, less surveillance, and often similar financial rewards? In this sense, the yakuza are caught in a double bind: the shrinking pool of eligible candidates is matched by a declining interest in joining at all.

In this context, ideology becomes more important than ever, not only as a source of legitimacy, but as an internal support structure. The group's mythology, rituals, and moral language offer members a sense of identity and purpose, even as material incentives erode. While the organisation still needs to make money, it increasingly survives on belief. As was shown throughout this book, the power of the yakuza has significantly declined in the past fifteen years. As one boss stated:

> We have to go back to the starting point, the *bushidō* spirit, the yakuza spirit (*yakuza no seishin*): from there you can't make any mistake. It's not about making money easily, that was in the 1980s. (C2)

There have been periods in time when the main driver to join the yakuza was money. But, as shown in Chapter 3, it is important to consider that the yakuza is ideologically driven, for reasons that go beyond internal coherence and group reputation. In 2023, I met a yakuza who had joined the group in his late thirties, with a family, who had closed his construction company to become a member of the local group. When I asked why, he said: 'Because I don't want to lower my head in front of anyone. When I had my company, customers would not pay me, they would disrespect me. But now I can keep my head high' (C18). His boss later confirmed that they have people in their thirties, forties, and even fifties who join their group. Cases like his underscore that in circumscribed spaces, for instance a neighbourhood where a group is still powerful, the yakuza's moral language can still have an appeal based on honour and a code of conduct that stands apart from mainstream society. As another senior member explained:

> In the past, you became a yakuza to make a lot of money, now you become a yakuza and make no money. But people who join the yakuza now do it because they believe in *ninkyō*, they have this old way of thinking about how to protect this area, they believe in *bushidō*. People who think becoming a yakuza means to drive a nice car and live the good life quit, people who believe in the *ninkyō* spirit remain, so that's good because there were many opportunistic yakuza... Nothing is forever... we have to adapt to the times: now we have to be frugal, once we could be gaudy. But the foundation of the yakuza does not need to change.... (C2)

While other groups have taken over segments of the illegal economy, none have adopted or replicated the ideological framework that once distinguished the yakuza. Their ability to enforce order, to frame illegality within a coherent value system, and to give members a sense of role and identity has not been matched. The reputation of the yakuza—fragile as it may now be—has not been completely eroded. And this is one of the last things that the yakuza can offer to its members. In this sense, ideology is not just a remnant, it is part of the residual governance that still legitimises the yakuza, even as their economic and organisational foundations erode.

Overall, these dynamics underscore the importance of reintegration policies, as the failure to reintegrate former members feeds directly into the fragmented criminal ecosystem described above. As noted in Chapter 4, only a fraction of people who officially leave the yakuza successfully enter legitimate employment. The great majority are only formally defectors who remain in the underworld, either working unofficially for the same groups or drifting towards loosely connected formations such as hangure. If the state wishes to eradicate organised crime, it must address this gap, as suppression alone is insufficient. Serious efforts to facilitate reintegration could start from simply not applying all the restrictions imposed by the YEO to former yakuza members for five years after they leave a group, as is currently the case. Even if a person exits the yakuza, the fact that they cannot have a phone or a bank account makes it nearly impossible to find a job. A former yakuza recounted this problem: because he couldn't find work, he opened his own shop. But not having a bank account, not being able to take out insurance for his shop, and being unable to register a phone in his name proved to be enormous burdens (C5). Furthermore, the state should offer viable employment alternatives, including state-sponsored options, as private companies are often reluctant to hire ex-convicts who remain heavily stigmatised, even when seeking to undertake socially valuable work such as nursing or care for the elderly (C14; C22). Otherwise, former members remain vulnerable to recidivism and the symbolic legitimacy of the yakuza, as an institution that still provides meaning, identity, and protection to those in the criminal underworld, persists.

New actors

The third argument of this book is that the exclusion and repression of the yakuza has contributed to the rise of fragmented, fluid, and less accountable forms of criminal activity. As Chapter 6 shows, these new actors do not offer informal regulation and rarely operate within clear norms or reputational hierarchies. While yakuza groups once acted as stabilisers in certain markets, their successors are more similar to action-sets rather than gangs. Fraud groups, hangure, and other unaffiliated actors operate through changing, loosely connected networks that resist identification and enforcement. Some invoke the symbolic legacy of the yakuza to intimidate or lend themselves credibility, but they do not replicate its internal organisation or normative discourse. Not only have yakuza groups mostly lost their capacity to govern, no other actor has stepped in to replace them. This absence has implications not just for public safety, but for how the state interacts with the underworld in the absence of a recognisable interlocutor.

The loss of yakuza authority has not resulted in greater security, rather, it has produced an environment in which new forms of criminality can emerge. The fragmentation of yakuza power has given rise to a constellation of actors who lack the formality, hierarchy, and internal regulation that once defined organised crime in Japan. Hangure—loosely connected networks of semi-affiliated criminals—can now occupy more space. As discussed in Chapter 6, these formations often include former motorcycle gangs, ex-yakuza, unemployed youth, and university students. They operate through flexible arrangements, connected more by opportunity than loyalty or shared identity. Unlike traditional yakuza groups, which cultivated a discourse of loyalty, obligation, and status, these networks are transactional. The emergence of tokuryū—fluid, anonymous networks—has made it harder to identify actors or patterns, and has increased the opacity of violence. Disputes in illegal markets still occur but they are less likely to be ritualised or mediated, as they once were under yakuza systems. At the same time, the visibility of organised crime has decreased. These groups avoid the public markers that once made the yakuza legible to the state. In eliminating the 'visible' mafia, the state has facilitated the proliferation of criminal forms that are harder to track, negotiate with, or contain.

The yakuza's claim to power was based on their functional role in the informal economy: they mediated disputes, enforced contracts, and imposed a certain order—not out of altruism but because order was profitable. Their territorial embeddedness, generational continuity, and capacity to enforce agreements gave them predictable authority. It was always partial, often violent, and exploitative, but their decline exposes a structural gap: governance is not easily replaced. The state has limited capacity or willingness to manage everyday underworld conflicts. In this vacuum, the field is increasingly occupied by actors who have no interest in maintaining order, only in maximising short-term gain. In such a landscape, the residual authority of the yakuza, however diminished, still matters. Their bureaucratic structure once allowed them to resolve internal disputes in an organised way, but their ability to enforce these decisions is shrinking. What replaces them is not another mafia, but a fragmented, faster, and ultimately more precarious version of the old system.

Violence

To understand how the dynamics of violence have changed, it is useful to consider the emblematic case of the Yamaguchi-gumi, Japan's largest yakuza syndicate. The Yama-ichi war of 1978, described in Chapter 4, started with violent confrontations between members of the Yamaguchi-gumi and the rebel faction Ichiwa-kai that, by the end of the war, had resulted in 317 violent incidents, twenty-five deaths, and seventy injuries. Other syndicates, such as the Inagawa-kai and the Sumiyoshi-kai, tried to intervene and mediate but the conflict ended only when the head of the rebel faction visited the Yamaguchi-gumi headquarters to offer an apology and formally admit defeat. The Ichiwa-kai was swept away and the Yamaguchi-gumi emerged from the war with its authority reaffirmed.

Contemporary internal conflict, however, looks markedly different. In August 2015, the Yamaguchi-gumi experienced a major schism: a rebel faction led by Kunio Inoue broke away to form the Kōbe Yamaguchi-gumi, composed primarily of Kansai-based affiliates. The split stemmed from growing dissatisfaction with the leadership of sixth-generation boss Shinobu Tsukasa, particularly the high rents, his centralisation of power, and the perceived favouring of Nagoya-based allies. In 2017, a further rupture occurred when a group seceded from the Kōbe Yamaguchi-gumi without returning to the main syndicate, instead establishing the Ninkyō-dantai Yamaguchi-gumi (Mizoguchi, 2017). The schism resulted in a ten-year-long low-intensity confrontation, with few incidents and casualties (Breuer and Baradel, 2025). However, the 2015–2025 conflict did not end through negotiation between factions but through external pressure and the growing cost of maintaining confrontation. As violence became more difficult to sustain, legally, financially, and reputationally, groups that had once tolerated or ignored the conflict began to push for its resolution. The Inagawa-kai played a central role, sending senior members across Japan with a joint petition to gather signatures in support of ending the hostilities. The Yamaguchi-gumi submitted a formal declaration of closure to the Hyōgo Prefectural Police in April 2025, presenting it as a response to nationwide appeals from '*ninkyō* organisations', that is, yakuza groups. The text included an apology to the public and bore the name of second-in-command Takayama Seiji, though notably not that of boss Tsukasa Shinobu. According to one source, 'The Yamaguchi-gumi wanted to unilaterally declare the end of the conflict, but that would not look good'. Framing the decision as a response to outside appeals allowed the group to save face (News PostSeven, 27/4/2025). The low-intensity conflict that persisted for a decade greatly weakened the secessionist Kōbe Yamaguchi-gumi, which is effectively the losing side but still survives. However, even the Yamaguchi-gumi is debilitated. As one source put it: 'It's because there are too many yakuza who can't make a living. Since the conflict intensified and was designated a "specific conflict", it's become even more difficult to survive. Even if there were already efforts to eliminate gangs, the police have started to pursue people for things they previously overlooked' (Shūpure News, 3/6/2025). The risks and costs of overt violence have become prohibitively high. A 2004 amendment to the 1992 Anti-Yakuza Law introduced the liability of bosses for violent acts committed by their affiliates during conflicts (NPA, 2012). Combined with broader regulatory pressure, this has created a landscape in which yakuza groups engage in what has been described as low-intensity warfare, without bursts of violence (JJ04/2016). An open conflict on the scale of the Yama-Ichi war in the 1980s would now result in the complete paralysis of both groups' activities (JJ12/2015).

The economic and legal costs of continued confrontation were clear. The conflict had produced no winner, only organisational fatigue. A decade of repression, shrinking revenues, and factional instability had made violence not only ineffective, but actively damaging. The war did not end with the victory of the strongest faction, it ended because no one could afford to keep fighting.

Moving abroad

An important area to monitor is the expansion of the yakuza abroad. This illustrates a broader point: repression does not always extinguish organised crime; it can displace it. Russian groups have sought to expand into Italy and Hungary, with mixed results: Taiwanese and Hong Kong Triads have moved into mainland China and the 'Ndrangheta has extended its presence to Germany (Hauser, 2025; Varese, 2011) and Australia (Sergi, 2015b). But cross-border expansion is fraught with obstacles. Relocation does not guarantee entrenchment. Organised crime groups attempting to operate in foreign jurisdictions must navigate cultural and linguistic barriers, as well as unfamiliar legal systems and enforcement environments. The capacity to adapt—socially, culturally, and strategically—becomes decisive. While the drivers of expansion have received scholarly attention, we know far less about the process itself: how groups navigate new terrain, what challenges they face, and which configurations prove most resilient.

In the case of Japan, the intensification of regulatory and legal pressures against the yakuza over the past fifteen years has also led to their migration. Trade relations with groups in Hong Kong, Taiwan, and China are well-documented (Baradel and Breuer, 2024) and recent reports indicate that Japanese organised crime syndicates are establishing branch-like operations in countries across East and Southeast Asia, including the Philippines, Thailand, and Malaysia (Suzuki, 2023). In certain contexts, these actors appear capable of replicating, at least partially, the governance-type functions they once exercised in Japan. The geographic proximity and historical connections between Japan and parts of East and Southeast Asia make this area a natural locus for transnational operations. A significant portion of methamphetamine trafficked into Japan originates from this region (Baradel and Breuer, 2024) and evidence points to an enduring yakuza presence in China. Fieldwork conducted with active members confirms the persistence of ties between Japanese syndicates and Taiwanese Triads. In Okinawa, for instance, the Kyokuryū-kai maintain longstanding relationships with Taiwan's largest Triad, the Bamboo Union (Taiwan News, 23/05/2023), and mutual visits have reinforced these connections (Taipei Times, 23/05/2023).

The Yamaguchi-gumi have been particularly active in forging alliances with Taiwanese groups. Close links have been documented with the Zhu Lian gang, the Si Hai gang, and the Yi Shin Hui gang—the latter reportedly operating as a branch of the Yamaguchi-gumi. These relationships have been made visible on multiple occasions: yakuza members attended the public funeral of Niu Bu boss Zhang Nai-Fu, and Liu Wei-Min, head of the Si Hai gang, brought his men to Tokyo to establish ties with their Japanese counterparts (News Sina, 03/11/2004). Akira Nemoto, a prominent figure within the Yamaguchi-gumi, played a key role in a gun-smuggling operation that sought to move firearms from the Philippines to Taiwan (Taipei Times, 05/06/2004). A separate case involved a member of the Osaka-based Isshin-kai who was arrested in Taiwan for running an illegal satellite pornography operation. Such cases underscore the persistence and depth of collaborations between Japanese and East Asian criminal networks (News Sina, 03/11/2004).

Southeast Asia, too, has become increasingly relevant. Japanese criminal groups have built trade relationships with criminal groups in Thailand, particularly in relation to cannabis importation (Japan Customs, 2023). Thailand's significance is further reinforced by the size and visibility of its Japanese population. Although official statistics list around 40,000 Japanese residents, actual estimates exceed 100,000. Bangkok, a hub for Japanese business and manufacturing, hosts a wide range of service industries catering to Japanese nationals, including those associated with the sex trade (Business Journal, 28/04/2015). Signs of yakuza involvement in this sector surfaced in a recent case in which the dismembered body of a man running Japanese restaurants and sex shops was discovered in Bangkok. Investigations linked the murder to two men allegedly affiliated with the yakuza (Higashi Spo Web, 26/04/2024; Newsclip, 07/12/2023).

When mafias move abroad, they can (although rarely) transplant, meaning they export their capacity for governance to a new territory (Varese, 2011). More commonly, they undergo functional diversification, in which they remain dependent on their territory of origin while overseas branches carry out specific trade-related activities without forming large-scale international alliances (Campana, 2011). Hauser (2025) introduces a third form of mobility: hibernation, where a group maintains a structural presence in the new territory but remains inactive. She suggests that groups may shift along a continuum of these three stages—transplantation, functional diversification, and hibernation—at different points in time. In the case of the yakuza, international expansion is a relatively recent phenomenon and the lack of systematic research makes it difficult to determine which stage yakuza groups occupy in each of the countries mentioned above. Moreover, the yakuza are not a single entity but a constellation of organisations, meaning that two groups active in the same country may be at different stages of development. Preliminary evidence suggests that international connections are becoming increasingly important for yakuza groups operating within Japan. Abroad, they appear to be in the functional diversification phase, though in some cases they may exert rudimentary forms of governance, particularly in neighbourhoods with a significant Japanese presence. In such contexts, where navigating foreign legal systems may be difficult or undesirable, the yakuza could provide basic coordination or informal dispute resolution for compatriot businesses.

What about the future?

Future research will need to follow several possible developments in the Japanese criminal underworld. How will newer formations—hangure, fraud rings, black-market job networks—evolve? Could they develop governance capacity? Will yakuza residuals continue to play a role or will they fade entirely?

Criminological theory suggests that criminal actors can evolve along a continuum: from action-sets to gangs (Sullivan, 2005), from gangs to organised crime (Densley, 2012; McLean, 2018), from organised crime to mafias, from mafias to insurgencies, and eventually even to state-like formations (Varese, 2017). These transitions are neither automatic nor common. To move along this continuum, groups must develop recognisable structures, reputational systems, and internal cohesion, and only a few succeed in progressing to the next stage. At present, hangure and tokuryū networks prioritise flexibility, concealment, and opportunism over reputation, regulation, or market stabilisation, as expected from groups involved in trade-based and predatory activities. Becoming a full-fledged mafia would entail greater repression and require the development of an organisational structure, internal coordination mechanisms, a credible capacity for violence, and some degree of social embeddedness. Most of these groups currently lack both the incentive and the conditions to undertake such a transformation. Nonetheless, in areas where extra-legal governance is in demand, some actors may begin to assume stabilising roles. After all, providing governance can be profitable. Such a shift would not occur overnight but the potential remains, especially in fragmented or opaque markets where regulation by the state is weak or inaccessible.

As for the yakuza, the future appears bleak. Outsourcing tasks to unaffiliated actors may ensure a degree of operationality but, in the absence of embedded networks and new recruits, their power continues to wane. What endures is increasingly ideological: a nostalgic identity anchored in values, hierarchy, and the symbolic remnants of authority. Their ability to function as a mafia-type organisation is likely to continue to decline. Instead, they may increasingly cling to titles, codes, and ideological narratives to differentiate themselves from groups like hangure and tokuryū, which they regard as disorganised and disreputable. What is left, however, is not a functioning mafia but rather, a symbolic authority with minimal operational capacity that can survive only through increased collaboration with non-yakuza groups, increasingly losing power, functionality, and reputation. Another possible trajectory is to shed the formal label of 'yakuza' altogether and revert to being categorised as ordinary organised crime, thereby evading the legal restrictions attached to designated groups. The case of the Ninkyō-dantai Yamaguchi-gumi (now rebranded as the Kizuna-kai) is illustrative. The group tried to replace formal titles with generic and legitimate-sounding labels—such as the boss being called 'representative'—and presented itself as a 'traditional fraternity'. Yet, ideological identity is not easily abandoned and, despite changing names, the group was evidently continuing in the yakuza tradition and soon found itself on the list of active yakuza groups. Ultimately, yakuza groups refuse to become common criminals, and tradition often becomes the last remaining source of cohesion. Whether abroad or in reconfigured domestic forms, the yakuza's influence is waning. This book began by asking what happens when a mafia begins to die. The answer, as Japan's case demonstrates, is not a safer society but disorder: more fragmented, more anonymous, and harder to govern. The yakuza's story is far from over, but what comes after them may prove more difficult to understand, and more difficult to control.

APPENDIX

List of Designated Yakuza Groups with Headquarter Location and Current Boss

No.	Organisation Name	Headquarters Location	Representative
1	Rokudaime Yamaguchi-gumi	4-3-1 Shinoharahonmachi, Nada-ku, Kobe-shi, Hyogo	Shinoda Kenichi
2	Inagawa-kai	7-8-4 Roppongi, Minato-ku, Tokyo	Kiyota Jiro (Shin ByonGyu)
3	Sumiyoshi-kai	7-26-7 Shinjuku, Shinjuku-ku, Tokyo	Ogawa Osamu
4	Goudaime Kudo-kai	1-8-8 Usa-machi, Kokurakita-ku, Kitakyushu-shi, Fukuoka	Nomura Satoru
5	Kyokuryu-kai	1362 Shimabukuro, Kitanakagusuku-son, Nakagami-gun, Okinawa	Itokazu Makoto
6	Hachidaime Aizukotetsu-kai	21-4 Ichijoji Tsukamoto-cho, Sakyo-ku, Kyoto-shi, Kyoto	Takayama Yoshiyuki
7	Rokudaime Kyosei-kai	18-10 Minamiokawa-cho, Minami-ku, Hiroshima-shi, Hiroshima	Arase Susumu
8	Shichidaime Goda-ikka	3-13-6 Takezaki-cho, Shimonoseki-shi, Yamaguchi	Suehiro Makoto (Kim Kyohwan)
9	Yondaime Kozakura-ikka	9-24 Kotsuki-cho, Kagoshima-shi, Kagoshima	Hiraoka Kiei
10	Goudaime Asano-gumi	615-11 Kasaoka, Kasaoka-shi, Okayama	Nakaoka Yutaka
11	Dojin-kai	247-6 Kyo-machi, Kurume-shi, Fukuoka	Kobayashi Tetsuji
12	Nidaime Shinwa-kai	2-14-4 Shiokami-cho, Takamatsu-shi, Kagawa	Kira Hirofumi

No.	Organisation Name	Headquarters Location	Representative
13	Soai-kai	1343-8 Uruidori, Ichihara-shi, Chiba	Shiizuka Noboru
14	Sandaime Kyodo-kai	3025-1 Yamanami-cho, Onomichi-shi, Hiroshima	Ikezawa Nozomu
15	Taishu-kai	1314-1 Yugeta, Tagawa-shi, Fukuoka	Hidaka Hiroshi
16	Ju-daime Sakaume-gumi	1-3-17 Taishi, Nishinari-ku, Osaka-shi, Osaka	Kinoshita Masahide (Lee JeongSoo)
17	Kyokuto-kai	2-18-12 Kabuki-cho, Shinjuku-ku, Tokyo	Takahashi Jin
18	Nidaime Azuma-gumi	1-11-8 Sanno, Nishinari-ku, Osaka-shi, Osaka	Takimoto Hiroshi
19	Matsuba-kai	2-9-8 Nishi-Asakusa, Taito-ku, Tokyo	Ito Yoshimasa
20	Yondaime Fukuhaku-kai	5-18-15 Chiyo, Hakata-ku, Fukuoka-shi, Fukuoka	Kaneshiro Kuniyasu (Kim Kuktae)
21	Nidaime Namikawa-kai	38-1 Yatsue-machi, Omuta-shi, Fukuoka	Umeki Kazuma
22	Kobe Yamaguchi-gumi	1379-10 Nakamura Ike-no-ato, Inami-cho, Kako-gun, Hyogo	Inoue Kunio
23	Kizuna-kai	1-14-14 Shimanochi, Chuo-ku, Osaka-shi, Osaka	Oda Yoshinori (Kim Jeonggi)
24	Kanto Sekine-gumi	4-10-13 Sakura-machi, Tsuchiura-shi, Ibaraki	Otsuka Itsuo
25	Ikeda-gumi	2-12-2 Ta-machi, Kita-ku, Okayama-shi, Okayama	Ikeda Takashi (Kim Hyoji)

Interviews

Criminals and former criminals

C1 Former criminal and convict, Tokyo, November 2017
C2 Yakuza boss, Tokyo, January 2018, March 2018, several occasions between March 2022 and December 2023
C3 Former yakuza boss, Tokyo, February 2018, April 2022, December 2022
C4 Former yakuza member, Yokohama, March 2018, June 2022, November 2023
C5 Former yakuza boss, Kyūshū, April 2018
C6 Former user and dealer, May 2023
C7 Former user, May 2023
C8 Former drug dealer, Tokyo, May 2023
C9 Hangure, Kobe, October, 2023
C10 Former yakuza boss, August 2023
C11 Former hangure, Kawaguchi, September 2023
C12 Former hangure, Kawaguchi, September 2023
C13 Yakuza ritual celebrant (*baishakunin*), Tokyo, June 2023
C14 Nishimura Mako, Gifu, several occasions between October 2023 and November 2024
C15 Yakuza boss, Okinawa, July 2023, July 2024
C16 Yakuza boss, Okinawa, July 2023
C17 Yakuza *wakagashira*, Okinawa, July 2023, July 2024
C18 Yakuza member, Okinawa, July 2023, July 2024
C19 Ringleader of fraud group, October 2024
C20 Former hangure, October 2024
C21 Former ringleader of fraud group, Tokyo, October 2024
C22 Former yakuza boss, June 2023
C23 Yakuza apprentice, July 2024
C24 Former yakuza member, February 2023

Journalists

J1 Hirosue Noboru, several occasions between March 2018 and November 2024
J2 Mizoguchi Atsushi, January 2018
J3 Miyazaki Manabu, February 2018
J4 Suzuki Tomohiko, several occasions between March 2018 and September 2023
J5 Hijikata Koji, December 2018
J6 Imanishi Noriyuki, several occasions between October 2023 and December 2024

Police and prosecutors

P1 Police Chief
P2 Prosecutor
P3–9 Police officers working on organised crime
P10–17 Police officers of the Narcotics and Firearms Department
P18–19 Aichi police
P20–21 Hyogo police

Various

V1 Yamanouchi Yukio, former lawyer of the Yamaguchi-gumi, several occasions between March 2018 and December 2023
V2 Murahashi Hiroshi, October 2024
V3 Collaborator Murahashi, October 2024
V4 NPO in San'ya, November 2018
V5 Owner of a bar near a big yakuza office, April 2023

Bibliography

Allison, A. (1994). *Nightwork: Sexuality, pleasure, and corporate masculinity in a Tokyo hostess club*. Chicago: The University of Chicago Press.

Allum, F. (2007). Doing it for themselves or standing in for their men? Women in the Neapolitan Camorra (1950–2003). In G. Fiandaca (ed.), *Women and the mafia: Female roles in organized crime structures* (pp. 9–17). New York: Springer.

Ames, W. L. (1981). *Police and community in Japan*. Berkeley and Los Angeles: University of California Press.

Anderson, N. (1923). *The hobo: The sociology of the homeless man*. Chicago: University of Chicago Press.

Araki, T. (1999). 1999 Revisions of employment security law and worker dispatching law: Drastic reforms of Japanese labor market regulations. *Japan labour bulletin* 38(9), 5–12.

Arduini, G. (2016). *Yakuza. Un'altra mafia*. Milano: Luni Editrice.

Arias, E. D. (2006). The dynamics of criminal governance: Networks and social order in Rio de Janeiro. *Journal of Latin American studies*, 38(2), 293–325.

Arias, E. D. (2017). *Criminal enterprises and governance in Latin America and the Caribbean*. Cambridge: Cambridge University Press.

Armao, F. (2015). Mafia-owned democracies. Italy and Mexico as patterns of criminal neoliberalism. *Tiempo devorado*, 2(1), 4–21.

Asahi Shinbun. (2017). *Kumichō to issho ni kome nado nanbiki yōgi. Kōbe Yamaguchi-gumi kei kumiinra taihō* [Charged with shoplifting rice with the boss: arrested a member of a group related to the Kobe Yamaguchi-gumi] Available at: https://web.archive.org/web/20170524013455/https://www.asahi.com/articles/ASK5R7CYPK5ROIPE02D.html[accessed 14 May 2019].

Asahi Shimbun. (2023). *Kōsoku Ī-Tī-Shī "bōryokudan haijo" kyōka: 6-sha ga kādo kiyaku o kaisei, 3-gatsu kara* [Expressway ETC "organized crime exclusion" strengthened: Six companies revise card terms from March]. Available at: https://www.asahi.com/articles/ASR2J3T0BR2JULFA005/ [Last accessed 28 February 2026].

Atkinson, R. and Flint, J. (2004). Snowball sampling. In M. Lewis-Beck, A. E. Bryman, and T. F. Liao (eds.), *The SAGE encyclopedia of social science research methods* (pp. 1043–4). London: SAGE Publications Ltd.

Baradel, M. (2021). The rise of shaming paternalism in Japan: Recent tendencies in the Japanese criminal justice system. *Trends in organized crime*, 24(1), 23–41.

Baradel, M. (2021). Yakuza grey: the shrinking of the Il/legal nexus and its repercussions on Japanese organised crime. *Global crime*, 22(1), 74–91.

Baradel, M. (2023). *Yakuza incarcerata: 'governance' e controllo nelle prigioni giapponesi* [Incarcerated yakuza: Governance and control in Japanese prisons]. *Annuario di diritto comparato e di studi legislativi*, 14, 235–58.

Baradel, M. (2024) 'I never lost a fight against a man': The story of the only woman to join Japan's notorious yakuza, The Conversation. Available at: https://theconversation.com/i-never-lost-a-fight-against-a-man-the-story-of-the-only-woman-to-join-japans-notorious-yakuza-220792 [Last accessed 27 February 2026].

Baradel, M. and Bortolussi, J. (2021). Under a setting sun: the spatial displacement of the yakuza and their longing for visibility. *Trends in organized crime*, 24(2), 209–26.

Baradel, M. and Breuer, N. (2024). Mapping drug smuggling networks in Japan: A social network analysis of trial documents. *Global crime*, 25(3–4), 220–41.

Barnes, N. (2025). *Inside criminalized governance*. Cambridge: Cambridge University Press.

Bayley, D. H. (1991). *Forces of order: Policing modern Japan*. Berkley: University of California Press.

Bellah, R. N. (2005). Durkheim and ritual. In J. C. Alexander and P. Smith (eds.), *The Cambridge companion to Durkheim* (pp. 183–210). Cambridge: Cambridge University Press.

Belousov, K. et al. (2007). Any port in a storm: Fieldwork difficulties in dangerous and crisis-ridden settings. *Qualitative research*, 7(2), 155–75.

Berik, G. (1996). Understanding the gender system in rural Turkey: Fieldwork dilemmas of conformity and intervention. In Wolf D.L. (ed.), *Feminist dilemmas in fieldwork* (pp. 56–71). Boulder, CO: Westview.

Bernasco, W. (2011). *Offenders on offending: Learning about crime from criminals*. London and New York: Routledge.

Bessatsu Takarajima Henshūbu (2017). *Nihon no yakuza hyakunin* [*One hundred Japanese yakuza*]. Tokyo: Takarajimasha.

Bichler, G. and Norris, A. (2024). Crossing lines: Structural advantages of inter-racial criminal street gang violence. *Trends in organized crime*, 27(3), 235–62.

Blattman, C., Duncan, G., Lessing, B., and Tobón, S. (2025). Gang rule: Understanding and countering criminal governance. *Review of economic studies*, 92(3), 1497–531.

Blok, A. (1974). *The mafia of a Sicilian village, 1860–1960: A study of violent peasant entrepreneurs*. Long Grove: Waveland Press.

Boissevain, J. (1971). Second thoughts on quasi-groups, categories and coalitions. *Man*, 6(3), 468–72.

Bōryokudan Taisaku Hōsei Kenkyūkai [Organized Crime Countermeasures Law Study Group] (ed.). (1995). *Chikujō: Bōryokudan-in ni yoru futō na kōi no bōshi tō ni kansuru hōritsu* [*Article-by-article commentary on the Act on Prevention of Unjust Acts by Organized Crime Group Members*]. Tōkyō: Tachibana Shobō.

Bourdieu, P. (1986). The forms of capital. In J. Richardson (ed.), *Handbook of theory and research for the sociology of education* (pp. 241–58). Westport: Greenwood.

Bōtaihō – Bōryokudan-in ni yoru futōna kōi no bōshi-nado ni kansuru hōritsu [Law for the prevention of improper conduct by members of the bōryokudan] (1991). Law no. 77. Available at: http://elaws.e-gov.go.jp/search/elawsSearch/elaws_search/lsg0500/detail?lawId=403AC0000000077_20171201_429AC0000000046&openerCode=1 [Last accessed 15 May 2019].

Boyd, J. and Williams, R. (1999). Artful means: An aesthetic view of Shinto purification rituals. *Journal of ritual studies*, 13(1), 37–52.

Breuer, N. and Baradel, M. (2025). Investigating the dynamics of yakuza violence using multilevel network analysis. *Social networks*, 82, 14–26.

Breuer, N. and Varese, F. (2023). The structure of trade-type and governance-type organized crime groups: A network study. *The British journal of criminology*, 63(4), 867–88.

Brewster, D. (2018). A critical assessment of indications of the national prevalence of illegal drug use in Japan. *Contemporary drug problems*, 45(4), 425–40.

Brunson, R. K. and Pegram, K. (2015). From the mouths of babes: Conducting qualitative research with youths. In H. Copes and J. M. Miller (eds.), *The Routledge handbook of qualitative criminology* (ch. 17). New York: Routledge.

Bryans, D. and Anema, F. J. (2018). Bitcoin and money laundering: Mining for an effective solution. In McKarty K.J. (ed.), *The money laundering market: Regulating the criminal economy* (pp. 139–179). Newcastle upon Tyne: Agenda Publishing.

Bryman, A. (ed.). (1988). *Doing research in organizations.* London: Routledge.

Bryman, A. (2012). *Social research methods* (4th ed). Oxford: Oxford University Press.

Business Journal. (2015). *Kaigai shinshutsu suru bōryokudan, Tai de akkapaji Keiyaku toraburu de jū tsukitsuke kyōhaku jūbusō guntai tōjō de shazai* [Yakuza expanding overseas, shame in Thailand: Threats at gunpoint over contract dispute, then apology as the army intervenes]. Available at: https://www.excite.co.jp/news/article/Bizjournal_mixi201504_post-3026/ [Last accessed 14 February 2026].

Business Journal. (2018). *'Kikenna hinkon yakuza' wo ryōsan shita bohaijorei de Nihon no chian akka . . . kaigai hanzai shūdan ga bakko* [The 'dangerous destitute yakuza' product of the yakuza exclusionary ordinances and the worsening of public order in Japan . . . foreign organised crime on the rise] Available at: https://www.excite.co.jp/news/article/Bizjournal_mixi201807_post-12838/ [Last accessed 15 May 2019].

Cabinet Office (2002) 'Bōryokudan ni kansuru yoron chōsa' [Public opinion survey on yakuza groups], Tokyo: Naikakufu. Available at: https://survey.gov-online.go.jp/h04/H05-01-04-15.html [Last accessed 27 February 2026].

Calderoni, F. (2011). Where is the mafia in Italy? Measuring the presence of the mafia across Italian provinces. *Global crime*, 12(1), 41–69.

Calderoni, F. (2012). The structure of drug trafficking mafias: The 'Ndrangheta and cocaine. *Crime, law and social change*, 58(3), 321–49.

Cao, L., Stack, S., and Sun, Y. (1998). Public attitudes toward the police: A comparative study between Japan and America. *Journal of criminal justice*, 26(4), 279–89.

Campana, P. (2011). Eavesdropping on the Mob: The functional diversification of Mafia activities across territories. *European journal of criminology*, 8(3), 213–28.

Campana, P. and Varese, F. (2013). Cooperation in criminal organizations: Kinship and violence as credible commitments. *Rationality and society*, 25(3), 263–89.

Campana, P. and Varese, F. (2018). Organized crime in the United Kingdom: Illegal governance of markets and communities. *The British journal of criminology*, 58(6), 1381–1400.

Catino, M. (2015). Mafia rules. The role of criminal codes in mafia organizations. *Scandinavian journal of management*, 31(4), 536–48.

Catino, M. (2019). *Mafia organizations. The visible hand of criminal enterprise.* Cambridge: Cambridge University Press.

Cheshire, C. (2011). Online trust, trustworthiness, or assurance? *Daedalus*, 140(4), 49–58.

Chin, K. L. (2007). Into the thick of it: Methodological issues in studying the drug trade in the Golden Triangle. *Asian journal of criminology*, 2(2), 96–117.

Chu, Y. K. (2000). *The Triads as business.* London: Routledge.

Chūō Chōsasha [Central Research Service]. (2018). *Giin, kanryō, daikigyō, keisatsy nado no shinraikan Chōsa* [Investigation on public's trust towards members of the Diet, bureaucrats, enterprises and the police] Tokyo. Available at: http://www.crs.or.jp/data/pdf/trust17.pdf [Last accessed 15 May 2019].

Chwe, M. S. Y. (2013). *Rational ritual: Culture, coordination, and common knowledge.* Princeton: Princeton University Press.

Clark, J. N. (2012). Fieldwork and its ethical challenges: Reflections from research in Bosnia. *Human rights quarterly*, 34(3), 823–39.

Clarke, M. (1975). Survival in the field: Implications of personal experience in field work. *Theory and society*, 2(1), 95–123.

Clifford, J. and Marcus, G. E. (1986). *The poetics and politics of ethnography.* Berkeley: University of California, Berkeley Press.

Daily Shincho. (2023). *6-daime Yamaguchi-gumi no saikō kanbu-ra mo "sūpā no pointo kādo" to "ETC kādo" no sagi yōgi de taiho sareru jidai ni* [How even top executives of the 6th-generation Yamaguchi-gumi are being arrested for supermarket point card and electronic toll card fraud]. Available at: https://www.dailyshincho.jp/article/2023/03100603/ [Last accessed 28 February 2026].

Deacon, T. (1997). *The symbolic species: The co-evolution of language and the brain.* New York: Norton.

Densley, J. A. (2012). Street gang recruitment: Signaling, screening, and selection. *Social problems*, 59(3), 301–21.

Densley, J. A. (2014). It's gang life, but not as we know it: The evolution of gang business. *Crime & delinquency*, 60(4), 517–46.

Diamond Online (2024) *'Rufi' ra yonin ga gōryū shita machi Susukino de 'shōbai no yarite' ga hanzai-sha ni narihate ta wake* [The reason why a 'business talent' in Susukino—the city where Luffy and the other three joined forces—ended up as a criminal] Available at: https://diamond.jp/articles/-/342194 [Last accessed 23 July 2024].

DeWalt, K. M. and DeWalt, B. R. (2002). *Participant observation: A guide for fieldworkers.* Walnut Creek: AltaMira.

Di Maria, F. and Lo Verso, G. (2007). Women in mafia organizations. In G. Fiandaca (ed.), *Women and the mafia: Female roles in organized crime structures* (pp. 87–101). New York: Springer.

Douglas, M. (1992). *Risk and blame: Essays in cultural theory.* London: Routledge.

Dower, J. W. (1999). *Embracing defeat: Japan in the wake of World War II.* New York: W.W. Norton & Company.

Durkheim, E. (2012). *The elementary forms of the religious life* (J. W. Swain, Trans.; Dover edition.). New York: Dover Publications.

Ellis, C. (2007). Telling secrets, revealing lives: Relational ethics in research with intimate others. *Qualitative inquiry*, 13(1), 3–29.

Evelyn, N. M. and Wang, P. (2025). Cooperation under anonymity: Extralegal governance and China's illegal online sexual fiction market. *Deviant behavior*, 1–20.

England, K. V. (1994). Getting personal: Reflexivity, positionality, and feminist research. *The professional geographer*, 46(1), 80–89.

Englander, M. (2012). The interview: Data collection in descriptive phenomenological human scientific research. *Journal of phenomenological psychology*, 43(1), 13–35.

Etherington, K. (2007). Ethical research in reflexive relationships. *Qualitative inquiry*, 13(5), 599–616.

Eurispes. (2019). *Eurispes rapport Italia 2019: I risultati* [Eurispes report 2019: the results] Available at: https://eurispes.eu/news/eurispes-rapporto-italia-2019-i-risultati/ [Last accessed 15 May 2019].

Fabian, J. (1991). Ethnographic objectivity: From rigor to vigor. *Annals of scholarship*, 8, 381–408.

Fernández-Planells, A., Orduña-Malea, E., and Feixa Pàmpols, C. (2021). Gangs and social media: A systematic literature review and an identification of future challenges, risks and recommendations. *New media & society*, 23(7), 2099–2124.

Fisher, M. (2009). *Capitalist realism: Is there no alternative?* Winchester: Zero Books.

Foote, D. H. (1992). The benevolent paternalism of Japanese criminal justice. *California Law Review*, 80, 317.

Fowler, W. (1996). *San'ya blues: Labouring life in contemporary Tokyo.* Ithaca: Cornell University Press.

FNN. (2022). *'Bōryokudan mo osoreru' Chainīzu Doragon – Hyaku-nin kibo 'shussho iwai' wa Furansu ryōriten – Dairantō ni 'yaritai hōdai' daga ano Marubō ga . . .* [The Chinese

Dragons: Feared even by the yakuza. A 100-person release party at a French restaurant ends in a massive brawl and chaos . . . but then the organized crime division stepped in] Available from: https://www.fnn.jp/articles/-/431668 [Last accessed 23 July 2025].
Fujinaga, K. (1992). *Bōryokudan Hanzai* [*Organized Crime*]. Tokyo: Tōkyō Hōrei Shuppan.
Fujita, G. (1983). *Ninkyo Daihyakka*. Tokyo: Ninkyō Kenkyūkai.
Fukurai, H. and Kurosawa, K. (2010). Impact of the popular legal participation on forced confessions and wrongful convictions in Japan's bureaucratic courtroom: A cross-national analysis in the US and Japan. *US–China Law Review*, 7(7), 1–18.
Fukuyama, F. (2001). Social capital, civil society and development. *Third world quarterly*, 22(1), 7–20.
Funabashi, Y. and Kushner, B. (2015). *Examining Japan's lost decades*. New York: Routledge.
Fūzoku-eigyō nado no kisei oyogi gyōmu tekiseika nadoni kansuru hōritsu [Law and regulations concerning the entertainment business and the suitability of businesses] (1948) Available at: http://elaws.e-gov.go.jp/search/elawsSearch/elaws_search/lsg0500/detail?lawId=323AC0000000122 [Last accessed 14 May 2019].
Gambetta, D. (1993). *The Sicilian mafia*. Cambridge, MA: Harvard University Press.
Gambetta, D. (2009). *Codes of the underworld: How criminals communicate*. Princeton, NJ: Princeton University Press.
Gani, J. K. and Khan, R. M. (2024). Positionality statements as a function of coloniality: Interrogating reflexive methodologies. *International studies quarterly*, 68(2), sqae038.
Geertz, C. (1973). *The interpretation of cultures*. New York: Basic Books.
Geertz, C. (1988). *Works and lives: The anthropologist as author*. Stanford: Stanford University Press.
Giddens, A. (1990). *The consequences of modernity*. Cambridge: Polity Press.
Ginsburg, T. and Hoetker, G. (2006). The unreluctant litigant? An empirical analysis of Japan's turn to litigation. *The Journal of Legal Studies*, 35(1), 31–59.
Gill, T. (2001). *Men of uncertainty: The social organization of day laborers in contemporary Japan*. Albany, NY: State University of New York Press.
Glick, P. and Fiske, S. T. (1996). The ambivalent sexism inventory: Differentiating hostile and benevolent sexism. *Journal of personality and social psychology*, 70(3), 491–512.
Gravel, J., Allison, B., West-Fagan, J., McBride, M., and Tita, G. E. (2018). Birds of a feather fight together: Status-enhancing violence, social distance and the emergence of homogenous gangs. *Journal of quantitative criminology*, 34(1), 189–219.
Gurney, J. N. (1991). Female researchers in male-dominated settings. In Pogrebin M.R. (ed.), *Qualitative approaches to criminal justice: Perspectives from the field*, (pp. 377–82). Thousand Oaks: Sage Publications.
Haggerty, K. D. (2004). Ethics creep: Governing social science research in the name of ethics. *Qualitative sociology*, 27(4), 391–414.
Hamamatsu City (2025). *Hamamatsu-shi no bōhan no ayumi* [*History of crime prevention in Hamamatsu City*] March 13. Available at: https://www.city.hamamatsu.shizuoka.jp/simink/boutsui/ayumi.html [Lastaccessed 11 March 2026]
Hamill, H. (2010). *The hoods: Crime and punishment in Belfast*. Princeton: Princeton University Press.
Hanson, R. and Richards, P. (2017). Sexual harassment and the construction of ethnographic knowledge. *Sociological forum*, 32(3), 587–609.
Hanzai ni yoru shūeki no iten bōshi ni kan suru Hōritsu [Law for the Prevention of the Transfer of Criminal Revenues] (2007) [online] Available at: http://elaws.e-gov.go.jp/search/elawsSearch/elaws_search/lsg0500/detail?lawId=419AC0000000022 [Last accessed 15 May 2019].

Hauser, Z. L. (2025). *Mafia expansion: The 'Ndrangheta in established democracies.* Oxford: Oxford University Press.

Heckathorn, D. D. (1997). Respondent-driven sampling: a new approach to the study of hidden populations. *Social problems*, 44(2), 174–99.

Hedgecoe, A. (2016). Reputational risk, academic freedom and research ethics review. *Sociology*, 50(3), 486–501.

Henshall, K. (1999). *Dimensions of Japanese society.* New York: St. Martin's Press.

Herber, E. D. (2009). Japanese sentencing practices: Creating an opportunity for 'formal' paternalism. *International journal of criminology and sociological theory*, 2(2), 303–13.

Hess, H. (1973). *Mafia and mafiosi.* Farnborough: Saxon House.

Hill, P. (2003). *The Japanese mafia.* Oxford: Oxford University Press.

Hill, P. (2005). The changing face of the yakuza. *Global crime*, 6(1), 97–116.

Hill, P. (2014). The Japanese yakuza. In L. Paoli (ed.), *The Oxford handbook of organized crime* (ch. 11). New York: Oxford University Press.

Hirosue, N. (2016). *Yakuza ni naru riyū* [*Why (some people) become yakuza*]. Tokyo: Shinchōsha.

Hirosue, N. (2017). *Yakuza to kaigo—bōryokudan ridatsusha-tachi no kenkyu* [*Yakuza and nursing—a research on withdrawn yakuza*]. Tokyo: Kadokawa.

Hirosue, N. (2019). *Bōryokudan ridatsusha ha ima, shūshokusaki de konna imeji ni atteiru* [Ex yakuza now at the workplace are facing these situations] *Gendai Business.* Available at: https://gendai.ismedia.jp/articles/-/60276?page=2 [Last accessed 14 May 2019].

Hirosue, N. (2023). *Yami Baito — Kyōakuka suru Wakamono no Riaru* [*Yami Baito: The grim reality of increasingly violent youth crimes*]. Tokyo: Shōdensha Shinsho.

Higashi Spo Web. (2024). *Tai Nihon no bōryokudan kankeisha barabara itai jiken koyoware untenshu wa gomanen no houshu* [Thai-Japanese gang member dismembered body case: Hired driver 'paid 50,000 yen'] Available at: https://www.tokyo-sports.co.jp/articles/-/300390 [Last accessed 14 February 2026].

Hobbs, D. (2001). Ethnography and the study of deviance. In P. Atkinson et al. (eds.), *Handbook of ethnography* (pp. 204–19). London: SAGE Publications Ltd.

Hobbs, D. and Antonopoulos, G. A. (2014). How to research organized crime. In L. Paoli (ed.), *The Oxford handbook of organized crime* (pp. 96–117). New York: Oxford University Press.

Hongo, J. (2008). Law bends over backwards to allow 'fuzoku'. *The Japan times.* Available at: https://www.japantimes.co.jp/news/2008/05/27/reference/law-bends-over-backward-to-allow-fuzoku/#.XNszzZMzb-Y [Last accessed 14 May 2019].

Hong Kong Free Press. (2017). Hong Kong police bust rare triad gang initiation ceremony, 4 arrested. Available at: https://hongkongfp.com/2017/11/29/hong-kong-police-bust-rare-triad-gang-initiation-ceremony-4-arrested/ [Last accessed 14 February 2026].

Hoshino, S. (1980). *Bōryokudan'in to ruihan* [Yakuza and recidivism]. *Hanzai shakaigaku kenkyū* [*Japanese journal of sociological criminology*], 5, 42–63.

Hoshino, T. and Kamada, T. (2021). Third-party policing approaches against organized crime: An evaluation of the Yakuza exclusion ordinances. *Journal of quantitative criminology*, 37(3), 791–811.

Hoshino, E., Gardner, C., Jennings, S., and Hartmann, K. (2015). Examining the long-run relationship between the prices of imported abalone in Japan. *Marine resource economics*, 30(2), 179–92.

Hughes, L. A. and Short, J. F. 2005. Disputes involving youth street gang members: Micro-social contexts. *Criminology*, 43(1), 43–76.

Huisman, W. and Nelen, H. (2007). Gotham unbound Dutch style: The administrative approach to organized crime in Amsterdam. *Crime, law and social change*, 48(3), 87–103.

Hunter, J. (2013). *The emergence of modern Japan: An introductory history since 1853.* Abingdon: Routledge.

Ingrascì, O. (2007). Women in the 'Ndrangheta: the Serraino-Di Giovine case. In G. Fiandaca (ed.) *Women and the mafia: female roles in organized crime structures.* (pp. 47–52). New York: Springer.

Igarashi, Y. (2000). *Bodies of memory: Narratives of war in postwar Japanese culture, 1945–1970.* Princeton, NJ: Princeton University Press.

Igarashi, Y. (2021). *Japan, 1972: Visions of masculinity in an age of mass consumerism.* New York: Columbia University Press.

Ino, K. (1999). *Yakuza to Nihonjin* [*The yakuza and the Japanese*]. Tokyo: Chikuma Bunko.

Ino, K. (2000). *Yakuza Sengoshi* [*History of Postwar Yakuza*]. Tokyo: Chikuma Bunko.

Iwai, H. (1963). *Byōri shūdan no kōzō* [*The structure of pathological groups*]. Tokyo: Seishin Shobō.

Jacobs, J. B., Friel, C., and Raddick, R. (2001). *Gotham unbound: How New York City was liberated from the grip of organized crime.* New York: NYU Press.

Jacobs, B. A. (2006). The case for dangerous fieldwork. In Hobbs, D. and Wright, R. (eds.) *The Sage handbook of fieldwork* (pp. 157–68). London: Sage Publications Ltd.

Jamieson, A. and Violante, L. (1999). *The antimafia.* London: Palgrave Macmillan.

Jankowski, M. S. (1991). *Islands in the street: Gangs and American urban society* (Vol. 159). Berkeley: University of California Press.

Japan Coast Guard. (2013). Kaijō hoan repōto 2013 [Japan Coast Guard Report 2013]. Chapter 2: Kokunai mitsugyo taisaku [Domestic poaching countermeasures]. Available at: https://www.kaiho.mlit.go.jp/info/books/report2013/html/honpen/1_04_1_chap2.html [Last accessed 28 February 2026].

Japan Customs. (2023). Enforcement Report. Available at: https://www.customs.go.jp/english/enforcement/report2023_e/2023haku02e.pdf.

Jiji. (2024). *Jun-bōryokudan kanren-saki kara mikajime-ryō yōgi de Sumiyoshikai-kei kanbu-ra taiho – Keishichō* [Sumiyoshikai-affiliated members arrested by Tokyo Metropolitan Police for allegedly collecting protection money from groups linked to quasi-gang organisations] Available at: https://www.jiji.com/jc/article?k=2024100400838&g=soc [Last accessed 28 July 2025].

Johnson, D. T. (2002). *The Japanese way of justice: Prosecuting crime in Japan.* Oxford: Oxford University Press.

Jones, T. Y. (2011). Yakuza among first with relief supply in Japan. Reuters [online] Available at: https://www.reuters.com/article/us-yakuza/yakuza-among-first-with-relief-supplies-in-japan-idUSTRE72O6TF20110325 [Last accessed 14 May 2019].

Kaplan, D. and Dubro, A. (2003). *Yakuza.* Berkeley: University of California Press.

Kawaguchi, E. (1985). *Meiji no Yokohama no Hito.* Tokyo: Seiunsha.

Keihō 185 jō [Criminal law Art. 185] (2017) Available at: http://elaws.e-gov.go.jp/search/elawsSearch/elaws_search/lsg0500/detail?lawId=140AC0000000045#801 [Last accessed 14 May 2019].

Kingsberg, M. (2014). *Moral nation: Modern Japan and narcotics in global history.* Berkeley: University of California Press.

Kloß, S. T. (2017). Sexual(ized) harassment and ethnographic fieldwork: A silenced aspect of social research. *Ethnography*, 18(3), 396–414.

Koch, G. (2021). Twenty-four ways to have sex within the law. *Journal of legal anthropology*, 5(2), 21–42.

Koonings, K. and Kruijt, D. (eds.). (2004). *Armed actors: Organised violence and state failure in Latin America.* London: Zed Books.

Komiya, N. (1999). A cultural study of the low crime rate in Japan. *British journal of criminology*, 39(3), 369–90.

Kryshtanovskaya, O. and White, S. (2003). Putin's militocracy. *Post-soviet affairs*, 19(4), 289–306.

Ladson-Billings, G. (2003). It's your world, I'm just trying to explain it: Understanding our epistemological and methodological challenges. *Qualitative inquiry*, 9(1), 5–12.

Landesco, J. (1968). *Organized crime in Chicago*. Chicago: University of Chicago Press.

Lane, J. (2019). *The digital street*. Oxford: Oxford University Press.

Lavorgna, A. (2015). Organised crime goes online: Realities and challenges. *Journal of money laundering control*, 18(2), 153–68.

Lee-Treweek, G. and Linkogle, S. (2002). Putting danger in the frame. In Lee-Treweek, G. and Linkogle, S. (eds.) *Danger in the field: Ethics and risk in social research* (pp. 18–22). London: Routledge.

Leonardsen, D. (2004). *Japan as a low-crime nation*. Basingstoke: Palgrave Macmillan.

Lessing, B. (2017) Counterproductive punishment: How prison gangs undermine state authority. *Rationality and society*, 29(3), 257–97.

Lessing, B. (2018). *Making peace in drug wars: Crackdowns, cartels, and consolidation*. Cambridge: Cambridge University Press.

Lessing, B. (2020). Conceptualizing criminal governance. *Perspectives on politics*, 19(3), 854–73.

Lessing, B. and Willis, G. D. (2019). Legitimacy in criminal governance: Managing a drug empire from behind bars. *American political science review*, 113(2), 584–606.

Lévi-Strauss, C. (1963). *Structural anthropology* (C. Jacobson and B. G. Schoepf, Trans.). New York: Basic Books. (Original work published 1949).

Lewis, K. and Papachristos, A.V. (2020). Rules of the game: Exponential random graph models of a gang homicide network. *Social forces*, 98(4), 1829–58.

Lincoln, J. R. and Gerlach, M. L. (2004). *Japan's network economy: Structure, persistence, and change*. Cambridge: Cambridge University Press.

Lindegaard, M. R. and Bernasco, W. (2018). Lessons learned from crime caught on camera. *Journal of research in crime and delinquency*, 55(1), 155–86.

Livedoor News. (2019). *Gendai yakuza ha ikidurai? Seikatsuku de nikkyū 5000 en no arubaito ni hagemu hibi* [Is livelihood hard for contemporary yakuza? Working part-time for 5,000 yen a day to get by] Available at: http://news.livedoor.com/article/detail/15925464/ [Last accessed 12 February 2019].

Lusthaus, J. (2012). Trust in the world of cybercrime. *Global crime*, 13(2), 71–94.

Lusthaus, J. (2018). *Industry of anonymity: Inside the business of cybercrime*. Cambridge, MA: Harvard University Press.

Lusthaus, J. and Varese, F. (2021). Offline and local: The hidden face of cybercrime. *Policing: A journal of policy and practice*, 15(1), 4–14.

MAFF [Ministry of Agriculture, Forestry and Fishery) (2023). *Mitsuryō wo Yurusanai – Suisanchō no Mitsuryō Taisaku* [Poaching is not permitted – The anti-poaching strategy of the Fisheries Agency] [online] Available at: https://www.jfa.maff.go.jp/j/enoki/mitsuryotaisaku.html [Last accessed 25 October 2022].

Massari, M. and Motta, C. (2007). Women in the Sacra Corona Unità. In G. Fiandaca (ed.), *Women and the mafia: Female roles in organized crime structures* (pp. 53–66). New York: Springer.

Mayaku Tokurei-hō. (1991). *Kokusaitekina kyōryoku no shita ni kisei yakubutsu ni kakawaru fusei kōi wo jochō suru kōi nado no bōshi wo hakaru tame no mayaku oyobi kōsei shinyaku torishimarihō nado ni kansuru hōritsu* [Law regarding the control of drugs and psychotic drugs, to prevent behaviours that foster wrongdoing in relation to drugs restricted by international cooperation] Law no. 94 [online] Available at: http://elaws.e-gov.go.jp/search/elawsSearch/elaws_search/lsg0500/detail?lawId=403AC0000000094 [Last accessed 12 February 2019].

Mayaku tsuihō kokudo jōka dōmei [Alliance for the banishment of drugs and clean-up of the country]. (2013). [online] Available at: http://mjyouka.web.fc2.com/index2.html [Last accessed 15 May 2019].

Merlino, R. (2012). From a man to a 'man of honour': The role of religion in the initiation ritual of the Sicilian mafia. *International journal of the humanities*, 9(11), 59–70.

McLean, R. (2018). An evolving gang model in contemporary Scotland. *Deviant behavior*, 39(3), 309–21.

Midford, P. (2011). *Rethinking Japanese public opinion and security: From pacifism to realism?* Stanford: Stanford University Press.

Milhaupt, C. J. and West, M. D. (2000). The dark side of private ordering: An institutional and empirical analysis of organized crime. *The University of Chicago law review*, 67, 41.

Miyazaki, M. (2008). *Yakuza to Nihon* [*The yakuza and Japan*]. Tokyo: Chikuma.

Miyazaki, M. (2010). *Kindai yakuza kōteiron* [*A positive theory of modern yakuza*]. Tokyo: Chikuma.

Miyazawa, S. (1992). *Policing in Japan*. Albany: State University of New York Press.

Miyazawa, S. (2008). The politics of increasing punitiveness and the rising populism in Japanese criminal justice policy. *Punishment & Society*, 10(1), 47–77.

Mizoguchi, A. (2011). *Bōryokudan*. Tokyo: Shinchōsha.

Mizoguchi, A. (2012). *Tsuduki – Bōryokudan* [*Bōryokudan Vol 2*]. Tokyo: Shinchōsha.

Mizoguchi, A. (2013). *Tokete iku bōryokudan* [*The disappearing bōryokudan*]. Tokyo: Kōdansha.

Mizoguchi, A. (2017). *Yamaguchi-gumi sangokushi* [*Yamaguchi-gumi: Annals of the three kingdoms*]. Tokyo: Kōdansha.

Mizoguchi, A. (2018). *Abe shushō no fuseina senkyo bōgai irai to Abe jimusho hōka jiken no tenmatsu* [Abe's request to illegal election hindrance and details about the arson incident at Abe's headquarters] *Nikkan Gendai* [online] Available at: https://www.nikkan-gendai.com/articles/view/news/233887 [Last accessed 15 May 2019].

Mizoguchi, A. (2019). *Keisatsu ga unen soshi? Roku-daime Yamaguchi-gumi Takayama wakagashira ni hayaku mo saitaiho setsu* [The police hinders administration? Lieutentant Takayama to be rearrested soon] *Nikkan Gendai* [online] Available at: https://www.nikkan-gendai.com/articles/view/news/245898 [Last accessed 15 May 2019].

Mizoguchi, A. (2026). *Yakuza wa hontō ni "hitsuyō aku" datta no ka* [Were the yakuza really a "necessary evil"?]. Tokyo: Kodansha.

Mizoguchi, A. and Suzuki, T. (2021). *Shokugyō to shite no yakuza*. Tokyo: Shōgakukan Shinsho.

Mizushima, K. (1986). Nihon no shakai byōri genshō [Social pathological phenomena in Japan]. *Seikatsu rigaku kenkyū*, 8, 1–16.

MoF [Ministry of Finance]. (2024). Reiwa 6-nen no zenkoku no zeikan ni okeru kanzeiho ihan jiken no torishimari jōkyō [Status of enforcement of customs law violations by customs offices nationwide in 2024]. Available at: https://www.mof.go.jp/policy/customs_tariff/trade/safe_society/mitsuyu/cy2024/index.htm [Last accessed 12 February 2026].

MoJ [Ministry of Justice]. (1985). Shōwa 60 Nenhan Hanzai Hankusho [White Paper on Crime Showa 60 Issue] [online] Available at: http://hakusyo1.moj.go.jp/jp/26/nfm/mokuji.html [Last accessed 14 May 2019].

MoJ [Ministry of Justice]. (1989). Heisei Moto Nenhan Hanzai Hankusho [White Paper on Crime Heisei 1 Issue] [online] Available at: https://hakusyo1.moj.go.jp/jp/30/nfm/mokuji.html [Last accessed 11 March 2026].

MoJ [Ministry of Justice]. (1991). Heisei 3 Nenhan Hanzai Hankusho [White Paper on Crime Heisei 3 Issue] [online] Available at: http://hakusyo1.moj.go.jp/jp/32/nfm/mokuji.html [Last accessed 12 February 2019].

MoJ [Ministry of Justice]. (1992). Heisei 4 Nenhan Hanzai Hankusho [White Paper on Crime Heisei 4 Issue] [online] Available at: http://hakusyo1.moj.go.jp/jp/33/nfm/mokuji.html [Last accessed 12 February 2019].

MoJ [Ministry of Justice]. (1993). Heisei 5 Nenhan Hanzai Hankusho [White Paper on Crime Heisei 5 Issue] [online] Available at: http://hakusyo1.moj.go.jp/jp/34/nfm/mokuji.html [Last accessed 12 February 2019].

MoJ [Ministry of Justice]. (1994). Heisei 6 Nenhan Hanzai Hankusho [White Paper on Crime Heisei 6 Issue] [online] Available at: http://hakusyo1.moj.go.jp/jp/35/nfm/mokuji.html [Last accessed 12 February 2019].

MoJ [Ministry of Justice] (1995). Heisei 7 Nenhan Hanzai Hankusho [White Paper on Crime Heisei 7 Issue] [online] Available at: http://hakusyo1.moj.go.jp/jp/36/nfm/mokuji.html [Last accessed 12 February 2019].

MoJ [Ministry of Justice]. (1997). Heisei 9 Nenhan Hanzai Hankusho [White Paper on Crime Heisei 9 Issue] [online] Available at: http://hakusyo1.moj.go.jp/jp/38/nfm/mokuji.html [Last accessed 12 February 2019].

Hōmushō [Ministry of Justice]. (1998). Heisei 10 Nenhan Hanzai Hankusho [White Paper on Crime Heisei 10 Issue] [online] Available at: http://hakusyo1.moj.go.jp/jp/39/nfm/mokuji.html [Last accessed 12 February 2019].

MoJ [Ministry of Justice]. (1999). Heisei 11 Nenhan Hanzai Hankusho [White Paper on Crime Heisei 11 Issue] [online] Available at: http://hakusyo1.moj.go.jp/jp/40/nfm/mokuji.html [Last accessed 12 February 2019].

MoJ [Ministry of Justice]. (2000). Heisei 12 Nenhan Hanzai Hankusho [White Paper on Crime Heisei 12 Issue] [online] Available at: http://hakusyo1.moj.go.jp/jp/41/nfm/mokuji.html [Last accessed 12 February 2019].

MoJ [Ministry of Justice]. (2001). Heisei 13 Nenhan Hanzai Hankusho [White Paper on Crime Heisei 13 Issue] [online] Available at: http://hakusyo1.moj.go.jp/jp/42/nfm/mokuji.html [Last accessed 12 February 2019].

MoJ [Ministry of Justice]. (2002). Heisei 14 Nenhan Hanzai Hankusho [White Paper on Crime Heisei 14 Issue] [online] Available at: http://hakusyo1.moj.go.jp/jp/43/nfm/mokuji.html [Last accessed 12 February 2019].

MoJ [Ministry of Justice]. (2003). Heisei 15 Nenhan Hanzai Hankusho [White Paper on Crime Heisei 15 Issue] [online] Available at: http://hakusyo1.moj.go.jp/jp/44/nfm/mokuji.html [Last accessed 12 February 2019].

MoJ [Ministry of Justice]. (2004). Heisei 16 Nenhan Hanzai Hankusho [White Paper on Crime Heisei 16 Issue] [online] Available at: http://hakusyo1.moj.go.jp/jp/48/nfm/mokuji.html [Last accessed 12 February 2019].

MoJ [Ministry of Justice]. (2005). Heisei 17 Nenhan Hanzai Hankusho [White Paper on Crime Heisei 17 Issue] [online] Available at: http://hakusyo1.moj.go.jp/jp/51/nfm/mokuji.html [Last accessed 12 February 2019].

MoJ [Ministry of Justice]. (2006). Heisei 18 Nenhan Hanzai Hankusho [White Paper on Crime Heisei 18 Issue] [online] Available at: http://hakusyo1.moj.go.jp/jp/52/nfm/mokuji.html [Last accessed 12 February 2019].

MoJ [Ministry of Justice]. (2007). Heisei 19 Nenhan Hanzai Hankusho [White Paper on Crime Heisei 19 Issue] [online] Available at: http://hakusyo1.moj.go.jp/jp/54/nfm/mokuji.html [Last accessed 12 February 2019].

Hōmushō [Ministry of Justice]. (2008). Heisei 20 Nenhan Hanzai Hankusho [White Paper on Crime Heisei 20 Issue] [online] Available at: http://hakusyo1.moj.go.jp/jp/55/nfm/mokuji.html [Last accessed 12 February 2019].

MoJ [Ministry of Justice]. (2009). Heisei 21 Nenhan Hanzai Hankusho [White Paper on Crime Heisei 21 Issue] [online] Available at: http://hakusyo1.moj.go.jp/jp/56/nfm/mokuji.html [Last accessed 12 February 2019].

MoJ [Ministry of Justice]. (2010). Heisei 22 Nenhan Hanzai Hankusho [White Paper on Crime Heisei 22 Issue] [online] Available at: http://hakusyo1.moj.go.jp/jp/57/nfm/mokuji.html [Last accessed 12 February 2019].

MoJ [Ministry of Justice]. (2011). Heisei 23 Nenhan Hanzai Hankusho [White Paper on Crime Heisei 23 Issue] [online] Available at: http://hakusyo1.moj.go.jp/jp/58/nfm/mokuji.html [Last accessed 12 February 2019].

MoJ [Ministry of Justice]. (2012). Heisei 24 Nenhan Hanzai Hankusho [White Paper on Crime Heisei 24 Issue] [online] Available at: http://hakusyo1.moj.go.jp/jp/59/nfm/mokuji.html [Last accessed 12 February 2019].

MoJ [Ministry of Justice]. (2013). Heisei 25 Nenhan Hanzai Hankusho [White Paper on Crime Heisei 25 Issue] [online] Available at: http://hakusyo1.moj.go.jp/jp/60/nfm/mokuji.html [Last accessed 12 February 2019].

MoJ [Ministry of Justice]. (2014). Heisei 26 Nenhan Hanzai Hankusho [White Paper on Crime Heisei 26 Issue] [online] Available at: http://hakusyo1.moj.go.jp/jp/61/nfm/mokuji.html [Last accessed 12 February 2019].

MoJ [Ministry of Justice]. (2015). Heisei 27 Nenhan Hanzai Hankusho [White Paper on Crime Heisei 27 Issue] [online] Available at: http://hakusyo1.moj.go.jp/jp/62/nfm/mokuji.html [Last accessed 12 February 2019].

MoJ [Ministry of Justice]. (2016). *Zairyū gaikokujin tōkei* [Statistics of foreign residents] [online] Available at: http://www.e-stat.go.jp/SG1/estat/List.do?lid=000001150236 [Last accessed 17 May 2019].

MoJ [Ministry of Justice]. (2016). Heisei 28 Nenhan Hanzai Hankusho [White Paper on Crime Heisei 28 Issue] [online] Available at: http://hakusyo1.moj.go.jp/jp/63/nfm/mokuji.html [Last accessed 12 February 2019].

MoJ [Ministry of Justice]. (2017). Heisei 29 Nenhan Hanzai Hankusho [White Paper on Crime Heisei 29 Issue] [online] Available at: http://hakusyo1.moj.go.jp/jp/64/nfm/mokuji.html [Last accessed 12 February 2019].

MoJ [Ministry of Justice]. (2018). Heisei 30 Nenhan Hanzai Hankusho [White Paper on Crime Heisei 30 Issue] [online] Available at: http://hakusyo1.moj.go.jp/jp/65/nfm/mokuji.html [Last accessed 12 February 2019].

MoJ [Ministry of Justice]. (2019). Reiwa Moto Nenhan Hanzai Hankusho [White Paper on Crime Reiwa 1 Issue] [online] Available at: https://hakusyo1.moj.go.jp/jp/66/nfm/mokuji.html [Last accessed 2 March 2026].

MoJ [Ministry of Justice]. (2020). Reiwa 2 Nenhan Hanzai Hankusho [White Paper on Crime Reiwa 2 Issue] [online] Available at: https://hakusyo1.moj.go.jp/jp/67/nfm/mokuji.html [Last accessed 2 March 2026].

MoJ [Ministry of Justice]. (2021). Reiwa 3 Nenhan Hanzai Hankusho [White Paper on Crime Reiwa 3 Issue] [online] Available at: https://hakusyo1.moj.go.jp/jp/68/nfm/mokuji.html [Last accessed 2 March 2026].

MoJ [Ministry of Justice]. (2022). Reiwa 4 Nenhan Hanzai Hankusho [White Paper on Crime Reiwa 4 Issue] [online] Available at: https://hakusyo1.moj.go.jp/jp/69/nfm/mokuji.html [Last accessed 2 March 2026].

MoJ [Ministry of Justice]. (2024). Reiwa 6 Nenhan Hanzai Hankusho [White Paper on Crime Reiwa 6 Issue] [online] Available at: http://hakusyo1.moj.go.jp/jp/65/nfm/mokuji.html [Last accessed 12 February 2026].

Monaghan, L. F. (2006). Fieldwork and the body: Reflections on an embodied ethnography. In Hobbs, D. and Wright, R. (eds.) *The SAGE handbook of fieldwork* (pp. 225–42). London: Sage Publications Ltd.

Moncada, E. (2021). *Resisting extortion: Victims, criminals, and states in Latin America. Cambridge Studies in Comparative Politics.* Cambridge: Cambridge University Press.

Morgan, W. P. (1960). *Triad Societies in Hong Kong.* Hong Kong: Government Press.

Morselli, C., Giguère, C., and Petit, K. (2007). The efficiency/security trade-off in criminal networks. *Social networks*, 29(1), 143–53.

Morselli, C. and Roy, J. (2008). Brokerage qualifications in ringing operations. *Criminology*, 46(1), 71–98.

Moyle, L. et al. (2019). # Drugsforsale: An exploration of the use of social media and encrypted messaging apps to supply and access drugs. *International Journal of Drug Policy*, 63, 101–10.

Murakami, K. (2005a). *Ninkyō • sakazukigoto no subete [ue]: Oyako ketsuen sakazuki • gikyōdai enkumi sakazuki* [*All about chivalry and sakazuki [Vol. 1]: Parent–child bonding cups and brotherhood alliance cups*]. Tokyo: Bunkasha.

Murakami, K. (2005b). *Ninkyō • sakazukigoto no subete [shita]:edachi wakiawase sakazuki • intai shūmei sakazuki* [*All about chivalry and sakazuki [Vol. 2]: Parting cups and retirement name-succession cups*] Tokyo: Bunkasha.

Mügge, L. M. (2013). Sexually harassed by gatekeepers: Reflections on fieldwork in Surinam and Turkey. *International journal of social research methodology*, 16(6), 131–47.

Nagata, T. (2011). *Sengo Yakuza Kōsō-shi* [*Postwar Yakuza Conflict History*]. Tokyo, Japan: East Press.

Nakamura, K. (1971). Twice a loser. *Far Eastern economic review*, 47, 12.

Nakamura, A. (2016). Mayaku jūaku hanzai no genjō to taisaku: Sono 2, Kakuseizai jihan [The current situation and countermeasures for serious drug crimes: Part 2, Stimulant offenses]. *Keisatsu Gaku Ronshū*, 69(6), 143–77.

Nakamura, K., Tita, G. E., and Krackhardt, D. (2020). Violence in the 'balance': A structural analysis of how rivals, allies, and third-parties shape inter-gang violence. *Global Crime*, 21(1), 3–27.

Nelson, J. K. (1996). *A year in the life of a Shinto Shrine.* Seattle: University of Washington Press.

News PostSeven. (2016). *Keisatsu ha bōryokudan ni ite morawanakute ha komaru jijō ari* [The reasons why the police is in trouble if the yakuza is not there] Available at: https://www.news-
postseven.com/archives/20160316_392131.html/2 [Last accessed 15 May 2019].

News PostSeven. (2018). *Moto kumichō, Chūgokujin hanzai no jittai akasu "Yatsu-ra to wa kumenaI"* [Former boss reveals the reality of Chinese crime: "We can't work with them"]. Available at: https://www.news-postseven.com/archives/20180907_756562.html [Last accessed 11 March 2026].

News PostSeven. (2022). *Bōryokudan no shinnen gyōji: 12-gatsu-chū ni 'koto-hajime-shiki', shōgatsu ni kinjo no kodomo ni 'otoshidama sanman-en' kubatta rei mo* [Yakuza New Year's 'Shigoto-me Ceremony' held in December; 30,000 yen otoshidama given to neighborhood children] Available at: https://www.news-postseven.com/archives/20221227_1825977.html?DETAIL [Last accessed 14 February 2026].

News PostSeven. (2024). *Kumichō o intai shite mo intai to naranai? Rokudaime Yamaguchi-gumi ga dōnyū shita 'Sōsai-seido' no nerai* [Retired but not really retired? The purpose behind the Sixth Yamaguchi-gumi's 'President System]. Available at: https://www.news-postseven.com/archives/20240114_1933912.html?DETAIL [Last accessed 14 February 2026].

News PostSeven. (2024). *Bōryokudan vs yami baito: 'Uchi no nawaba ri de gōtō o shitara danko taru shochi o torimasu'—Yūmei yakuza soshiki ga gōtōdan ni gifunbun o kakagete* *ita—kanbu ga kuchi ni shita keiji no riyū** [Violent groups vs. under-the-table part-time workers: 'If robbery is committed in our territory, we'll take decisive action'—a famous yakuza group posted a 'righteous indignation statement'; a senior member explained the rationale]. Available at: https://www.news-postseven.com/archives/20241107_2003080.html?DETAIL [Last accessed 14 February].

News PostSeven. (2025). *'Jūnen kōsō ga naze totsuzen?' Rokudaime Yamaguchi-gumi ga Kōbe Yamaguchi-gumi to no kōsō shūketsu o sengen—zenchō toshite kake-megutta uwasa to chokugo ni tōkō sareta kaibunsho* ['Why did the 10-year war suddenly end?' The Sixth-Generation Yamaguchi-gumi declares an end to the conflict with the Kobe Yamaguchi-gumi—Rumours that spread as a prelude and the bizarre document posted immediately afterward] Available at: https://www.news-postseven.com/archives/20250427_2037520.html?DETAIL [Last accessed 14 February 2026].

News PostSeven (2026) *Rokudaime Yamaguchi-gumi ga hatsumode ni "Butōha Herumēsu wakagashira no dōkō" ni keisatsu ga kanshin. . . Tsukasa Shinobu kumichō fujōzai no sanpai de chūmoku atsumaru "shichidaime tanjō jiki"'* [The Rokudaime Yamaguchi-gumi's New Year shrine visit: police interest in the movements of the "hard-line Hermès lieutenant"—with boss Shinobu Tsukasa absent, attention turns to the timing of the seventh-generation succession] Available at: https://www.news-postseven.com/archives/20260119_2087874.html?DETAIL [Last accessed 27 February 2026].

Newsclip. (2023). *Bankoku de Nihonjin 2 nin taiho bouryokudan kankeisha ka* [Two Japanese arrested in Bangkok, possibly gang-related] Available at: https://newsclip.be/thai-news/thai-local/8543 [Last accessed 14 February 2026].

News Sina. (2004). *Rì běn hēi bang shān kǒu zǔ chā shǒu tái wān lì wěi zuǎn* (Japanese yakuza Yamaguchi-gumi intervene in Taiwan's legislative council election campaign.) Available at: https://news.sina.cn/sa/2004-11-03/detail-ikkntiam1560188.d.html [Last accessed 15 May 2024].

NHK. (2018). *Hinkon bōryokudan ga aratana kyōi* [Poor yakuza are the new menace] Available at: https://www.nhk.or.jp/gendai/articles/4136/index.html?1527575911 [Last accessed 14 May 2019].

Nikkan SPA. (2017). *Hangure yori mo kasegenai: Yakuza ga merukari sagi ni made te wo someta wake* [Earning less than hangure: The yakuza is getting involved with merkari frauds] Available at: https://nikkan-spa.jp/1335965 [Last accessed 14 May 2019].

Nikkei Shimbun. (2013). *Kudō-kai, tokutei kiken shitei o arasou: Saiban de kenpō-jō no kenri shingai o shuchō* [Kudō-kai disputes special dangerous group designation, argues it violates constitutional rights]. Available at: https://www.nikkei.com/article/DGXNASJC18029_Y3A110C1ACY000/ [Last accessed 18 February 2026]

Ninkyōdō. (2016). Ninkyodo English version [online] Available at: https://web.archive.org/web/20160617024447/http://ninkyoudou-english-version.jimdo.com/ [Last accessd 7 May 2016].

Ninkyō suishin iinkai [Committee for the promotion of ninkyō]. (2015). *Yamaguchigumi: hōdō sarenai ura no seigi. Shinsai kyūen katsudō* [Yamaguchi-gumi: The justice from the other side that doesn't get reported. Earthquake disaster relief work] [Video file] Available at: https://www.youtube.com/watch?v=6CqctZzAy8o [Last accessed 17 May 2019].

Nippon. (2017). The upstart gangs filling the yakuza power vacuum. Available from: https://www.nippon.com/en/features/c04205/ [Last accessed 23 July 2025].

Nishioka, K., Suzuki, T., Ito, H., and Natsuhara, T. (2016). *Yamaguchi-gumi: Bunretsu kōsō no zen naimaku* [*Yamaguchi-gumi: The complete inside story of the split conflict*]. Tokyo: Takarajima SUGOI Bunko.

Nordstrom, C. and Robben, A. C. (eds.). (1995). *Fieldwork under fire: Contemporary studies of violence and culture.* Berkeley and Los Angeles: University of California Press.

Norma, C. (2016). *The Japanese comfort women and sexual slavery during the China and Pacific wars*. New York: Bloomsbury Academic.

Norman, J. (2017). Confidence in police back at historical average. *News Gallup* [online] Available at: https://news.gallup.com/poll/213869/confidence-police-back-historical-average.aspx [Last accessed 15 May 2019].

NPA. (1991). Heisei 3 Nenhan Keisatsu Hakusho [White Paper of the Police Heisei 3 Issue] [online] Available at: https://www.npa.go.jp/hakusyo/h03/h03index.html [Last accessed 14 May 2019].

NPA. (1993). Heisei 5 Nenhan Keisatsu Hakusho [White Paper of the Police Heisei 5 Issue] [online] Available at: https://www.npa.go.jp/hakusyo/h05/h05index.html [Last accessed 14 May 2019].

NPA. (1999). Heisei 11 Nenhan Keisatsu Hakusho [White Paper of the Police Heisei 11 Issue] [online] Available at: https://www.npa.go.jp/hakusyo/h11/h11index.html [Last accessed 14 May 2019].

NPA. (2004). *Nihon keisatsu 50nen no saseki to aratanaru tenkai* [The trajectory and future developments of 50 years of Japanese police] [online] Available at: http://www.npa.go.jp/hakusyo/h16/hakusho/h16/pdf/F0200000.pdf [Last accessed 18 May 2019].

NPA. (2010). Heisei 22 Nenhan Keisatsu Hakusho [White Paper of the Police Heisei 22 Issue] [online] Available at: https://www.npa.go.jp/hakusyo/h22/index.html [Last accessed 14 May 2019].

NPA. (2012). Heisei 24 Nenhan Keisatsu Hakusho [White Paper of the Police Heisei 24 Issue] [online] Available at: https://www.npa.go.jp/hakusyo/h24/index.html [Last accessed 14 May 2019].

NPA. (2015a). Heisei 27 Nenhan Keisatsu Hakusho (White Paper of the Police 2015) [online] Available at: https://www.npa.go.jp/hakusyo/h27/honbun/index.html [Last accessed 28 August 2016].

NPA. (2015b). Heisei 27 Nenhan Keisatsy Hakusho-Gaiyō (Summary of the White Paper of the Police 2015) [online] Available at: https://www.npa.go.jp/hakusyo/h28/gaiyouban/gaiyouban.pdf [Last accessed 28 August 2016].

NPA. (2021). Reiwa 3 Nenhan Keisatsu Hakusho (White Paper of the Police 2021) Available at: https://www.npa.go.jp/hakusyo/r03/index.html [Last accessed 11 March 2026].

NPA. (2022). Reiwa 3 Nenhan Keisatsu Hakusho (White Paper of the Police 2022) Available at: https://www.npa.go.jp/hakusyo/r03/index.html [Last accessed 2 March 2026].

NPA. (2022). Reiwa 4 Nenhan Keisatsu Hakusho (White Paper of the Police 2022) Available at: https://www.npa.go.jp/hakusyo/r04/index.html [Last accessed 11 March 202].

NPA. (2023). Reiwa 5 Nenhan Keisatsy Hakushō (White Paper of the Police 2023) [online] Available at: https://www.npa.go.jp/hakusyo/r05/index.html [Last accessed 12 February 2026].

NPA. (2025). Reiwa 4 Nenhan Keisatsu Hakusho Hakusho (White Paper of the Police 2022) Available at: https://www.npa.go.jp/hakusyo/r04/index.html [Last accessed 12 February 2026].

NPA. (2025). Reiwa 7 Nenhan Keisatsu Hakusho (White Paper of the Police 2025) Available at: https://www.npa.go.jp/hakusyo/r07/index.html [Last accessed 10 February 2026].

Ojima, M. (2020). *'Sagi wa yamero': Inagawa-kai ga sanka ni dashita 'fushizen' na tsūchi no uragawa (Bōryokudan kanbu kokuhaku)* ['Stop the fraud': The unsettling notice issued within Inagawa-kai's affiliates—organised crime executive confession]. Bunshun Online. Available at: https://bunshun.jp/articles/-/37995 [Last accessed 14 February 2026].

Okita, G. (2018). *Roku-daime Yamaguchi-gumi. Takayama Kiyoshi wakagashira no shakaifukki made 1nen wo kiri, ano soshiki no seiryoku ga kakudaichū* [6th generation Yamagichi-gumi. Less than one year to the social rehabilitation of lieutentat Takayama Kiyoshi, the increased power of the group] *Business Journal*. [online] Available at: https://web.archive.org/web/20240225110549/https://biz-journal.jp/2018/10/post_25310.html [Last accessed 15 May 2019].

Okita, G. (2019). *Yakuza ga yūbinkyoku de ichinichi baito shita dake de taihō no hamon. Gendai kanbu ga kataru, jiken no tokushusei* [A yakuza was arrested just for working one day at the post. An active yakuza lieutenant speaks about these particular issues] *Business Journal* [online] Available at https://web.archive.org/web/20190206054903/https://biz-journal.jp/2019/02/post_26554.html [Last accessed 14 May 2019].

Olson, M. (1993). Dictatorship, democracy, and development. *American political science review*, 87(3), 567–76.

Ostrom, E. (2000). Social capital: A fad or a fundamental concept? In Dasgupta, P. and Serageldin, I. (eds.) *Social capital: A multifaceted perspective* (pp.172–214). Washington, DC: The World Bank.

Ovetz, R. F. (1996). Entrepreneurialization, resistance and the crisis of the universities: A case study of the University of Texas at Austin. PhD dissertation.

Paoli, L. (2002). The paradoxes of organized crime. *Crime, law and social change*, 37(1), 51–97.

Paoli, L. (2003). *Mafia brotherhoods*. Oxford: Oxford University Press.

Paoli L. (2007). Mafia and organised crime: The unacknowledged successes of law enforcement. *West European politics*, 30(4), 854–80.

Paoli, L. (2008). The decline of the Italian mafia. In D. Siegel and Nelen, H. (eds.), *Organized crime: Culture, markets and policies* (pp. 15–28). New York: Springer.

Papachristos, A. V. (2009). Murder by structure: Dominance relations and the social structure of gang homicide. *American journal of sociology*, 115(1), 74–128.

Patai, D. (1994). When method becomes power. In A. Gitlen (ed.), *Power and method: Political activism and educational research* (pp. 61–76). London: Routledge.

Piacentini, L. (2004). Penal identities in Russian prison colonies. *Punishment & Society*, 6(2), 131–47.

Pidd, H. (2015). Funeral for Salford's 'Mr Big' takes place with armed police on standby. *The Guardian* [online] Available at: https://www.theguardian.com/uk-news/2015/aug/28/funeral-salfords-mr-big-paul-massey-armed-police-on-standby [Last accessed 21 October 2022].

Pillow, W. S. (2010). Dangerous reflexivity rigour, responsibility and reflexivity in qualitative research. *The Routledge doctoral student's companion* (pp. 288–300). Abingdon: Routledge.

Pimenta, M. C. B. S., Suarez, M. A. G., and Ferreira, M. A. (2021). Hybrid governance as a dynamic hub for violent non-state actors: examining the case of Rio de Janeiro. *Revista Brasileira de Política Internacional*, 64(2), 1–21.

Pizzini-Gambetta, V. (2006). Becoming visible: Did the emancipation of women reach the Sicilian mafia? In A. Cento Bull and A. Giorgio (eds.), *Speaking out and silencing: Culture, society and politics in Italy in the 1970s* (pp. 201–211). London: Routledge.

Pizzini-Gambetta, V. (2008). Women and the mafia: A methodology minefield. *Global crime* 9(4), 348–53.

Pyrooz, D. C., Decker, S. H., and Moule, R. K. (2015). Criminal and routine activities in online settings. *Justice quarterly*, 32, 471–99.

Pyrooz, D. C. and Moule Jr, R. K. (2019). Gangs and social media. In N. Rafter and M. Brown (eds.), *Oxford research encyclopedia of criminology and criminal justice* (pp. 1–21). Oxford: Oxford University Press.

Qiu, P., Su, Z., and Chen, L. (2013). *Chinese comfort women: Testimonies from Imperial Japan's sex slaves*. Vancouver: UBC Press.

Ramseyer, J. M. and Nakazato, M. (1989). The rational litigant: Settlement amounts and verdict rates in Japan. *The Journal of Legal Studies*, 18(2), 263–90.

Ramseyer, J. M. and Rasmussen, E. (1998). Why is the Japanese conviction rate so high? Harvard Law School M. Olin Centre for Law, *Economics and Business Discussion Paper Series*, paper 240.

Randle, J. and Bichler, G. (2016). Uncovering the social pecking order in gang violence. In *Crime prevention in the 21st century: Insightful approaches for crime prevention initiatives* (pp. 165–86). Cham: Springer International Publishing.

Rankin, A. (2012). 21st-Century yakuza: Recent trends in organized crime in Japan – Part 1. *The Asia Pacific journal*, 10(7-2), 1–27.

Rappaport, R. A. (1999). *Ritual and religion in the making of humanity*. Cambridge: Cambridge University Press.

Rawlinson, P. (2008a) Look who's talking: Interviewing Russian criminals. *Trends in Organized Crime*, 11(1), 12–20.

Rawlinson, P. (2008b). Researching organized crime. In R. King and E. Wincup (eds.), *Doing research on crime and justice* (ch. 10). New York: Oxford University Press.

Reuter, P. (1983). *Disorganized crime: The economics of the visible hand*. Cambridge, MA: MIT press.

Reuter, P. (1985). *The organization of illegal markets: An economic analysis*. Washington, D.C.: US National Institute of Justice.

Reuter, P. (1995). "The Decline of the American Mafia." *The public interest*, 120, 89–99.

Riegelsberger, J. (2005). *Trust in mediated interactions*. PhD dissertation. University of London, University College London.

Roks, R. A., Leukfeldt, E. R., and Densley, J. A. (2021). The hybridization of street offending in the Netherlands. *The British journal of criminology*, 61(4), 926–45.

Rorty, R. (1979). Transcendental arguments, self-reference, and pragmatism. In P. Bieri, R. P. Horstmann, and L. Krüger (eds.) *Transcendental arguments and science: Essays in epistemology* (pp. 77–103). Dordrecht: Springer Netherlands.

Russell, C., Touchard, D., and Porter, M. (2002). What's rapport got to do with it? The practical accomplishment of fieldwork relations between young female researchers and socially marginalised older men. *The qualitative report*, 7(1), 1–21.

Sagaken keisatsu [Saga prefectural police] (2018) *Bōryokudan jōsei* [*Situation of bōryokudan*]. Available at: https://www.police.pref.saga.jp/kurashi/boutai/_1619/_1624.html [Last accessed 14 February 2026].

Saiten (2019). [Ninkyō] Yondaime Yamaguchi-gumi Keishō Sakazuki [Video]. YouTube. https://www.youtube.com/watch?v=mx0tzFvVFxo&list=PLV5SKHxexgJopB5LP6pwxgli5WoUl_sU7&index=6 [Last accessed 20 June 2020].

Sánchez De La Sierra, R. (2020). On the origins of the state: Stationary bandits and taxation in Eastern congo. *Journal of political economy*, 128(1), 32–74.

Sankei News. (2014). *Bōryokudan fūatsu no kage de abaremawaru 'Kantō Rengō' ōbī to 'Doraken' ōbī no mukidō* [The reckless rampage of former 'Kantō Rengō' and 'Dragon' members in the shadow of the crackdown on yakuza groups] 21 December. Available at: https://www.sankei.com/article/20141221-XYREVZTC3ZJNBIPYKNR4ZNUN4Y/ [Last accessed 14 February 2026].

Sankei News. (2023). *Suitai suru 'bōryokudan' to anyaku suru 'hangure'—Sugata kae hisomu chika saishin seiryokuzu* [The declining yakuza and the secret operations of hangure: A map of the latest underground power structures in disguise] Available at: https://www.sankei.com/article/20230808-246OQR6MKBI3ZOIBM5UWYZBVAY/ [Last accessed 22 July 2025].

Sankei Shimbun. (2011). *Zenkoku de bōhai jōrei shikō "Iyō na jidai ga kita" (jō)* [Nationwide enforcement of anti-yakuza ordinances: "A strange era has arrived" (Part 1)]. Available at: https://web.archive.org/web/20111001154843/http://sankei.jp.msn.com/affairs/news/111001/crm11100112010000-n1.htm [Last accessed 11 March 2026].

Sankei Shimbun. (2017). *Shimizu Ryotaro, ihō kajino-ten deiri de katsudo jishuku... sangatsu myūjikaru mo kōban* [Shimizu Ryotaro suspends activities due to visits to illegal casino, also withdraws from March musical]. Sankei Shimbun. Available at: https://www.sankei.com/article/20170211-ZKMEP6YY7BPILBGSAJGHSHBJ7M/ [Last accessed 11 March 2026].

Sankei Shimbun. (2020). *"Yamaguchi-gumi Harowīn" kinshi jōrei ga hiita seija no kyōkaisen* ["Yamaguchi-gumi Halloween" prohibition ordinance draws the boundary between right and wrong]. Available at: https://www.sankei.com/article/20201016-EDP5B5WKXZOXDL53MH4ZUZU3TU/ [Last accessed 28 February 2026].

Sankei West. (2015). *Rokudaime Tsukasa Shinobu Kumichō tandoku intabyū* [Interview to 6th leader Tsukasa Shinobu] Available at: https://web.archive.org/web/20151006061155/https://www.sankei.com/west/news/150831/wst1508310022-n1.html [Last accessed 11 March 2026].

Sankei West. (2017). *Yamaguchi-gumi moto-kanbu ni chōeki 6 nen, 7dome banri de hatsu no yuuzai juutōhō ihan sashimodoshi-ban* [Ex Yamaguchi-gumi leader sentenced to 6 years imprisonment with labour, first conviction after 7 trials for violation of Swords and Firearm Control Act] Available at: https://www.sankei.com/west/news/170324/wst1703240044-n1.html [Last accessed 29 January 2019].

Sberna, S. and Vannucci, A. (2019). Mafia and political corruption in Italy. In F. Allum, I.C. Marinaro, and R. Sciarrone (eds.) *Italian mafias today* (pp. 92–110). Cheltenham: Edward Elgar.

Schelling, T. C. (1971). "What Is the Business of Organized Crime?" *The American Scholar*, 40(4), 643–52.

Schneider, J. and Schneider, P. T. (2003). Reversible destiny: Mafia, antimafia, and the struggle for Palermo. Berkeley: University of California Press.

Schwedler, J. (2006). The third gender: Western female researchers in the Middle East. *PS: Political Science & Politics*, 39(3), 425–28.

Sciarrone, R. (1998). *Mafie vecchie, mafie nuove.* Roma: Donzelli.

Sciarrone, R. and Storti, L. (2014). The territorial expansion of mafia-type organized crime. The case of the Italian mafia in Germany. *Crime, Law and Social Change*, 61(1), 37–60.

Schimmenti, A., Giunta, S., and Verso, G. L. (2014). Mafia women: A study on language and mental representations of women engaged with mafia members. *International journal of criminology and sociology*, 3, 267–74.

Seiron Chōsa—Naikakufu [Public opinion poll—Cabinet office] (1964). *Keisatsukan no kyōyō nado ni kansuru seiron chōsa* [Public opinion poll on the education of policemen and related matters] Available at: https://survey.gov-online.go.jp/s39/S39-09-39-03.html [Last accessed 15 May 2019].

Seiron Chōsa—Naikakufu [Public opinion poll—Cabinet office] (1971). *Bōryokudan hanzai and shakai kankyō nado ni kansuru seiron chōsa* [Public opinion poll on the organised crime and social environment and related matters] Available at: https://survey.gov-online.go.jp/s46/S46-08-46-07.html [Last accessed 15 May 2019].

Seiron Chōsa—Naikakufu [Public opinion poll—Cabinet office] (1978). *Keisatsu ni kansuru seiron chōsa* [Public opinion poll on the police] Available at: https://survey.gov-online.go.jp/s53/S53-11-53-13.html [Last accessed 15 May 2019].

Sela-Shayovitz, R. (2012). Gangs and the web: Gang members' online behavior. *Journal of contemporary criminal justice*, 28(4), 389–405.

Sergi, A. (2015). The Italian anti-mafia system between practice and symbolism: Evaluating contemporary views on the Italian structure model against organized crime. *Policing: A journal of policy and practice*, 10(3), 194–205.

Sergi, A. (2015b). The evolution of the Australian 'ndrangheta. An historical perspective. Australian & New Zealand journal of criminology, 48(2), 155–74.

Sheldon, C.D. (1983). 'Merchants and Society in Tokugawa Japan'. *Modern Asian studies*, 17(3), 477–88.

Shirayanagi, S. (1916). *Oyabun Kobun Rōninhen* [*Oyabun Kobun Rōnin Chapter*]. Tokyo: Tōadō Shobō.

Shiroshita, Y. (2009). Current trends and issues in Japanese sentencing. *Federal sentencing reporter*, 22(4), 243–48.

Shūkan Asahi Geinō (2026). 'Kanzen mitchaku satsu! Rokudaime Yamaguchi-gumi no "kinga shinnen" (1): Kōbe Gokoku Jinja de shinnen no kigan wo . . .', [Full exclusive coverage: the Rokudaime Yamaguchi-gumi's New Year greetings (1): New Year prayers at Kōbe Gokoku Shrine] Available at: https://www.asagei.com/excerpt/346006 [Last accessed 27 February 2026].

Shūpure News. (2025). *Yamaguchi-gumi bunretsu kōsō shūketsu de 'kuenai yakuza' no tairyou ridatsu ga hajimaru?* [With the end of the Yamaguchi-gumi split conflict, will a mass exodus of 'unprofitable yakuza' begin?] 3 June, Available at: https://web.archive.org/web/20250603092754/https://news.yahoo.co.jp/articles/562bd96e94372f057a43f15c2afe25e3819ce025 [Last accessed 14 February 2026].

Siebert, R. (2007). Mafia women: The affirmation of a female pseudo-subject. The case of the 'Ndrangheta. In G. Fiandaca (ed.), *Women and the mafia: Female roles in organized crime structures* (pp. 19–45). New York: Springer.

Siniawer, E. M. (2008). *Ruffians, yakuza, nationalists: The violent politics of modern Japan, 1860–1960.* Ithaca and London: Cornell University Press.

Siniawer, E. M. (2012). Mediated democracy. Yakuza and Japanese political leadership. In P. Allum and R. Siebert (eds.), *Organized crime and the challenge to democracy* (ch. 12.). London and New York: Routledge.

Skarbek, D. (2008). Putting the 'con' into constitutions: The economics of prison gangs. *The journal of law, economics & organization*, 26(2), 183–211.

Skarbek, D. (2011). Governance and prison gangs. *American Political Science Review*, 105(4), 702–16.

Skarbek, D. (2014). *The social order of the underworld: How prison gangs govern the American penal system.* Oxford: Oxford University Press.

Skarbek, D. (2024). The political economy of criminal governance. *Public choice* 200(1), 1–24.

Skarbek, D. and Wang, P. (2015). Criminal rituals. *Global Crime*, 16(4), 288–305.

Soshiki Hanzai Shobatsu-hō [Law on punishment of organised crime] [online] Available at: http://elaws.e-gov.go.jp/search/elawsSearch/elaws_search/lsg0500/detail?lawId = 411AC0000000136_20180410_430AC0000000007&openerCode=1 [Last accessed 12 February 2019].

Soshiki hanzai shobatsu-hō – Soshikitekina hanzai no shobatsu oyobi hanzai shūeki no kisei nado ni kansuru hōritsu [Law regarding punishment of organised crime and restrictions of criminal proceeds]. (1999). Law no. 136. Available at: http://elaws.e-gov.go.jp/search/elawsSearch/elaws_search/lsg0500/detail?lawId=411AC0000000136 [Last accessed 15 May 2019].

SPN Journal. (2024). *Bōryokudan no 'jikai' no saki o misueyo – Bōryokudan kara Tokuryū e* [Anticipating what comes after the yakuza's collapse: From syndicates to tokuryū] Available from: https://www.sp-network.co.jp/column-report/column/bouhi/candr0347.html?curr=column [Last accessed 23 July 2025].

Stark, D. H. (1981). The yakuza: Japanese crime incorporated (Ph.D. Thesis). University of Michigan.

State Department. (2018). Japan 2018 human rights report. [online] Available at: https://www.state.gov/reports/2018-country-reports-on-human-rights-practices/japan [Last accessed 14 May 2019].

Stevens, C. (1995) Day laborers, volunteers and welfare in contemporary Japan. *Urban anthropology and studies of cultural systems and world economic development*, 24(3/4), 229–53.

Sullivan, M. L. (2005). Maybe we shouldn't study 'gangs'. Does reification obscure youth violence?. *Journal of contemporary criminal justice*, 21(2), 170–90.

Suzuki, T. (2005) *Densetsu no Yakuza-tachi: Nihon Outlaw Retsuden* [*Legendary Yakuza: Japan Outlaw Biographies*]. Tōkyo: Yōsensha.

Suzuki, T. (2011). *Sennyū rupo: yakuza no shuraba* [*Infiltration reportage: The yakuza scene of carnage*]. Tokyo: Bunshun Shinsho.

Suzuki, T. (2014). *Yakuza to genpatsu* [*Yakuza and nuclear power*]. Tokyo: Bunshun Shinsho.

Suzuki, T. (2018). *Sakana to yakuza: Bōryokudan no kyodai shikingen "mitsuryō bijinesu" o ou* [*Fish and yakuza: Tracking the violent gang's massive funding source "poaching business"*]. Tokyo: Shogakukan.

Suzuki, T. (2023). *Wakai shuu o uchikoroshi, jibun no atama o uchi nuite shinda Yakuza ga nokoshita saigo no hitokoto* [The last words left by a yakuza who shot a youngster to death and then shot himself in the head] Shukan Bunshun. Available at: https://bunshun.jp/articles/-/39695?page=2. [Last accessed 14 February 2026]

Suzuki, T. (2025). Yūmei yakuza soshiki ga futatabi "gigibun" "sutōkā o bokumetsu suru kakugo" haridashita riyū o chokugeki suruto. . . Hantoshi mae ni wa "yami baito gōtō ni dankotaru shochi" de wadai ni [Famous Yakuza organization posts 'righteous indignation statement' again: 'Determination to eradicate stalkers']. NEWS Post Seven. Available at: https://www.news-postseven.com/archives/20250517_2041718.html [Last accessed11 March 2026].

Suzuki, T. and Mizoguchi, A. (2019). *Kyōyō to shite no yakuza* [*Yakuza as general knowledge*]. Tokyo: Shogakukan.

Taipei Times. (2004). Japanese gun-smuggling suspect nabbed in Manila. Available at: https://www.taipeitimes.com/News/taiwan/archives/2004/06/05/2003173803 [Last accessed 16 June 2023].

Taipei Times. (2023). Police on alert after suspected yakuza arrive. Available at: https://www.taipeitimes.com/News/front/archives/2023/05/23/2003800259 [Last accessed 18 June 2023].

Taiwan News. (2023). Okinawan yakuza in Taiwan on China unification party's invitation. Available at: https://www.taiwannews.com.tw/news/4899665 [Last accessed 16 June 2023].

Takeshi, M. and Goodwin, J. (1993). Early kami worship. In Brown DM (ed.), *The Cambridge History of Japan* (Volume 1; pp. 317–58). Cambridge: Cambridge University Press.

takahashi hiroki. (2015). *Kudōkai tai Fukuoka kensatsu* [Kudōkai vs Fukuoka prefectural police] [video file]. Available at: https://www.youtube.com/watch?v=anVSpw-j5XE [Last accessed 15 May 2019].

Tamura, M. (1992). The yakuza and amphetamine abuse in Japan. In H. H. Traver and M. S. Gaylord (eds.), *Drugs, law and the state* (ch. 6). New Brunswick and London: Transactions Publishers.

Tanaka, Y. (2002). *Japan's comfort women: Sexual slavery and prostitution during World War II and the US occupation.* London: Routledge.

Taya, K. (2007). Gyogyō to keizai maruwakari (1): Awabi no mitsuryō no genjō to kadai—Saibai gyogyō to shigen kanri o obiyakasu mitsuryō [Fisheries and the economy explained (1): The current situation and challenges of abalone poaching—Poaching that threatens stock-enhancement fisheries and resource management]. *Yōshoku: Aqua culture magazine*, 44(8), 80–83.

Taylor, B. D. (2011). *State building in Putin's Russia: Policing and coercion after communism.* Cambridge: Cambridge University Press.

ter Haar, B. J. (2000). *Ritual and mythology of the Chinese Triads: Creating an identity.* Leiden/Boston: Brill.

Tetsu. (2023). "Washi ga zeni nai no shittotte, nomi ni itton no yaro ga!!" to teshita wo bokoboro ni shita koto mo . . . 18-sai no shinmai yakuza ni gokudō intai wo kakugo saseta "oyabun no nasakenai saifu jijō" ["Even when knowing I had no money, going out drinking!!" The pitiful financial situation of the boss that made an 18-year-old rookie yakuza decide to quit]. Bunshun Online. Available at https://bunshun.jp/articles/-/64965.

The Economist. (2017). Japan's government has legalised casinos, but they are not popular. Available at: https://www.economist.com/asia/2017/02/02/japans-government-has-legalised-casinos-but-they-are-not-popular [Last accessed 14 May 2019].

The Huffington Post Japan. (2016). *Nishimura Kenta senshu, ihō kajino dehiri, Nihon daihyō jogai badminton* [Athlete Nishimura Kenta went to an illegal casino and was excluded from the badminton national team] [online] Available at: https://www.huffingtonpost.jp/2016/04/19/kenta-nishimoto-badminton_n_9725960.html [Last accessed 14 May 2019].

Thrasher, F. M. (1963) [2013]. *The gang: A study of 1,313 gangs in Chicago.* Chicago: University of Chicago Press.

Tilly, C. (1985). War making and state making as organized crime. In Evans, P., Rueschemeyer, D., and Skocpol, T. (eds), *Bringing the state back* (pp. 169–191). Cambridge: Cambridge University Press.

Time (1974). The Godfather-san. Available at: https://web.archive.org/web/20080304002852/http://www.time.com/time/magazine/article/0,9171,944948,00.html [Last accessed 27 February 2026].

Tokyo Metropolitan Police Department. (2022). *Tokyo-to bōryokudan haijo jōrei ni tsuite* [About the Tokyo Metropolitan Ordinance for Elimination of Organized Crime Groups]. Available at: https://www.keishicho.metro.tokyo.lg.jp/kurashi/anzen/tsuiho/haijo_seitei/haijo_jourei.html [Last accessed 11 March 2026].

Tokyo Metropolitan Government. (2011). *Tokyo-to bōryokudan haijo jōrei* [Tokyo Metropolitan Ordinance for Elimination of Organized Crime Groups] (Ordinance No. 54, as amended through Ordinance No. 159 of 2024). Available at: https://www.reiki.metro.tokyo.lg.jp/reiki/reiki_honbun/g101RG00004199.html [Last accessed 11 March 2026].

Tsuneki, A. and Matsunaka, M. (2011). Labor relations and labor law in Japan. *Pacific Rim law & policy journal association*, 20(3), 529–61.

Tsūshin bōju-hō-Hanzai sōsa no tame no tsūshin bōju ni kansuru hōritsu [Law regarding the monitoring of communicaions for the investigation of crimes]. (2016). Available at: http://elaws.e-gov.go.jp/search/elawsSearch/elaws_search/lsg0500/detail?lawId=411AC0000000137&openerCode=1 [Last accessed 16 May 2019].

Turner, V. (2011). *The ritual process: Structure and anti-structure.* New Brunswick and London: Aldine Transaction.

Tung, G. (2021). Technology as a tool for transnational organized crime: Networking and money laundering. *The journal of intelligence, conflict, and warfare*, 4(1), 118–27.

Ueno, C. (2003). Self-determination on sexuality? Commercialization of sex among teenage girls in Japan 1. *Inter-Asia cultural studies*, 4(2), 317–24.

Uyeda, Y. (1991). Rites of passage and purification in Japanese society, PhD dissertation, University of Oregon.

van den Ende, L. and van Marrewijk, A. (2018). The point of no return: Ritual performance and strategy making in project organizations. *Long range planning*, 51(3), 451–62.

van Gennep, A. (1960). *The rites of passage*. Chicago: University of Chicago Press.

Van Hellemont, E. (2012). Gangland online: Performing the real imaginary world of gangstas and ghettos in Brussels. *European journal of crime criminal law & criminal justice*, 20, 165.

Van Uhm, D. P. (2016). *The illegal wildlife trade: Inside the world of poachers, smugglers and traders*. New York: Springer.

Van Wolferen, K. (1989). *The enigma of Japanese power*. New York: A.A. Knopf.

Varese, F. (2001). *The Russian mafia: Private protection in a new market economy*. Oxford: Oxford University Press.

Varese, F. (2010). General introduction. What is organized crime? In F. Varese (ed.), *Organized crime* (Vol. 1). London and New York: Routledge.

Varese, F. (2011). *Mafias on the move. How organized crime conquers new territories*. Princeton and Oxford: Princeton University Press.

Varese, F. (2014). Protection and extortion. In L. Paoli (ed.) *The Oxford handbook of organized crime* (pp. 343–58). Oxford: Oxford University Press.

Varese, F. (2017). What is organized crime? In S. Carnevale, S. Forlati, and O. Giolo (eds.) *Redefining organised crime: A challenge for the European union?* (pp. 25–56). London: Bloomsbury Publishing.

Varese, F. (2018) *Mafia Life: Love, death and money at the heart of organized crime*. London: Profile Books.

Varese, F. (2021). Ethnographies of Organized Crime. In S. M. Bucerius, K. D. Haggerty, and L. Berardi (eds.), *The Oxford handbook of ethnographies of crime and criminal justice* (pp. 340–60). Oxford: Oxford University Press.

Varese, F. (2022). Rigorous ethnography. In K. Gërxhani, N.D. de Graaf, and W. Raub (eds.) *Handbook of sociological science* (pp. 215–31). Cheltenham: Edward Elgar Publishing.

Varese, F. (2025). Introduction to special issue production, trade and governance: A new definition of organized crime. *European journal of sociology/archives Européennes de Sociologie*, 66 (2), 117–38.

Vigna, P. L. (2006). Fighting organized crime, with particular reference to mafia crimes in Italy, *Journal of international criminal justice*, 4(3), 522–27.

Villa, R. D., Braga, C. de M., and Ferreira, M. A. S. V. (2021). Violent nonstate actors and the emergence of hybrid governance in South America. *Latin American research review*, 56(1), 36–49.

Vogel, S. K. (1996). *Freer markets, more rules: regulatory reform in advanced industrial countries*. Ithaca: Cornell University Press.

Vogel, S. K. (2006). *Japan remodeled: How government and industry are reforming Japanese capitalism*. Ithaca and London: Cornell University Press.

Volkov, V. (2002). *Violent entrepreneurs: The use of force in the making of Russian capitalism*. Ithaca and London: Cornell University Press.

Volkov, V. (2014). The Russian mafia: Rise and extinction. In L. Paoli (ed.) *The Oxford handbook of organized crime* (pp. 159–76). Oxford: Oxford University Press.

Waldram, J. B. (2007). Everybody has a story: Listening to imprisoned sexual offenders. *Qualitative health research*, 17(7), 963–70.

Warburton, J. (2025). Subcontracted violence amongst London's drug gangs. *Global crime*, 26(3-4), 173–91.

Wax, R. H. (1979). Gender and age in fieldwork and fieldwork education: No good thing is done by any man alone. *Social problems*, 26(5), 509–22.

Weitzdörfer, J., Shiroshita, Y., and Padfield, N. (2018). Sentencing and punishment in Japan and England: A comparative discussion. In J. Liu and S. Miyazawa (eds.), *Crime and justice in contemporary Japan, Springer series on Asian criminology and criminal justice research* (pp. 189–214). Cham: Springer International Publishing.

Whyte W. F. (1993). *Street corner society: The social structure of an Italian slum* (4th ed.). Chicago: University of Chicago Press.

Wong, R. W. (2015). A note on fieldwork in 'dangerous' circumstances: Interviewing illegal tiger skin suppliers and traders in Lhasa. *International journal of social research methodology*, 18(6), 695–702.

Wong, R. W. (2019). *The illegal wildlife trade in China.* London: Springer International Publishing.

Yakuzanet. (2016). *Kumamoto jishin: Kōbe Yamaguchi-gumi no shien katsudō ha imēji senryaku?* [Kumamoto earthquake: Are the relief activities of the Kobe Yamaguchi-gumi just an image strategy?] [online] Available at: https://web.archive.org/web/20240226071757/http://xn--pcko0l.net/archives/10719 [Last accessed 17 May 2019].

Yakuza893 (2023). *Sanpo saserarete ita inu no fun o hōchi, Rokudaime Yamaguchi-gumi "Kyokudōkai" kumiin o taiho* [Yakuza member from the 6th-generation Yamaguchi-gumi "Kyokudōkai" arrested for leaving dog poop uncollected]. Available at: https://yakuza893.blog.jp/rokukei403.html [Last accessed 28 February 2026].

Yamadaira, S. (1988). *Hamamatsu Ichiriki Ikka Shimatsuki: Sendō sareta jūmin to ikenie ni sareta bōryokudan [The Chronicle of Hamamatsu's Ichiriki-ikka - The Incited Residents and the Sacrificed Yakuza]*. Tokyo, Japan: Daisan Shokan.

Yamadaira, S. (2003). *Yakuza ni manabu shidōryoku [Leadership skills that can be learned from the yakuza]*. Nagoya: Gentōsha.

Yamanouchi, Y. (2016). *Yamaguchi-gumi kōmon bengoshi [The lawyer of the Yamaguchi-gumi]*. Tokyo: Kadokawa.

Yamanouchi, Y. (2017). *Nihon yakuza "zetsumetsu no hi" [The day of Japanese yakuza "extinction"]*. Tokyo, Japan: Tokuma Shoten.

Yanagi, H. (2017). *Nippon keizai no seisui kara miru Yamaguchi-gumi 100nen no rekishi to bunretsu* [The Yamaguchi-gumi's 100 years' history and split from the perspective of the economic rise and fall] *Bessatsu saizō*, 5, 8–15.

Yomiuri Shinbun. (1890). *Asakusabashi fukin de bakuto no nawabari arasoi. Ichiji wa ōsawagi de kayaku ga naka ni hairi kaiketsu / Tōkyō* [Territorial dispute among gamblers near Asakusabashi—at one point it turned into a big commotion, but a gang mediator stepped in and resolved it / Tokyo].

Yomiuri Shimbun. (2024). *Mizukara "yubitsume" shita bōryokudan kanbu, "kashitsu de fushō" to shinkoku shi kenkō hoken de chiryō. . . mezurashii akuyō no sagi yōgi de taiho* [Yakuza executive who self-amputated finger claims "injured by negligence" and receives treatment under health insurance; arrested on rare fraud charges]. Available at: https://www.yomiuri.co.jp/national/20241010-OYT1T50156/ [Last accessed 28 February 2026].

Yomiuri Shimbun. (2025). *Sashukin senjō ni 'sōkin daikō' ōkō, yami baito no kōza keiyu . . . Keisatsuchō ga hō kisei o kentō* ['Remittance agents' help launder fraud proceeds via black market job accounts—NPA considers legal regulation].

Yomiuri Shinbun. (2025). *'Rufi' soshiki bōchō no hate sagi kyoten kounyū 12 oku-en, wairo 1 oku-en, sōkan manugare* ['Luffy' organisation's expansion reaches its limit: Scam base purchased for 1.2 billion yen, 100 million yen bribe paid, deportation avoided].

Yomiuri Shimbun. (2026). *Tōkyō Dōmu de puro yakyū kansen, bōryokudan kanbu-ra 4-nin taiho. . . kenzōbutsu shinnyū yōgi* [Four yakuza executives arrested for trespassing while watching professional baseball at Tokyo Dome]. Available at: https://www.yomiuri.co.jp/national/20260209-GYT1T00444/ [Last accessed 28 February 2026].

Yōsensha-Jitsuwa Jidai Henshūbu. (2004). *Gendai Yakuza Daijiten*. Tokyo: Yōsensha.
Yoshimi, Y. (2000). *Comfort women: Sexual slavery in the Japanese military during World War II*. New York: Columbia University Press.
Zhang, S. and Chin, K. L. (2003). The declining significance of triad societies in transnational illegal activities. A structural deficiency perspective. *British journal of criminology*, 43(3), 469–88.

Index

For the benefit of digital users, indexed terms that span two pages (e.g., 52–53) may, on occasion, appear on only one of those pages.

Note: Tables and figures are indicated by an italic *t* or *f.*